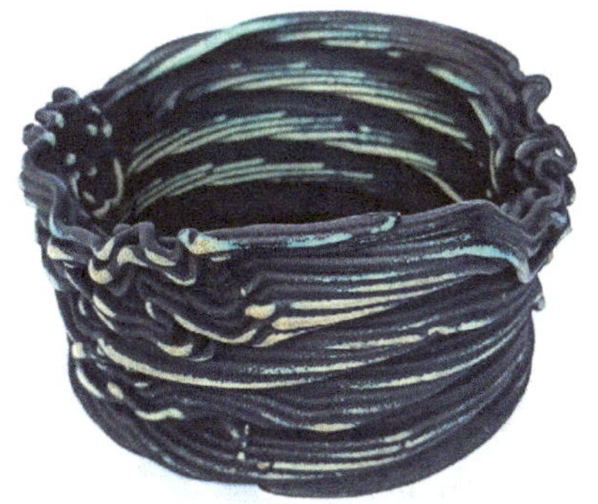

For all those who helped me on my journey, I will be forever grateful.

Let's Clay 3D Print! A Guidebook by Hendrien Horn.

www.hendrienhorn.com

@hendrienhorn

ISBN: 978-0-7961-9510-4

LET'S CLAY 3D PRINT!

A GUIDEBOOK

Hendrien Horn

CONTENTS

CONTENTS

FOREWORD

MADELEINE HENNING

Clay 3D printing is a relatively new technology within the arts. This book is an ideal introduction for those who want to try their hand at clay 3D printing or who simply want to learn more about it. It combines the thrill of learning new techniques with the know-how of traditional pottery to provide the reader with background information - a roadmap of how to kickstart their own journey in clay 3D printing.

This book takes an interesting and informative look at the history of clay 3D printing and introduces the reader to those artists and technicians involved in its evolution. With its comprehensive overview, as well as valuable tips and techniques gleaned from the author's own experience, it is the ideal point from which to enter the world of clay 3D printing.

As a pioneer in the field, Hendrien Horn has received several accolades for her 3D printed ceramic art, one of which is the prestigious 2022 South African National Corobrik Award that celebrates studio artists who showcase the evolution of ceramics.

Being the first contemporary clay 3D printing artist in South Africa, her passion and expertise in design and clay 3D printing makes her the ideal guide into this vibrant and versatile art form.

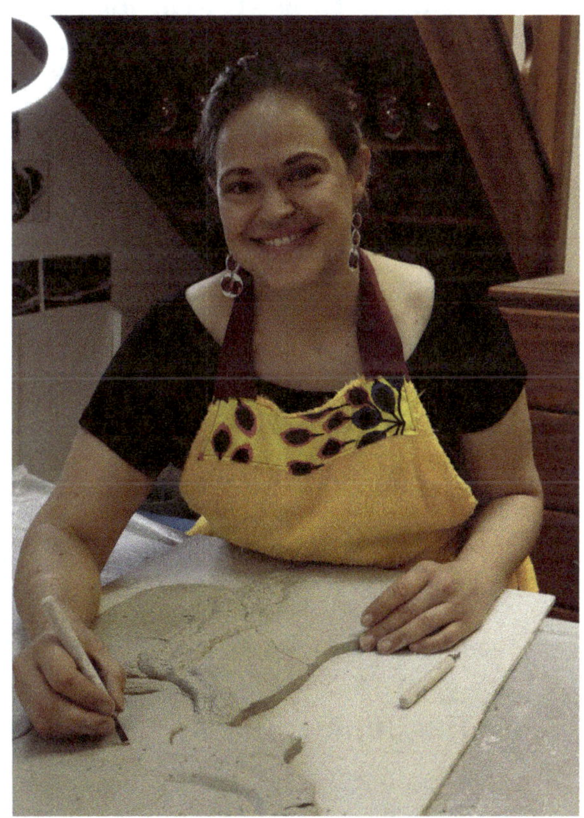

Madeleine Henning working on a ceramic wall panel for the Chateau des Tesnières in France / 2024.

OVERVIEW

Following a brief introduction to the author's narrative of entering the world of clay 3D printing, the book is divided into the following chapters:

---

1. What Is Clay 3D Printing?

A straight dive into what the process involves, Chapter 1 briefly explores the history of the industry.

2. Industry Leaders

The leading companies designing and building clay 3D printers tell their stories and showcase their quality 3D printers on the market.

3. Start With A Plan

Chapter 3 considers the question: What should prospective clay 3D makers focus on before investing in materials and equipment? The discussion includes references to the benefits of clay 3D printing and the range of possibilities within the industry.

4. 3D Printer Builds

Chapter 4 focuses on important considerations when either building or buying a clay 3D printer and how the different printer models compare with one another.

5. The Outline

An outline of the full clay 3D printing process that will be discussed in the book.

6. 3D Design (CAD)

Chapter 6 considers some of the applications currently available for first- time 3D makers and the various processes involved in preparing a 3D model for 3D printing.

7. Think Clay

Which type of clay should beginners use when 3D printing and why? This question and how clay should be prepared for 3D printing are addressed.

8. Clay 3D Printing

Chapter 8 shares the step-by-step process from setup to the full clay 3D printing procedure.

9. Pottery

The 'lingo' that potters often use and how the pottery process works is discussed. Various decorating materials and techniques are also explained, including how to calculate the shrinkage rate of a clay 3D print.

10. My Tips & Tricks

Setting up a design for success is important as we look at how to design in clay as the material of choice. Tips on glaze decorating and how to deal with cracks in your clay forms are shared, including health and safety considerations.

11. Clay Artists From Around The World

Chapter 11 introduces and shares the work from some of the artists who are making an impact within the clay 3D printing industry.

12. A South African Perspective

Considering how the industry has developed, we chat to those who are exploring this new field in the author's home country.

13. Final Thoughts

As you are now ready for the next leg in your clay 3D printing journey, we conclude with a few guidelines and final tips.

14. Additional Research

Want to learn more? All the featured guests share information on past projects, articles, interviews, and published books.

FROM THE AUTHOR

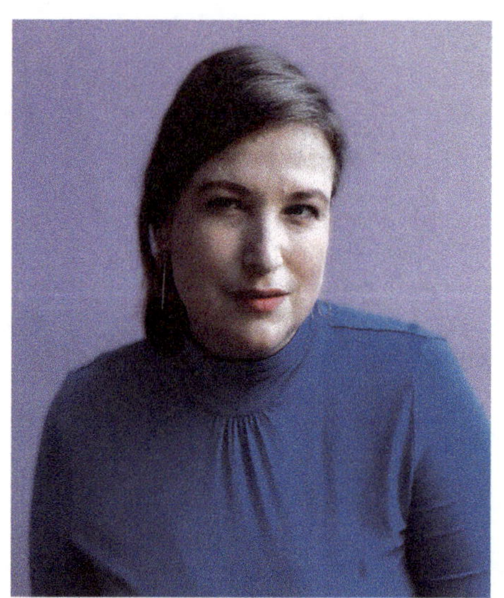

HENDRIEN HORN

3D printing, together with the wider application of this type of technology, is already an established practice across multiple industries. Clay 3D printing, however, has only started gaining traction within these industries over the past few years. In a world where the materials we use matter, clay has become a natural resource that is often used for prototyping and the testing of products, in architecture, and in design.

Would it surprise you to learn that some of the first 3D printers adapted to print in clay were modified and built by designers and artists and not only by engineers? Clay 3D printing is still considered a relatively new extension of ceramic art… AND AN ART IT IS, as becomes evident from the testimonies of several leaders in the field that are presented in this book.

There are four components to 3D printing at all scales: material, design, technology, and application.

Clay, as a 3D printed material, often requires multiple pottery processes before it becomes a finished product.

Designing for 3D printing requires foresight and knowledge on how an initial idea can be brought into existence in the concrete form of a 3D model.

Technologies such as 3D design software and equipment such as a clay 3D printer are the tools that you will need to bring your 3D model to life.

Lastly, how you apply these tools and processes is important as you streamline and adapt your workflow process to work for you.

I have been through the entire process, having discovered clay 3D printing whilst I was still practising conventional pottery in 2019. Initially, I decided to do some research. I started this by jump starting the "old school" process - by cutting and pasting four large posters of inspirational people, projects, and the clay 3D printers available across the globe. I stuck these pages onto my studio walls and just stared at them for weeks on end!

To be honest, though, my mind had already been made up even before the posters were attached to the wall, but I needed to envision the process clearly, because at the end of the day, taking up clay 3D printing was going to be a huge investment.

Very soon it became apparent that there were no clay 3D printers available in South Africa. At the time, the 3D printer companies I contacted had never heard of a "clay" 3D printer, and pretty much thought I had lost my mind for enquiring about one!

The next step was to teach myself how to design using 3D software. I watched YouTube tutorials and used various teaching platforms, and also tried to figure out how to get a clay 3D printer into a country that was in lockdown. Once I had gained confidence in my 3D designing capabilities and the importation restrictions had been lifted, I finally placed my order.

When the massive wooden crate arrived with its precious cargo it was quite an ordeal getting it off the courier truck as the driver had forgotten to bring the ramp for moving large crates. Luckily, all that was needed was an old trustworthy trolley, one exceptionally strong delivery driver, and a few loud sound effects - mainly from me. I am forever grateful to that delivery driver.

As a potter who had a full understanding of clay as a material, I still had some hurdles to cross as I started using my clay 3D printer. Having never operated a large robotic machine before, I can admit it was rather intimidating. I had to follow set procedures, and honestly, my "go with the flow" type of personality certainly proved to be my saving grace.

During the hand-made design and sculpting process, the fact that I could work with clay and use my hands meant that I could change my mind at any point in time.

With clay 3D printing, your 3D design predetermines the outcome, and thinking ahead is the name of the game. When I finally grasped this concept, I was able to streamline my processes and create clay 3D prints that as an artist, I was proud to share with the world.

Finding inspiration from international 3D creators across the world, I often felt that the world of clay making where all the action was happening was very far away. At times, I found myself struggling to understand and sort through all the online information. However, I'm so glad that I persevered, essentially teaching myself in the process. This journey is one of the main reasons why I wanted to write this book. I wish to give clay makers an easier path to understanding and enjoying what the clay 3D printing process requires whilst learning from the current experts who have helped build up the industry around the world.

I hope this book inspires you, much like the people in it who have inspired me – many of whom were present on my studio walls all those years ago!

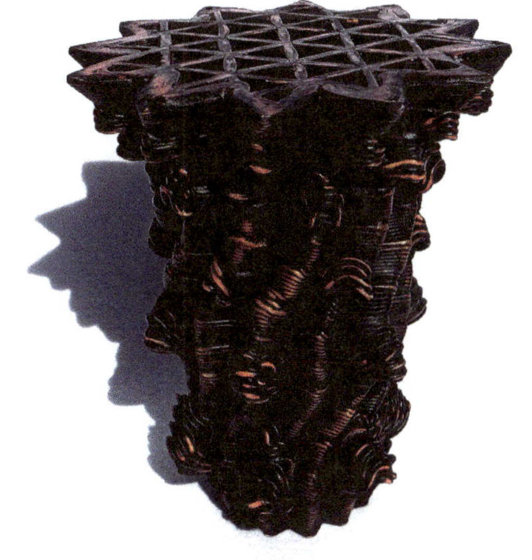

Fire Fossil / Hendrien Horn / 22.5cm (h) / 3D printed earthenware clay / 2023.

WHAT IS CLAY 3D PRINTING?

Clay 3D printing is an additive manufacturing technique that involves building up clay material in layers with the use of a 3D printer that has been modified to print a three-dimensional design with clay.

Natural clay is formed when minerals, dissolved plants, and animal matter are turned into silt that settles into beds of clay. Pottery is the art of making objects out of naturally found or synthetic clay and involves the hardening of this material at high temperatures through either fire or an electric kiln.

Widely used in the making of crockery and sculptures throughout the centuries, the art of pottery has fascinated countless people because of the ability of the clay material to be moulded and decorated in many different ways.

Clay 3D printing is a tool that can be used to create unique pottery items – much like the case of the artistic forms from the electric pottery wheel, which was introduced in the early 1900's.

Experimenting with the movement of clay during the clay 3D printing process / Hendrien Horn / 2021.

Moreover, working with clay requires a potter to acquire knowledge about the material and the firing procedures, which I refer to as the pottery process.

Clay is a fragile material when it is dry and must be kiln fired at high temperatures to make it hard and durable. Understanding the basic procedures of the pottery process is paramount to building and developing the skills of a clay maker. Many potters spend years building up their knowledge, and in so doing, perfecting their sculpting and decorating techniques. I would like to encourage you to do the same.

The process whereby the 3D printer prints is known as the coiling method. Clay is extruded and pushed through the nozzle mechanism of the 3D printer, with the clay coils 3D printed on top of one another as the printer follows its computational coded path. 3D printing enables you to print exceptionally detailed clay forms, offering you the opportunity to experiment with intricate designs.

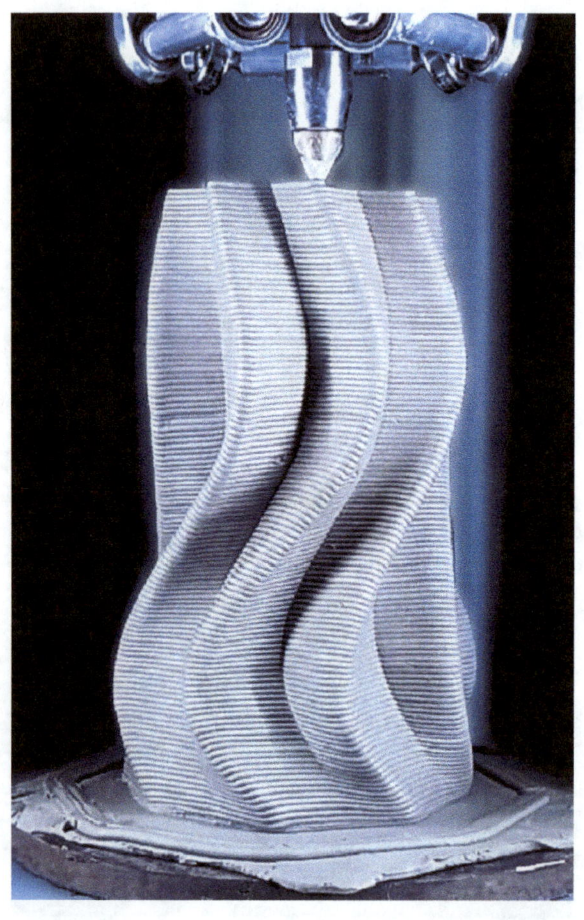

As it happens, coiling is one of the oldest clay pottery techniques! Hand coiled vessels dating back thousands of years have been found in many different cultural regions across the world. Even with the abundance of the new technologies available today, the clay 3D printer creation process uses this most tried and tested pottery technique.

Clay 3D printing a spiral vase / Hendrien Horn.

A BRIEF HISTORY

Let's look at some of the pioneers within the industry.

David Herrold

Although the name of the late David Herrold may not be widely recognisable in the clay 3D printing community, it should be.

David Herrold was a professor at DePauw University, in Indiana. His interests in combining technology and art did not only include the use of clay, but also, digital photography and animation. In 1986, he created a frame-by-frame animation using 3D modelling software on the Macintosh Plus (Apple computers).

In 2000, David was inspired to use 3D printing technologies after witnessing a demonstration of a 3D printer in England. In 2001, with no knowledge of computer systems relating to 3D printers, he proceeded to build his own analogue machine based on a mechanised pottery wheel. He called it the Slip Jet Printer. It was a manually controlled machine that could control the flow of extruded clay whilst creating a complex shape on a rotating pottery wheel. The idea was to help the maker create forms on the wheel not usually achievable by hand.

The Slip Jet Printer was loosely based on the early industrial Jacquard Loom (1801), a weaving machine that greatly advanced textile weaving. Interestingly, the inventor of the first mechanical computer namely, Charles Babbage, was also inspired by the Jacquard Loom.

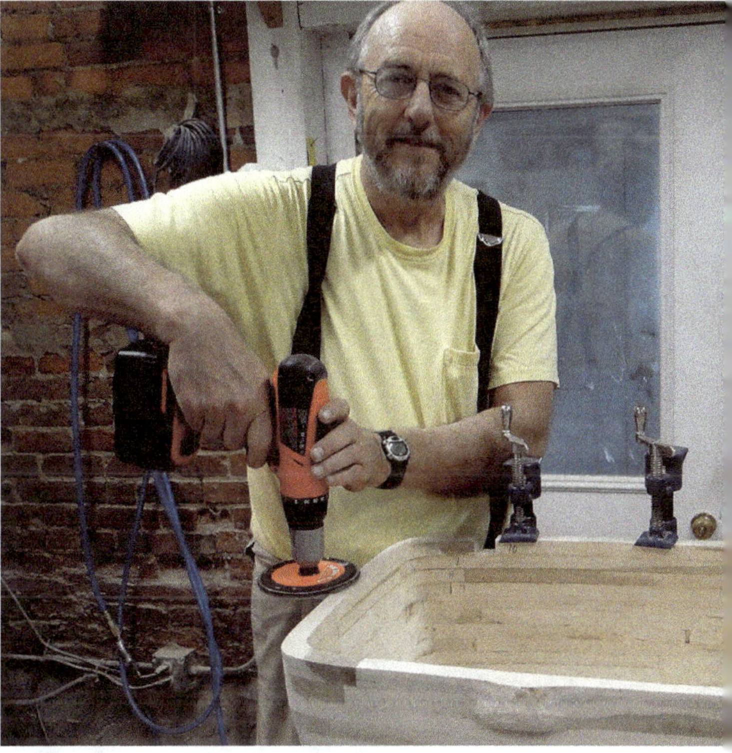

David Herrold in his workshop / Photo by Ryan Herrold.

David intended his printer to be an artist's tool, but remarked on how slow, along with its limited capabilities, the process actually was. He summed up his impressions as follows:

"It demonstrates a half step forward from the ancient potter's wheel to a future of digital 3D ceramic printers with vastly greater capabilities."

- David Herrold / 2007.

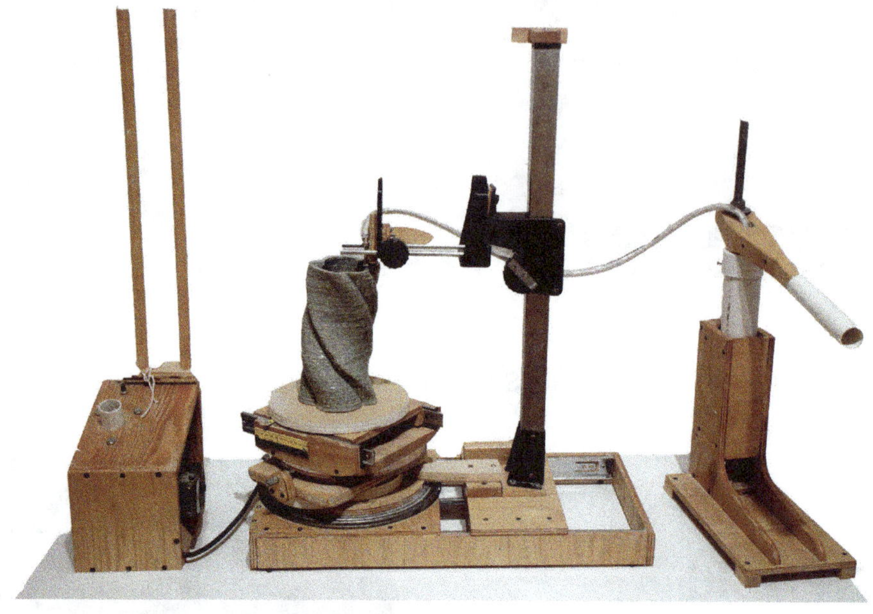

The Slip Jet Printer / Photo by David Herrold.

David created a complex shape by cutting it out of a flat piece of wood that he fitted on top of his pottery wheel. The guide that he used followed the outline of the shape and employed the use of a spring while the wheel was being turned manually. This contraption was connected to the nozzle of the Slip Jet Printer and mounted on a drawer rail which enabled it to move backwards and forwards. The flow of the clay was managed by manually pumping air into a clay container, pushing the clay through the pipe, and finally extruding it through the nozzle.

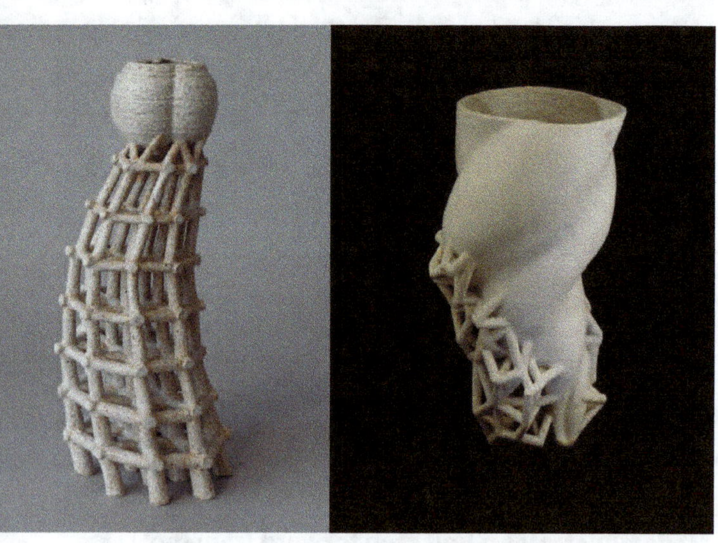

"Distressed Water Tower with Trestle" - 18 in (h) / "Seashell as Stressed Water Tower" - 18 in (h) / Porcelain and Slip Jet construction / 2004 / David Herrold.

Taken from David Herrold's Retrospective Exhibition Catalogue, these are to date some of the only images available of his artwork created with his Slip Jet Printer. David's artworks are revolutionary, drawing your eye in as you follow the sculpted stilts up to the extruded form. They seem to defy gravity with a quiet elegance, leaving the viewer with a lingering sense of intrigue.

"In graduate school, I figured if I was to achieve fame, I needed to be on the lookout for a signature style like Warhol's screen prints or Van Gogh's dots and dashes, or maybe even something huge like Cubism. I never found it. Eventually, just about everything becomes redundant. The age of 'isms' is over anyway".

- David Herrold / 2007.

Dr Adrian Bowyer

In 2007, Dr Adrian Bowyer and his team in Bath, England, created a machine that could 3D print and produce 60% of itself in parts. It was called the RepRap – Replicating Rapid Prototyper.

It is important to note that Dr Bowyer's printers were built for rapid prototyping in that they used various filament materials, none of which were intended for alternative materials such as clay. He, however, had laid the next foundation for paste extrusion enthusiasts (in this case, clay) to take the lead in digital coil building.

The RepRap was cost effective. In fact, if you already had such a machine, one could easily 3D print and build another. Dr Bowyer's team also made sure that the spare parts, (which were not 3D printed by the machine) but that were required in the building of the RepRap were easily attainable all over the world.

The designs for this self-replicating machine were released and made freely available to the public in the same year of manufacture, 2007.

The focus was to make manufacturing accessible to the poorest of nations which could then use their local resources to print, create and produce the items that they needed.

Variations of the design started popping up all over the world, and companies started selling "kits" to help individuals build and reproduce their own 3D printers.

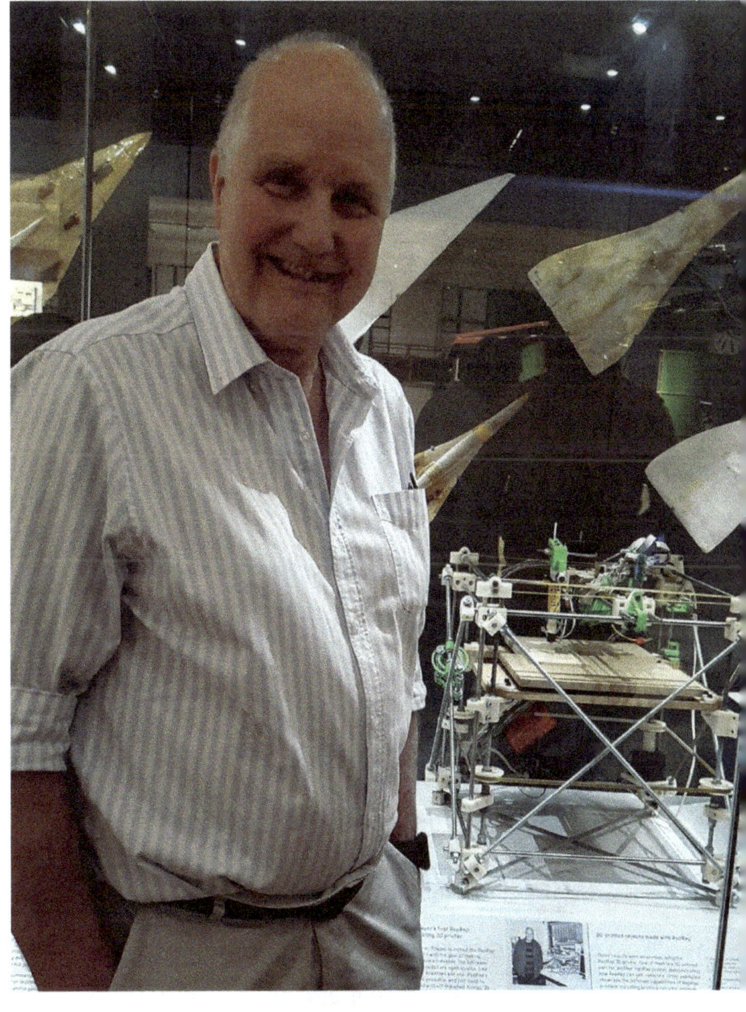

Dr Adrian Bowyer with the first RepRap machine in its display case at the London Science Museum / Photo by Mrs Bowyer.

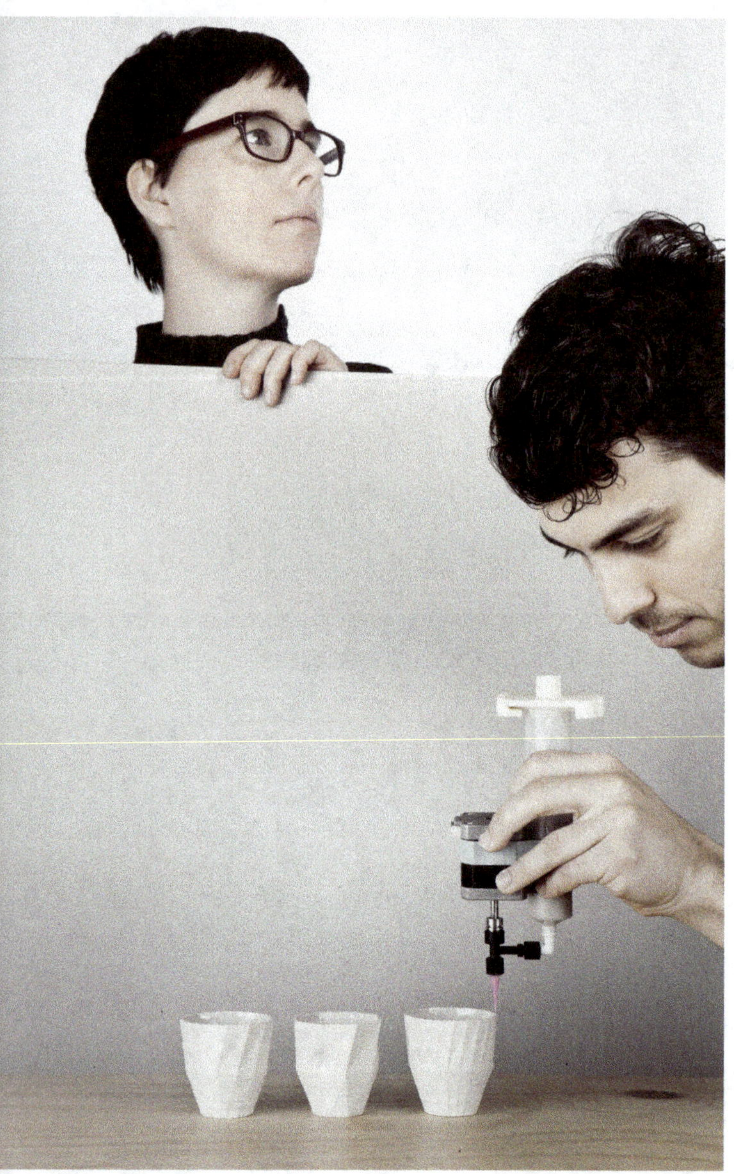

Photo by Kristof Vrancken / UNFOLD© / 2012.

Claire Warnier & Dries Verbruggen

This duo from UNFOLD, a design studio in Belgium, used one of the "kits" to build the 3D printer known as the RapMan (one of the many early modified versions of the RepRap). Looking at the future possibilities of paste extrusion, their relentless trial and error testing had finally paid off.

Their printer was the first digitally controlled extrusion ceramic 3D printer that could regulate the flow of clay by using compressed air pressure.

After both graduating from the Design Academy in Eindhoven, Claire and Dries founded UNFOLD in 2002. Here, they explored the "role of the designer and how it is changing at a time when design and manufacturing are becoming increasingly more digitized." - UNFOLD.

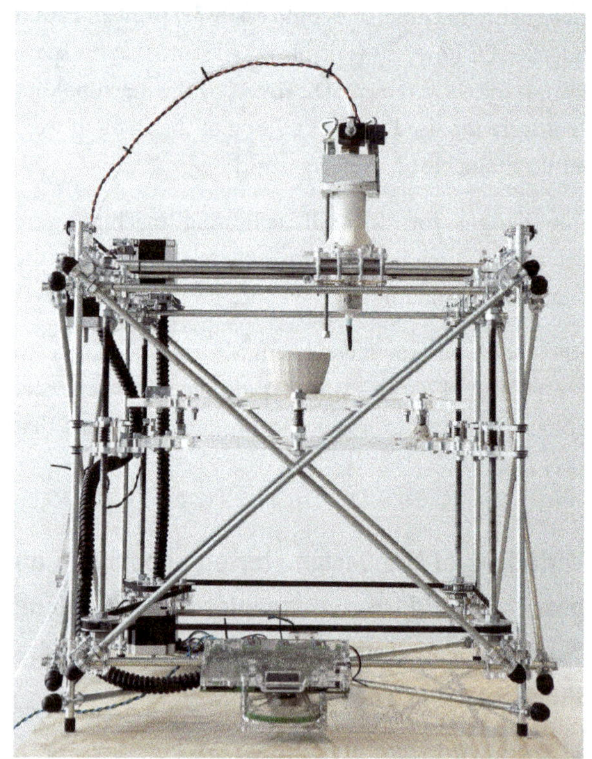

Ceramic 3D printer / Photo by Kristof Vrancken / Z33© / 2010.

Dries noted in an article that ceramists initially warned him that his prints would explode during the kiln firing process because of all the trapped air in the clay. His first completed firing, consisting of various tester prints, was achieved in early 2010. They had made it easily through all the firings!

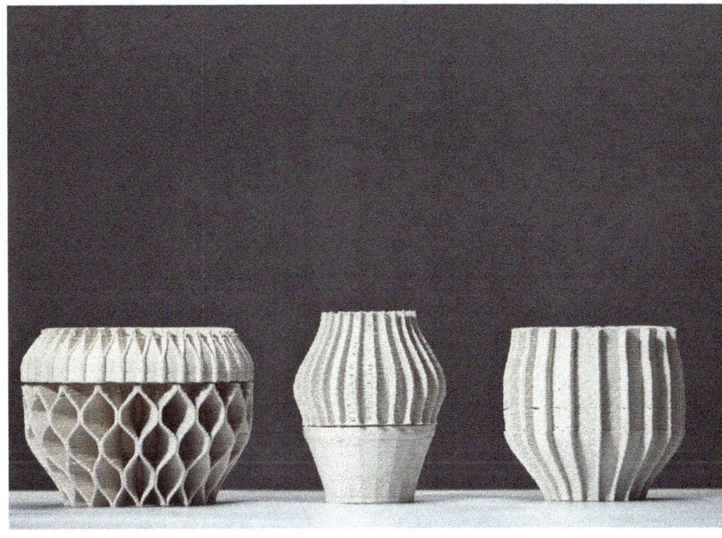

Clay 3D prints / Photo by Kristof Vrancken / UNFOLD© / 2012.

They were among the first to propose different extrusion models for clay; one such was a mechanised auger attached above the extruder nozzle. This type of attachment assists in regulating the movement of the clay through the nozzle and has to date greatly influenced the design of many clay 3D printers.

Claire and Dries went on to develop the first software tools to design and create toolpaths specifically designed for ceramic 3D printing. This experimental software, called G-code Stacker, was developed in conjunction with Tim Knapen. The toolpaths are designed in a vector drawing programme (e.g. Adobe Illustrator). From there they are loaded into the G-code Stacker, which allows for each 2D layer to be converted into a 3D layer. This enables the user to 3D print complex designs with intersecting lines that are usually difficult to achieve with the traditional slicing software.

If you are unfamiliar with the 3D design process, G-code, and the slicing software applications, you can learn more about these aspects in Chapter 6.

Clare and Dries's ceramic 3D printed works, including large interactive and collaborative installations, have been exhibited by and have acquired international fame through well-known institutions, some of which include the New Museum, New York (USA); the Yingge Ceramics Museum, Taipei (TW); the Design Museum, London (UK); Abu Dhabi Art (AE); the Istanbul Design Biennial (TR); the Jerusalem Museum (IL); and the Zuiderzeemuseum, Enkhuizen (NL).

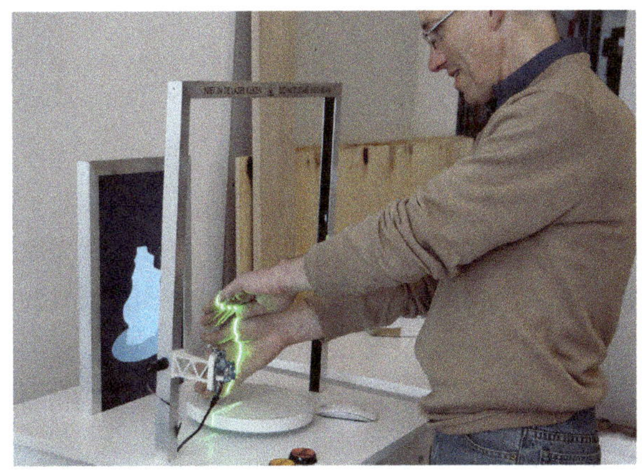

Jonathan Keep visiting UNFOLD in 2010, trying his hand at their Digital Pottery Wheel / UNFOLD©.

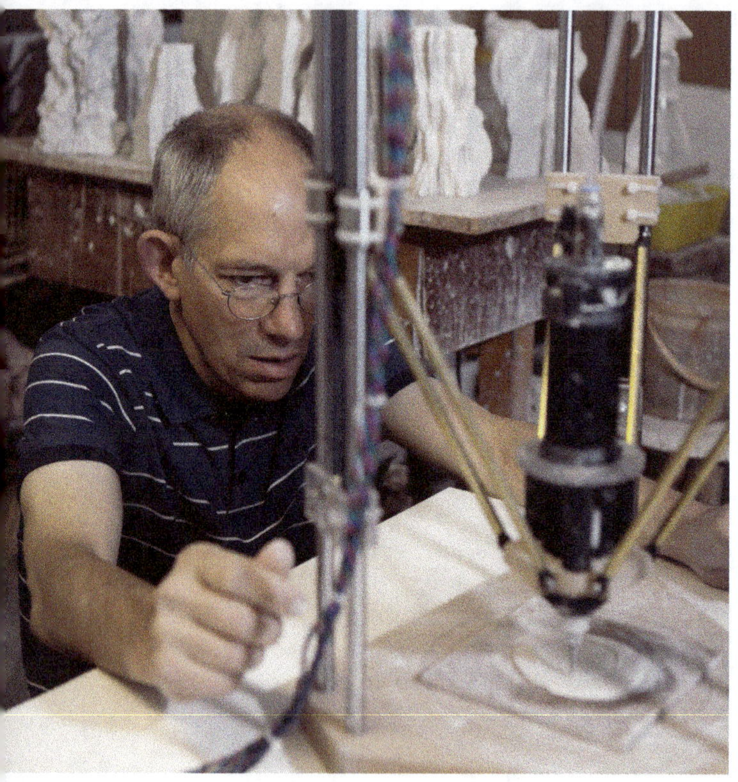

Jonathan Keep in his studio 3D printing with his custom-built ceramic 3D printer / 2016.

Jonathan Keep

Working primarily with form, Jonathan became increasingly frustrated with the limitations of the pottery wheel. In 1999, he first used 3D modelling software, opening the doors to exploring new ways of creating.

Jonathan is currently one of the most influential artists when it comes to clay 3D printing. He is classically trained in the art of pottery and in his later years started experimenting with the use of advanced technologies to create ceramic works that he says, "question the reality we create for ourselves."

Currently residing in the UK, he was born in South Africa, but moved abroad in 1986, where he went on to be awarded his MA from the Royal College of Arts in 2002.

"Normalising" these new ways of working, he is "quietly" getting these new techniques accepted as how traditional ceramics has moved on.

Knowing what the late David Herrold had achieved and awaiting Dr Bowyer's 3D printer, he started experimenting with analogue printing and paste extrusion by simply using a syringe!

Initially, he had first copied the UNFOLD RapMan kit conversion, and then proceeded to build his own ceramic 3D printer and mechanical ram extruder. Rather than use air pressure, it pushes the clay through the nozzle mechanically. Along with many of his other articles and research, he made all the building instructions freely available online. His knowledge of clay and the pottery process has made a huge impact on the industry, with some commercial companies even asking him to test their clay printers and to give feedback on their performance.

Jonathan Keep's ceramic 3D printer / 2013.

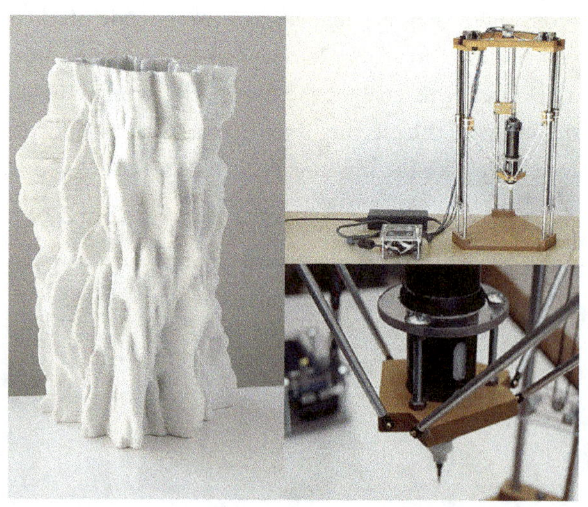

Danny Defelici

After retiring, Danny discovered clay 3D printing when it was still very much in its infancy. He decided to design and build an alternative approach when it came to building clay 3D printers – one that involved a mechanical extrusion system.

Living in Florida, in the United States of America, he is a self-taught artist, engineer, pilot, and inventor. An entrepreneur from the age of nineteen, he established and built-up companies in yacht building, aircraft manufacturing and robotics.

In 2015, he created the first manufactured direct drive clay extruder, which worked without air pressure. This type of machine allowed for thicker clay material to be pushed through the extruder, enabling larger print builds. His first manufactured printer was shipped early that same year.

Danny was not really interested in starting a new career. However, the huge demand for this new type of technology soon found him starting another business.

Having created 13 different machine designs for the ceramics 3D printing industry, 3D Potter is currently the only large-scale manufacturer of clay printers in the United States of America. Many of these are cartesian-type printers, with the Scara robotic arm being released in 2017. It has become one of their most successful machine designs to date. The various types of 3D printer builds and the differences between them are discussed in Chapter 4.

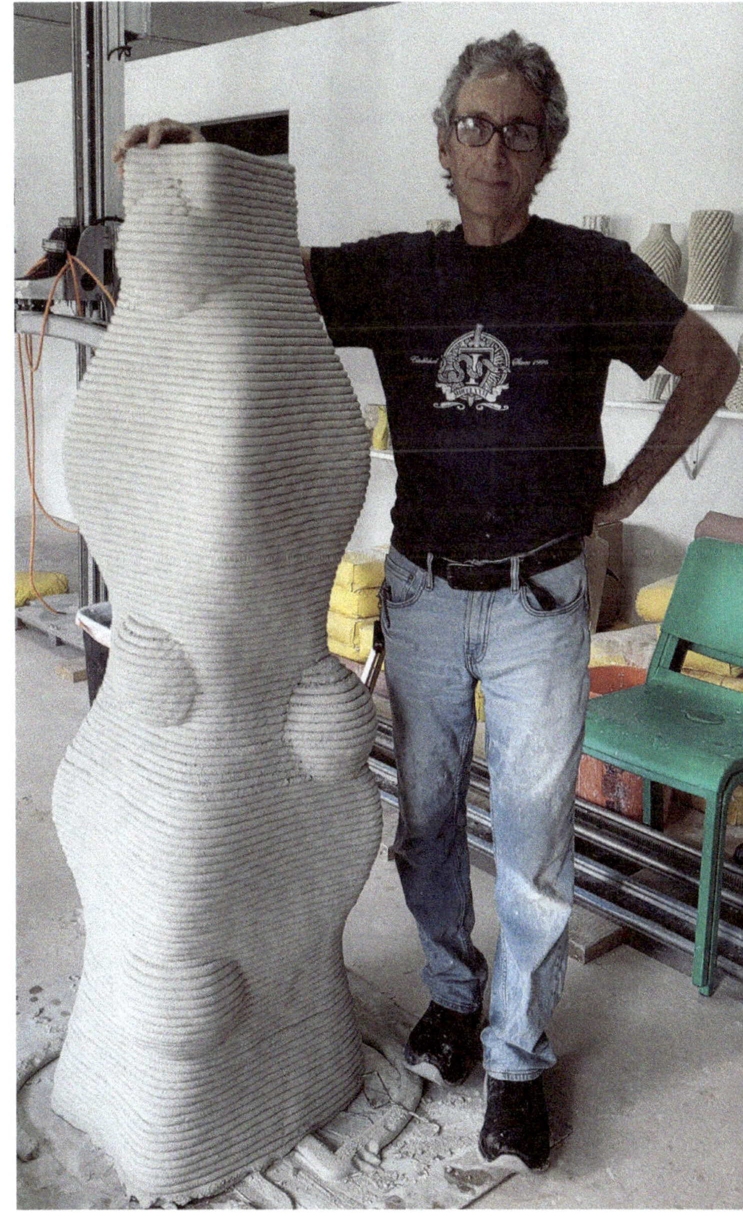

Danny Defelici / 3D Potter / 2023.

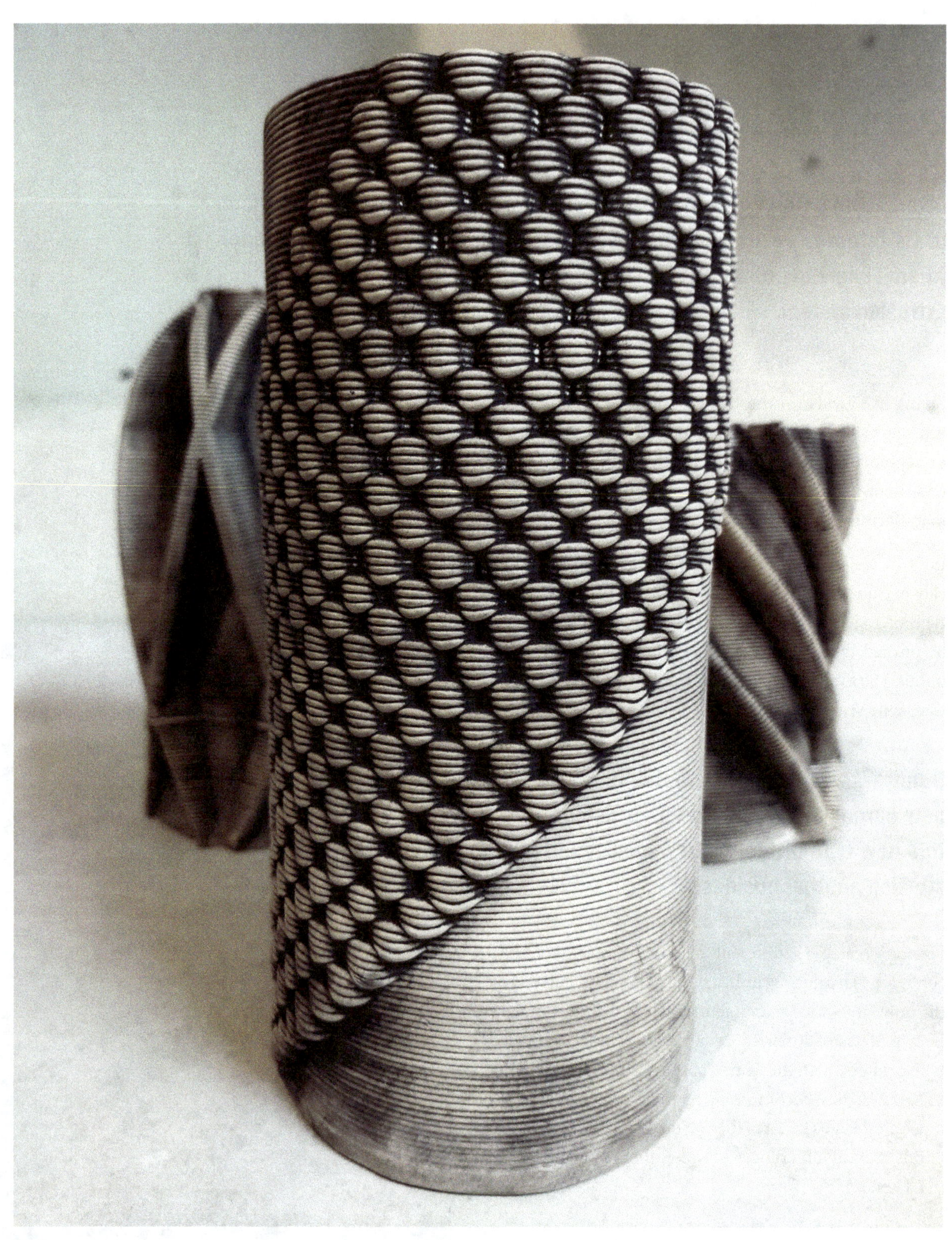

Vases / Hendrien Horn / 2021.

INDUSTRY LEADERS

Many of the companies that are building clay 3D printers for distribution around the world are continually involved in new and exciting technologies, innovative projects, and collaborations. Being interested in learning more about their 3D printer technology and processes, I decided to dive a bit deeper into their stories.

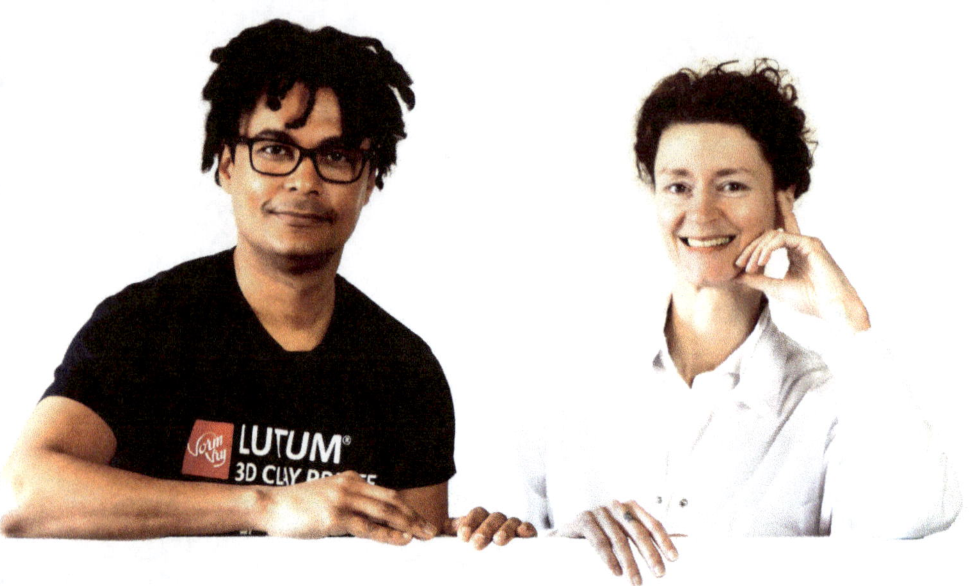

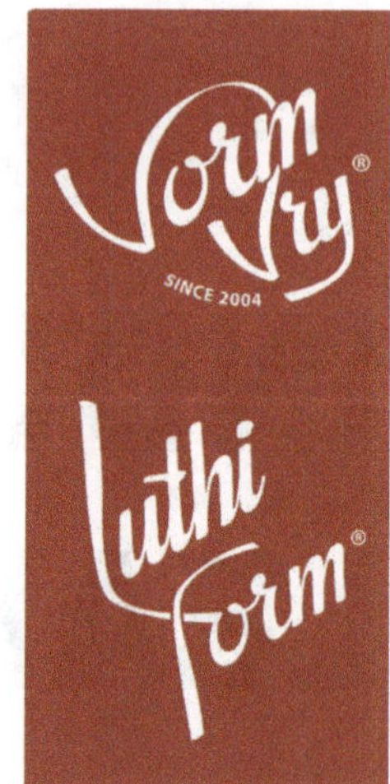

Yao van den Heerik and Marlieke Wijnakker / VormVrij® / 2020.

VORMVRIJ® & LUTHIFORM®

Yao van den Heerik & Marlieke Wijnakker

VormVrij® was formally established by Yao, and his wife, Marlieke Wijnakker, in 2017. After studying at the Design Academy in The Netherlands, they went abroad to do developmental work in West Africa. When it was time to move back home, they observed an increased interest in the 3D printing industry.

Intrigued by this concept, they bought their first plastic filament printer, but found it frustrating to use with its slow mechanics, along with the smell of heated plastic. Marlieke at the time had developed a growing interest in exploring pottery, but with not enough space for both a pottery wheel and a 3D printer in their home, Yao suggested that he build a clay 3D printer.

The couple enjoyed printing and selling their creations at fairs, always taking the machine along to do demonstrations. To their surprise, more interest was paid to the machine itself than to the 3D printed objects that they were selling. They decided to shift their focus to the equipment and related mechanics rather than to the actual clay 3D printing.

Their first fifty odd 3D printers were built for clients who were fully aware that each 3D printer produced would be improved upon with the next production build. Companies with industrial sized printers that were very slow and difficult to manage also started asking for assistance. At this time, various extrusion materials were being used by these companies in their 3D printers.

This flow of income enabled VormVrij® to modify and produce the LUTUM® 4M, as it is known today. "We refocused on - how do I want to use it, rather than how can I construct it best?"

- Yao van den Heerik / 2023.

With the global distribution and growth of VormVrij® over the past ten years, the company is now celebrating the rebrand of their company name, as LuthiForm®. This will make it easier for people from all over the world to be introduced to their products and workshops.

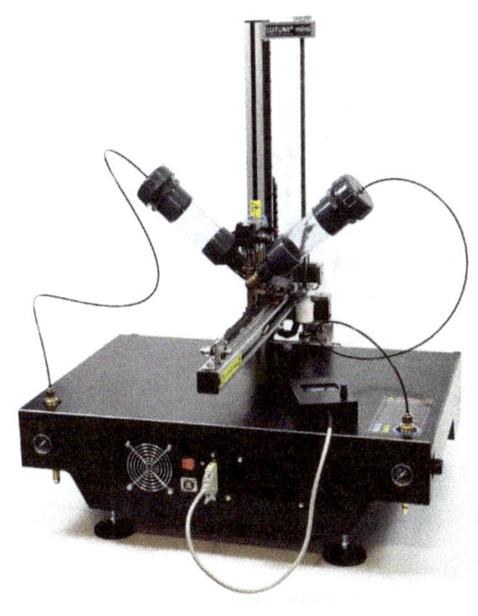

Prototype of the LUTUM® 2 / VormVrij® / 2016.

Design Features of the LUTUM®

Their background in design is evident in the features that VormVrij® has introduced, such as the touchscreen. You may think that a touchscreen could never work because working with clay can be messy. As an experienced clay maker, I can honestly say that your hands can to a large extent stay clean as long as you understand your workflow. Yao does not shy away from mentioning that this addition does indeed increase the price of the printers.

For this reason, they decided to include a base on the LUTUM® 4M printer that can at a later stage be used to attach the touchscreen as an extra add on. Depending on your budget and taking the small-time maker into consideration, you can buy the LUTUM® v4.6 that has the touchscreen already attached.

One of the defining features of the LUTUM® range of 3D printers is that the clay is held in a sealed container on top of the extruder. This allows the clay to be near the exit point and in a stable condition, thus allowing for detailed and precision printing. The 3D printer uses air pressure, allowing the compression of the clay in the container above the extruder to stabilise.

A unique capability of the LUTUM® 5M is that it can scan the surface (e.g. a plaster tile), on which it needs to print in advance. Often these tiles may look straight and flat, but as you print, you may notice that they are not perfect. After scanning the surface, the printer adjusts the first clay print layer automatically according to the surface, which keeps your hands clean!

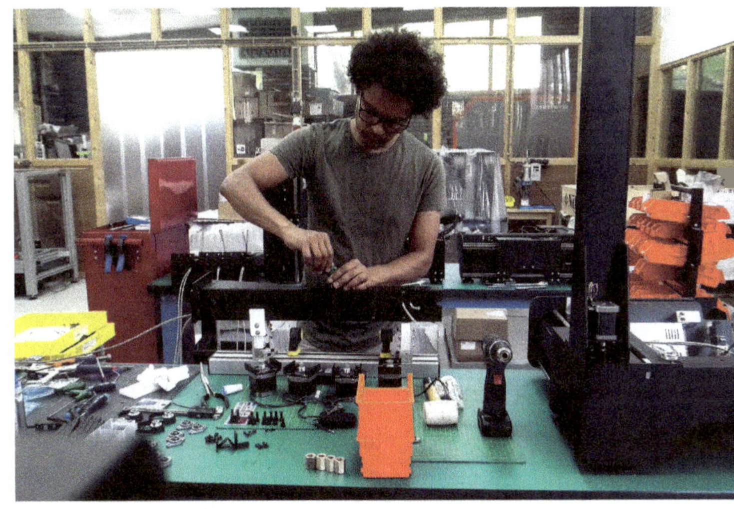

Yao in his workshop / VormVrij® / 2022.

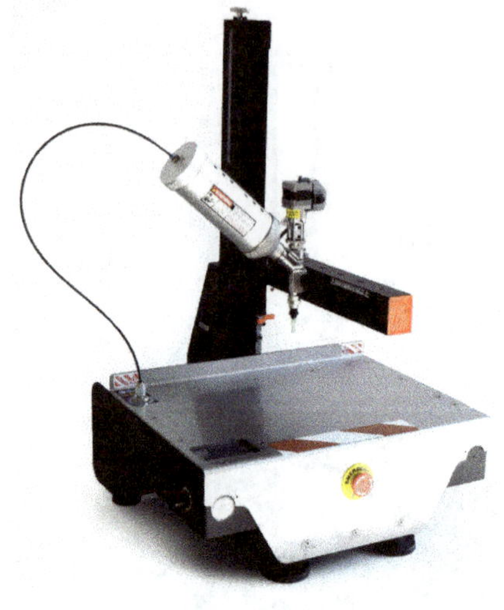

LUTUM® 4M Pro / VormVrij® / 2023.

Yao recommends the LUTUM® 4M and LUTUM® v4.6 for both hobbyists and those working with the printer daily. The LUTUM® 5M is built as an industrial grade printer, allowing for precision printing when it comes to creating exceptionally detailed objects. It is very stable and prints quickly.

The LUTUM® Eco Clay Extruder

The extruder used on all LUTUM® 3D printers is made of stainless steel. This makes it durable and able to print higher quality prints. The addition of the stainless-steel auger in 2019, which replaced the old steel-bronze auger, improved the tolerance levels of the extruder. Striving to make extruders more affordable, the Eco Clay Extruder is perfect for makers creating smaller DIY projects that require high quality printed results.

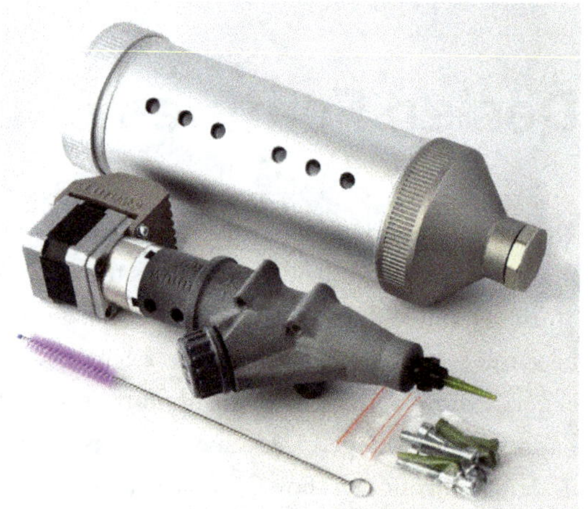

LUTUM® Eco Clay Extruder / VormVrij® / 2020.

Schools

VormVrij® collaborates with certain schools in The Netherlands to integrate clay 3D printing into the curriculum. An interesting point that Yao commented on was that it is common knowledge that all children have different capabilities when it comes to creating something from scratch. Clay 3D printing levels out the playing field, allowing children with different skill sets to participate, appreciate, and learn, making it an inclusive process for everyone.

VormVrij® intuitively designed and added a cup to their 3D printer package for schools. After a day of 3D printing, the steel extruder can be placed in a cup of water, which makes clean-ups a breeze! Often, teachers, who do not have the time to waste on cleaning can merely remove the extruder from the water the next day and start 3D printing immediately.

In conjunction with the wide overview of the process pertaining to their printers, VormVrij® provides workshops and training for individuals and groups. Their demonstrations show how their printers can be finetuned to create different shapes. Furthermore, they share tips and tricks that are invaluable to any apprentice clay 3D maker.

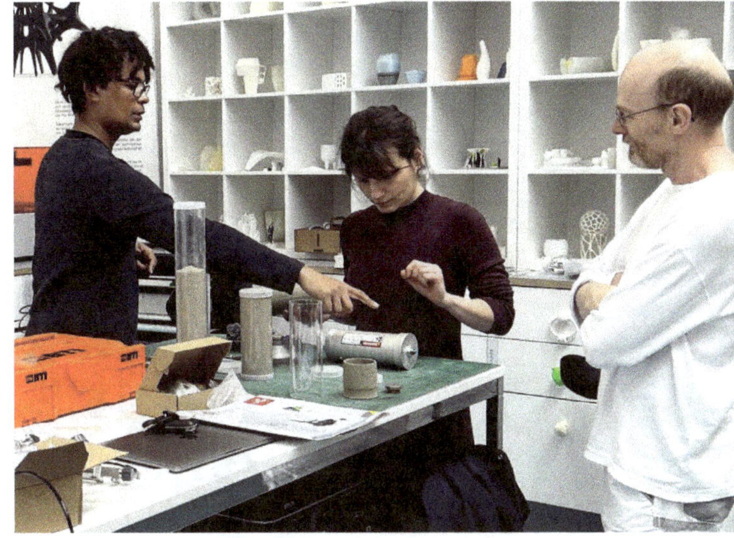

Presenting a workshop / Photo by Lisa Freyschmidt / 2023.

Clay Busts

Along with their printers, VormVrij® also print and sculpt clay busts on request. This all started when a well-established doctor ordered a bust to be displayed in his offices after his retirement. He did not want to sit for the sculpture and instead requested a 3D print. After a 3D scan of his features, the clay print was completed in only a few days. At the time, the final clay prints were rather rough because of the limited technical capabilities of the 3D printer. at the time. However, Marlieke was able to perfect the bust by sculpting the rest of it by hand.

VormVrij® soon found themselves with an influx of requests from businessmen and even parents, who wanted sculptures of their children, who couldn't sit still for long periods of time. The display window at their office allows passers-by to observe the detailed sculptural work created by Marlieke.

The many changes and add-ons that VormVrij® have introduced to their machines, have resonated with me as an artist. There is an in-depth thought process supporting each modification. With the clay maker constantly in the back of their minds, I appreciate their end-user mindset.

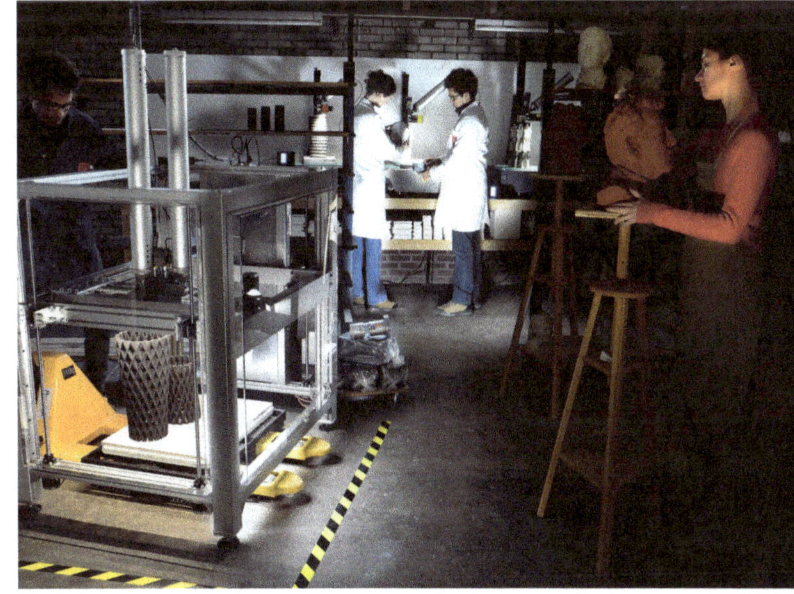

VormVrij® / 2020.

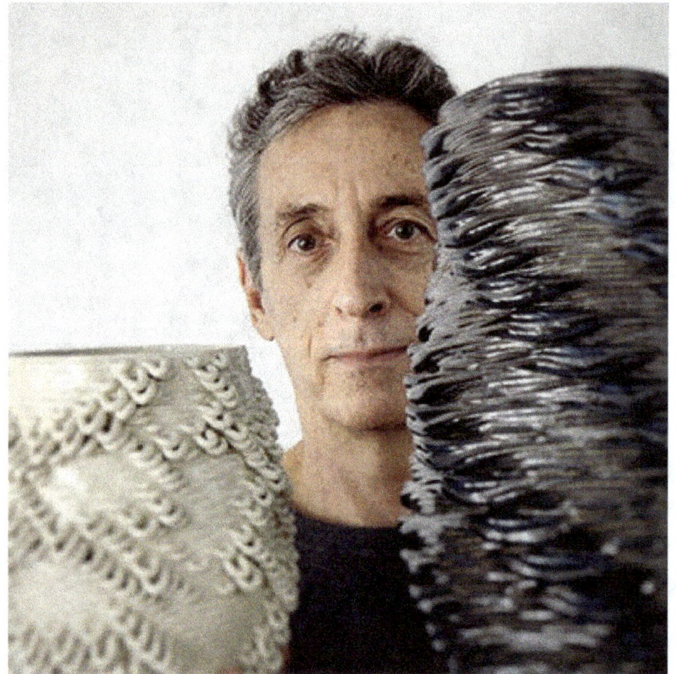

Danny Defelici / 3D Potter / 2021.

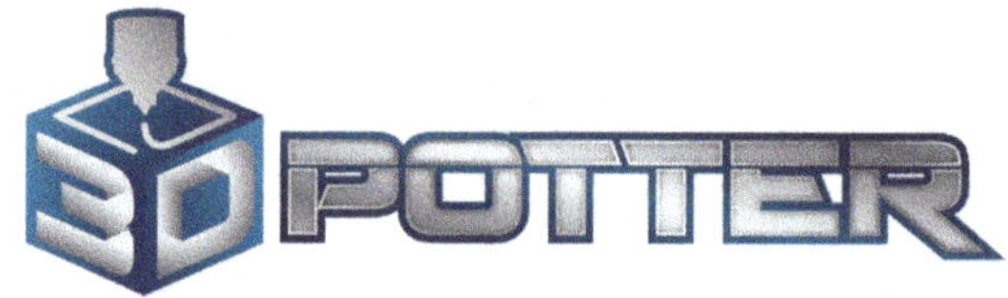

3D POTTER

Danny Defelici

Danny Defelici established 3D Potter in 2015, with the launch of his direct drive extruder. The business started growing largely through word of mouth, universities, private institutions, inventors from across the globe, and all those individuals and institutions interested in experimenting with 3D printing technologies.

Clay as a material must contain water for it to attain a consistency that allows for 3D printing. A strong force is required in extruding drier clays, with air pressure not always being sufficient in this regard. The mechanical extruders of the 3D Potter printers can, however, exert a strong force, thus enabling a tube of drier and heavier clay to be 3D printed. In so doing, the clay material can be printed at a faster rate, with more stable layer adhesion, and allowing for the printing of larger objects in less time.

The consistency of the clay used during the 3D printing process is similar to that used by potters on their pottery wheels. The clay tube is placed in a cannister above the nozzle, which allows for the direct flow of the clay. The use of the mechanical extruder does not cause the clay flow to fluctuate. This ensures for a consistent outflow which in turn creates clay layers of equal thickness from the start to the end of the print.

The design of the 3D printers makes it possible for the clay maker directing the operation to move around the 3D printers during the printing process - making it easier to adjust or modify the clay body mid-print.

The PotterBot Pro / 3D Potter.

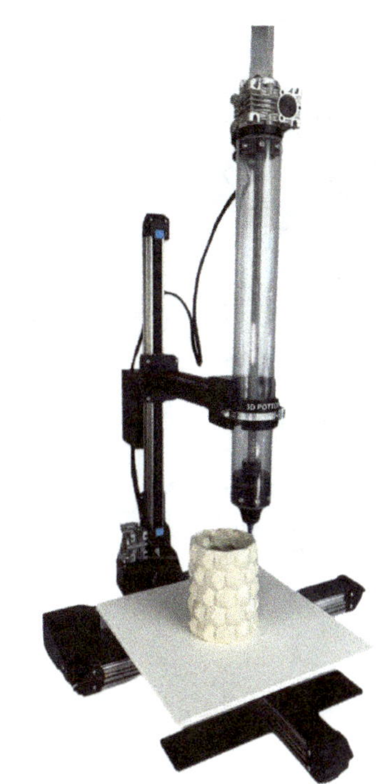

PotterBot printers

As a beginner hobbyist, Danny suggested that one should start with one of these two printers - naturally, with your budget having an impact on the final decision. The PotterBot Micro is small and capable of extruding 1 000ml of clay since the extruder is driven by a stepper motor. The PotterBot Pro, on the other hand, is more expensive but has more advanced capabilities than the Micro. It has a heavy duty closed loop stepper motor that exerts more pressure. Thus, it can print with even thicker clay and can extrude up to 2 000ml in one print run. These clay 3D printers are often sold to laboratories where they are used for experiments in material testing.

Other printers include the PotterBot Super (3 600ml) and the PotterBot XL (4 000ml). The PotterBot Super can also be purchased with the Auger System that ensures a continuous flow of material to the printer, allowing for accelerants to be added during the printing process.

Scara printers

The line of Scara (Selective Compliance Robotic Arm Assembly) 3D printers does not have a print bed, allowing for the printer to stand on a table or on the floor, depending on the size and weight of the printed object. Many of the print beds for 3D printers have a weight limit, which influences how much material can be extruded for a single print. This was the main reason why the Scara printer was developed. It can print 360°, thus enabling it to be placed on the inside of the object it prints. With its continuous feeding system, multiple prints can be completed during a single print run.

Scara printers use the same procedures and software as the PotterBot 3D printers, and anyone who understands the basics of 3D printing will be able to operate it. Two industrial grade harmonic drives (like the robotic arms used in car manufacturing) are built into the Scara to help with the rotation of the arm during the printing process. These also allow the printer to run at high speeds, with accuracy and precision, and for long periods of time. The Scara printers are built for industrial use and, to their credit, even their first-generation machines have not needed replacement.

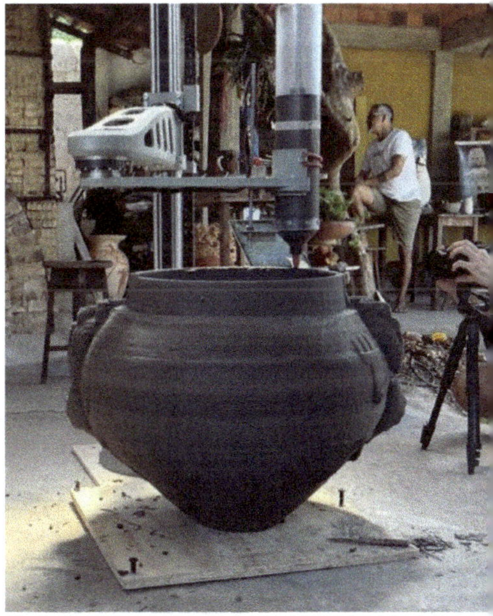

The Scara printing large pot / Barcelona 3D Ceramics / Atlas of lost finds / 2022.

"Even though the Scara looks like a complex robotic machine, you do not need an engineering degree to operate it." - Denis Graaf / Tech. Support.

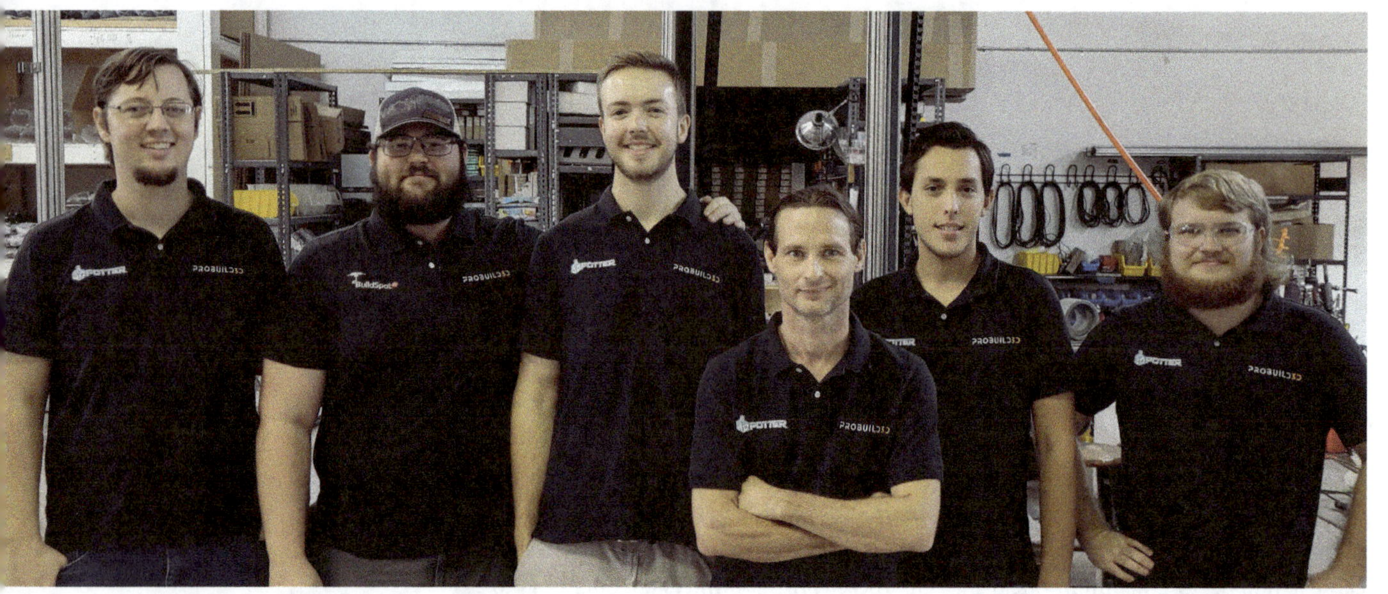

The 3D Potter Team / 3D Potter / 2023.

Training and distribution

3D Potter has distribution centres in the United States of America, Australia, Europe and the United Kingdom, with expansions on the horizon as their customer base progressively expands across the globe. Apart from being used by the small-time hobbyist and maker, their printers are used in numerous industries, including NASA, a large chocolate manufacturer, US Aerospace and Defence companies, as well as in various tertiary institutions.

3D Potter is gearing up to move into a new space that is four times larger than their current premises. The company is splitting in two. One part will be dedicated to the construction industry, while the other will focus on new types of 3D printing technologies.

In-house training for the large-scale printers will be available on site, whereas in the past they had to travel to clients if required. Currently, these printers have a dedicated YouTube channel where they post tips for first-time clay makers (e.g. How to 3D design and to use the slicing software paired with their line of printers). They also produce videos responding to questions and upload them for the public.

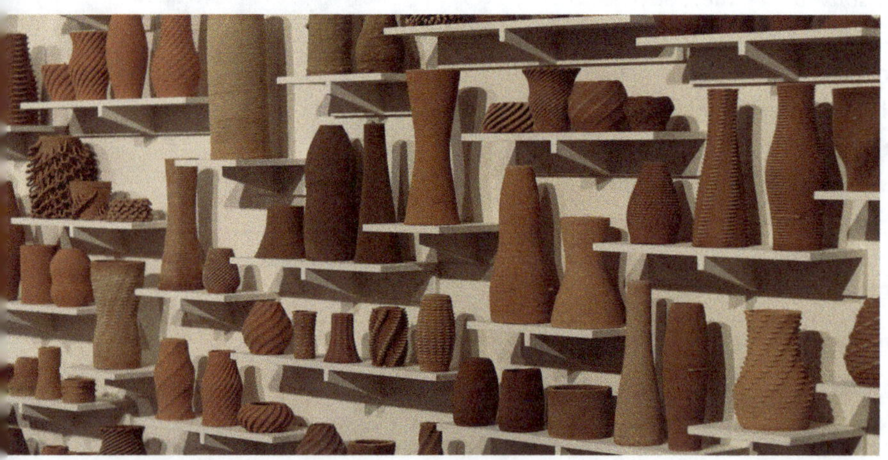

Clay wall / University of Texas at El Paso / Olalekan Jeyifous / 2019.

Innovation within construction

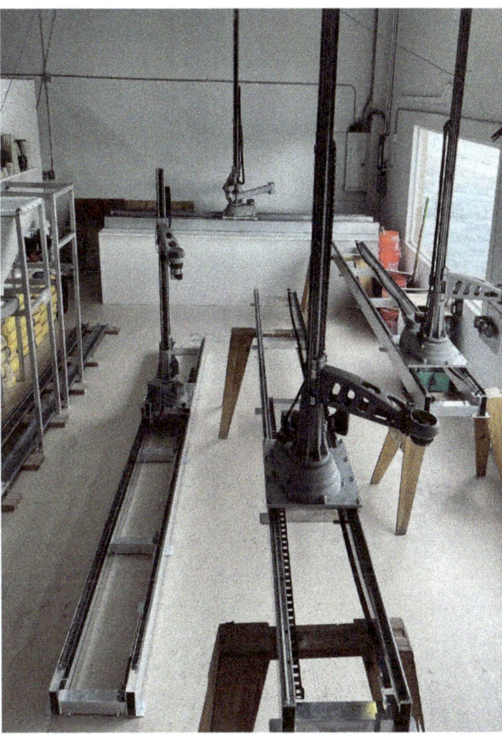

The Roadrunner system / 3D Potter / 2023.

3D Potter is exploring cost-effective strategies to develop low-income housing for working class or impoverished people. Together with Sika, a construction company that has developed environmentally friendly cementitious materials for large scale 3D printing, they are cutting the cost of supplying this type of technology and machinery. Some of these large-scale industrial machines for 3D printing houses cost well over one million dollars (USA) each.

The large robotic arms used for construction take several days to set up. Cranes and a handful of people are in fact needed to operate them. This can be a costly process, to the effect that PotterBot, in conjunction with a sister company, has developed the Roadrunner System.

The Roadrunner System allows for the Scara printer to run on a set of rails covering a large area when 3D printing parts.

By mobilising the printer, it is uniquely positioned to cut the cost of production, leaving many in the construction industry surprised at the low cost of approximately $30 000 (USA) for the developed system. It has been stated that the ability to produce parts of printed interiors, both on and off site, goes beyond continuous pumping; "it goes into continuous assembly."

Some of the materials produced by Sika harden much faster, allowing parts to be 3D printed and assembled in real time, thus reducing the time needed for construction. Compared to the days required to dismantle some of the larger robots, the dismantling of this system takes only a few hours. I believe this is a viable system for countries such as South Africa, where theft is a daily occurrence. Large robots would require extra security and push up construction costs when not in operation and if left to stand in remote areas.

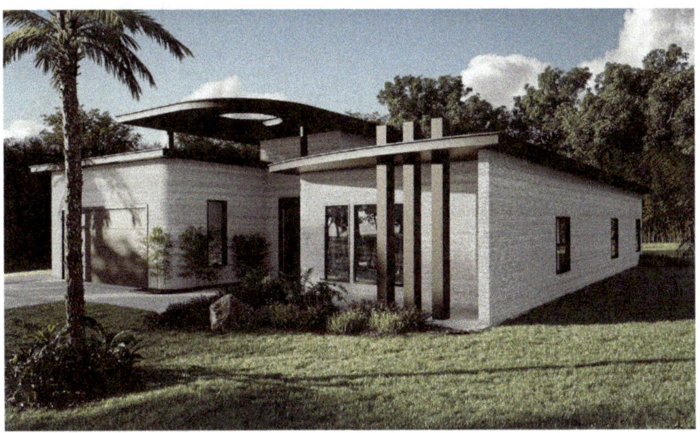

An architectural rendering for a 3D printed house / 3D Potter / 2023.

"I am a habitual adventurer, and, in the future, there will be more and more iterations of these amazing machines."

- Danny Defelici / 2023.

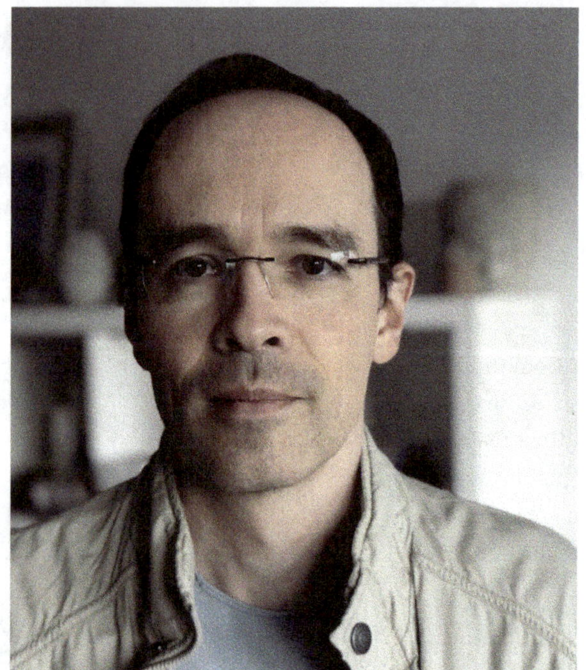

Anatoly Berezkin / Photo by Gabriel Steinmann / 2020.

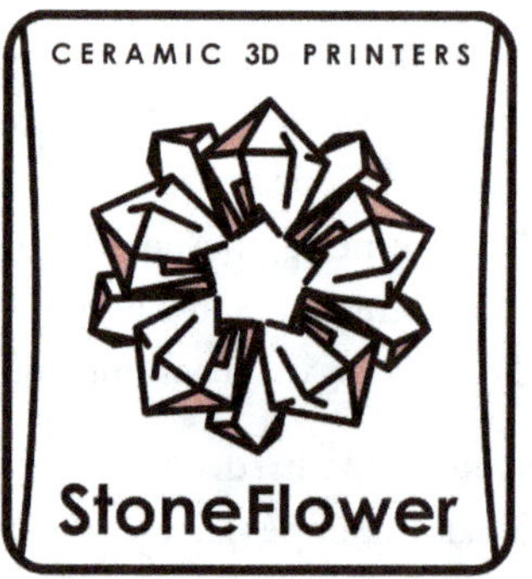

STONE FLOWER

Anatoly Berezkin

Whilst working in the field of theoretical and experimental physics, Anatoly Berezkin has also been professionally involved with the development of novel 3D printing technologies since 2011. Interested in generative design while studying at university, he had a great appreciation for art. He also witnessed firsthand what a custom-built clay 3D printer could do when he saw artworks 3D printed from clay by Olivier van Herpt - an artist from Eindhoven in The Netherlands.

"It was so impressive and unusual because as a material scientist if you told me that a material that tends to flow can be 3D printed, I would say, of course not! It would just fall into a pile and won't work, but it did, and it was like magic." - Anatoly Berezkin / 2023.

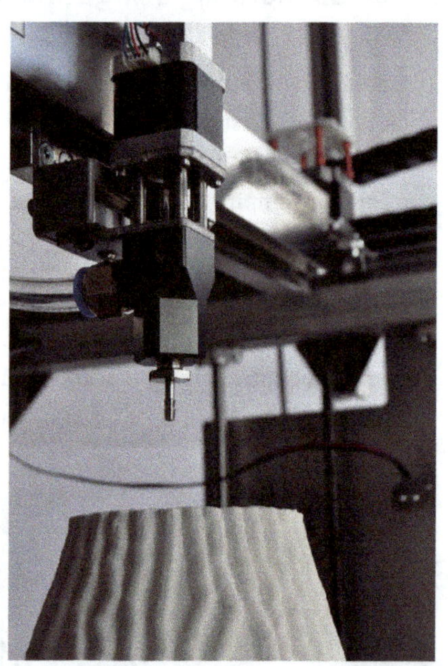

Stone Flower 4.0.

Anatoly started to experiment with clay and built his first cartesian clay 3D printer in 2017. He noted that it was a very exciting time, yet contraptions such as an exploding air pressure canister quickly made him rethink his safety measures and he proceeded to build a mechanical extruder system that required no air pressure. His first prototype was a "polished clone" of Jonathan Keep's design.

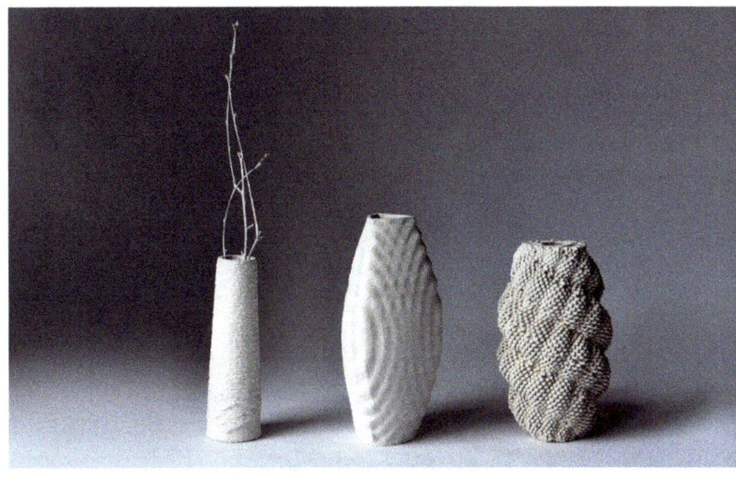
Intricate vases / Stone Flower / 2018.

This re-design made the printer easily portable as the extra machinery did not include an air compressor.

Anatoly enjoyed the newfound technology that he developed. Wanting to show his love of art by building a machine that could print with precision, he determined that the cartesian printer setup and build was cost-effective and could achieve the level of accuracy he desired.

Taking the first steps towards commercialising this technology, he started off with a "Ceramic 3D Printing KIT", a clay printing add-on for desktop FDM 3D printers, that gained notoriety after a Kickstarter campaign in 2018. A year later, in 2019, his clay 3D printer, the Stone Flower 3.0, started to be distributed and sold globally.

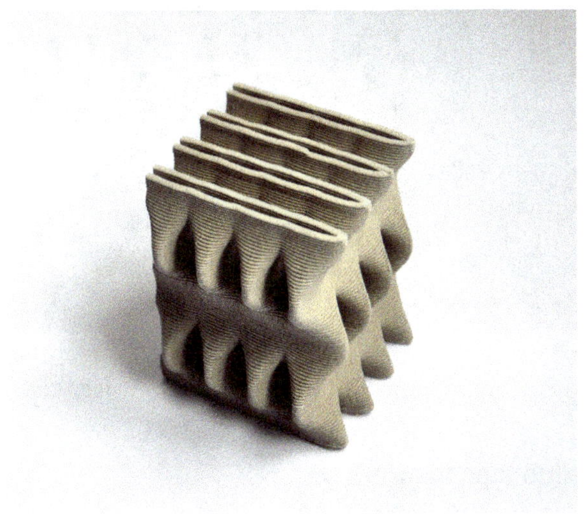
Vibrations / Stone Flower / Anatoly Berezkin.

Anatoly's efforts were widely supported by the maker community of the ceramic 3D printing forum on the Google Plus platform.

"At Google Plus, weak and strong points of new technologies were discussed and shared in real time, as they were being developed. Makers were receiving unbiased information about the advantages and disadvantages of technically complex solutions and products. The degree of presence of various companies on the forum reflected their willingness to play fair. For technically complex products, this was an unusually transparent situation, and probably the first time in human history where this has happened. Unfortunately, at a later stage, Google Plus ceased to exist. The clay 3D printing forum now continues on Wikifactory."

- Anatoly Berezkin / 2023.

Stone Flower 4.0

In April, 2021, the new Stone Flower 4.0 was released with a larger build volume. Built from stronger and more durable parts, the upgraded safety features allows for prints with multiple extrusion pastes, and not just clay.

The Stone Flower 4.0 has a print volume of 50cm x 50cm x 50cm, with a height that can be extended to 80cm on request. It also features a touchscreen that can be orientated on a table or a floor during the installation process making the setup so much easier.

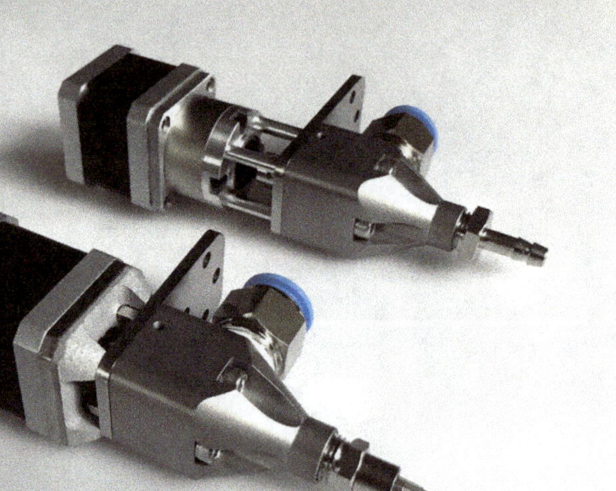

Print head / Stone Flower / 2023.

Concrete 3D Printer

The Stone Flower Concrete 3D Printer comes with a 50l continuous mortar pump. It can print up to widths of 150cm, depths of 300cm and heights of 120cm. The print head is capable of depositing rapidly hardening two-component mixtures, with a grain size of up to 7mm.

Custom builds and starter kits

I asked Anatoly if he does custom builds, and he said "Yes, in fact I am busy with one right now." He turned his laptop towards a cartesian printer standing in the nearby corner that had rather a large build volume. He remarked that concrete printing is starting to show more promise and that his next generation of printers will be more focused on extruding larger volumes of material.

Stone Flower also sells various components and starter kits to makers all over the world, enabling them to build their own printers. The Print Head 6 and 6R are manufactured from stainless steel, making them more durable and corrosion-resistant, and allowing them to be used with more abrasive pastes, such as concrete. They include a durable and chemical resistant two-flute auger screw with a variety of metallic nozzles.

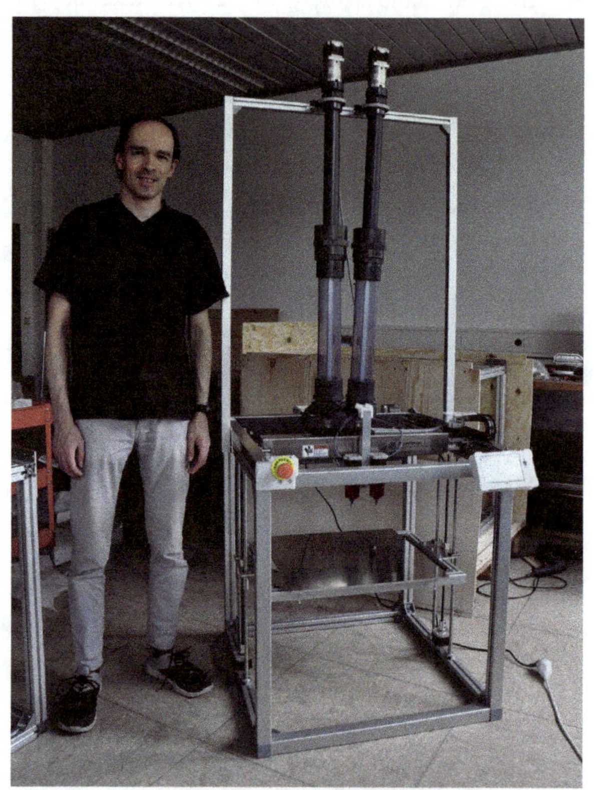

A dual extrusion 3D printer / Stone Flower.

Anatoly's admiration and respect for those who influenced his work when he started building his own machines is notable. He continues to adapt the existing technologies to compliment his printer builds.

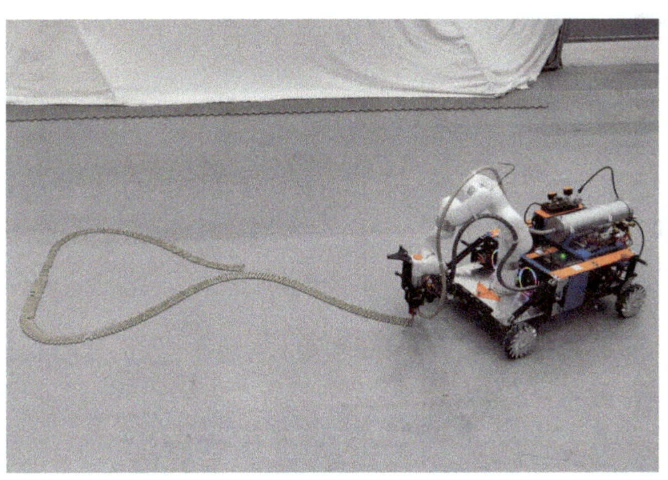

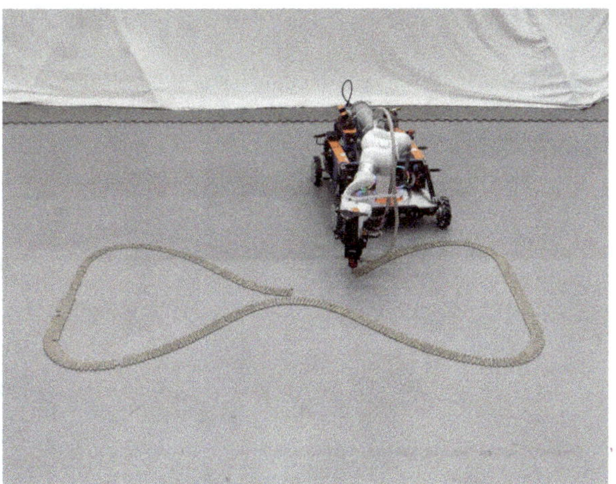

The "Armstone" robot was built by Julius Sustarevas in 2022. Originally from Lithuania, Julius completed his studies and doctoral degree at the University College of London where he built the robot for autonomous mobile 3D printing.

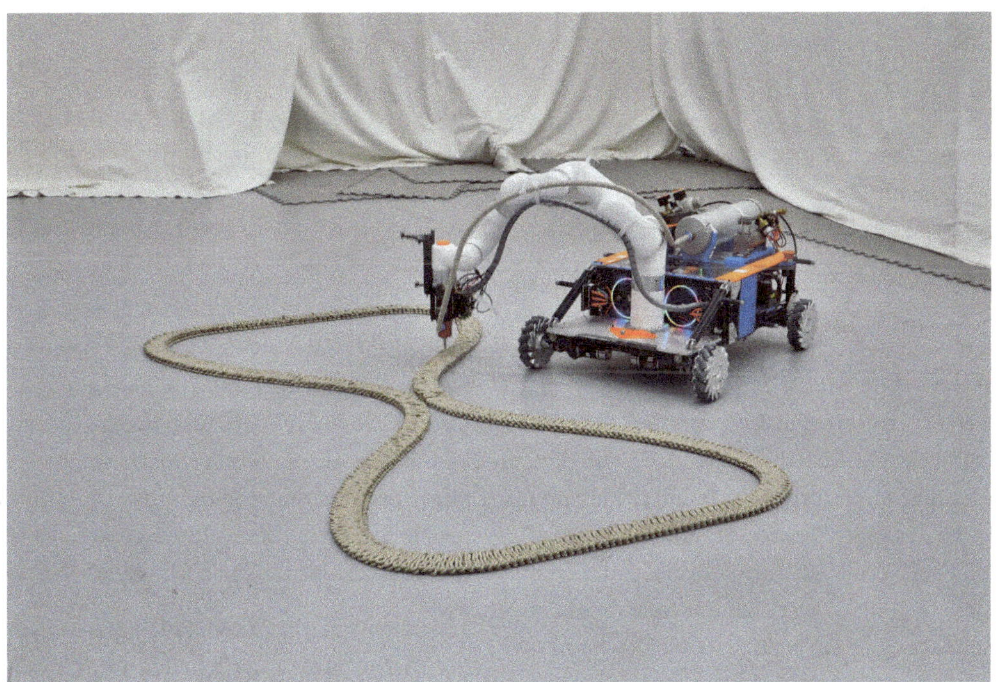

The "Armstone" robot / Julius Sustarevas / 2022.

The "Armstone" robot is a mobile manipulator that features the print head from Stone Flower. The robot is given a pre-coded nozzle path and computes how to achieve this path whilst avoiding collisions (e.g. with the already printed material).

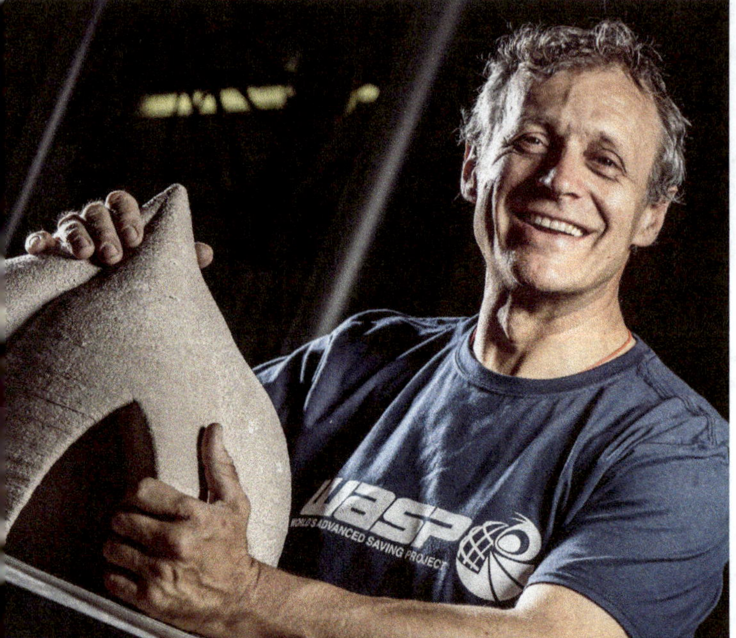

Massimo Moretti / WASP®.

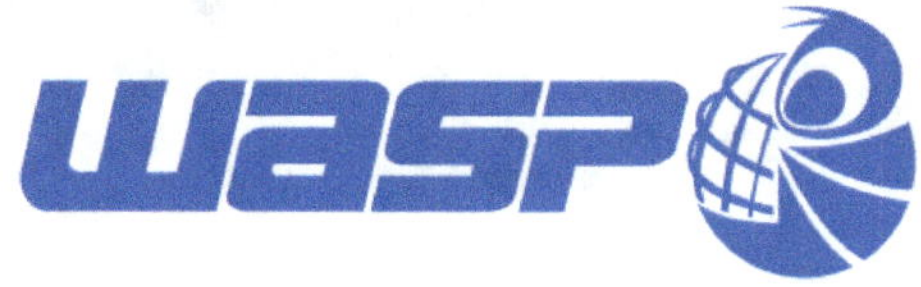

WASP®

Massimo Moretti

Massimo grew up enjoying his early years in the mechanical workshop of his father, at their home, as he built items that brought his peers together. He graduated as an electronics technician in 1974 and then began developing various products. In 2012, Massimo along with his daughter, Francesca, and a group of young designers, founded the World's Advanced Saving Project (WASP®). Their goal was to address the fundamental needs of people. Aspects such as homes/ shelters, access to food to promote energy levels and good health, employment, and fulfilment through art and culture were targeted through technology.

With the world's population growing rapidly and concerns of CO2 emissions emanating from concrete construction, the need for innovative solutions for housing is more pressing than ever.

Millions of people worldwide are still without housing, and natural disasters and conflict exacerbate an already dire situation. WASP® first began by designing and building small printers, using these proceeds to fund larger printers that could be used in projects to help people live better, in healthier conditions, and to lead more sustainable lives in harmony with nature.

The potter wasp, an insect which gets its name from the pot-shaped nests that it builds from locally available materials, served as the inspiration for WASP® to develop large 3D printers to create low-cost housing modules, using natural materials. Initially perceived as a far-fetched idea, the method of using local wet earth additive columbine techniques, and sun drying provided an answer to reliable sustainable building.

40100 Clay Production System

WASP® introduced an innovative automated system in 2021 that enables the serialised production of ceramic materials using additive technology. The system was inspired by the need to print 3 000 pots in a short period of just over three months. It features a continuous material supply system that allows for uninterrupted printing and an automatic part removal system, making it possible to carry out large production runs with ease. Thanks to this breakthrough, WASP® are now able to push the boundaries of additive manufacturing, enabling the mass production of clay parts.

In 2023, WASP® introduced their "Digital Factory", a comprehensive system that, in conjunction with 3D printing, allows for mass production where even small-time artisans can become manufacturers. To make it even more accessible, they have developed the WASP® App. By simplifying the design and export processes, WASP® are empowering small manufacturers to design and produce items, helping them to develop their business capacity.

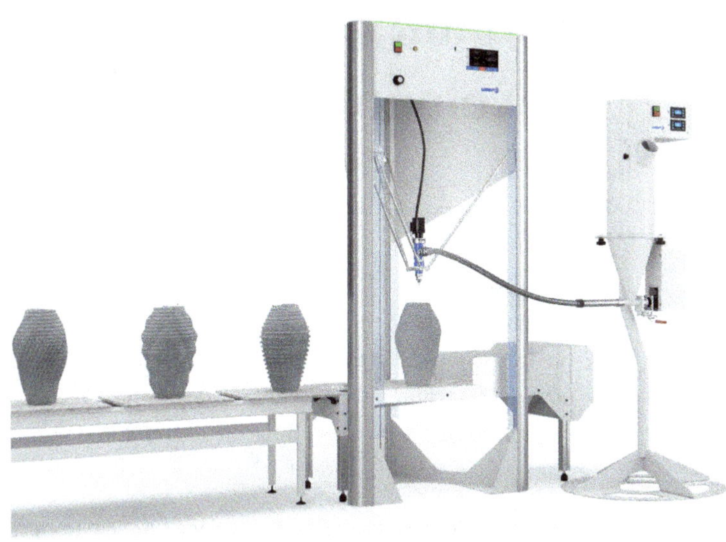

40100 Clay Production System / WASP® / 2023.

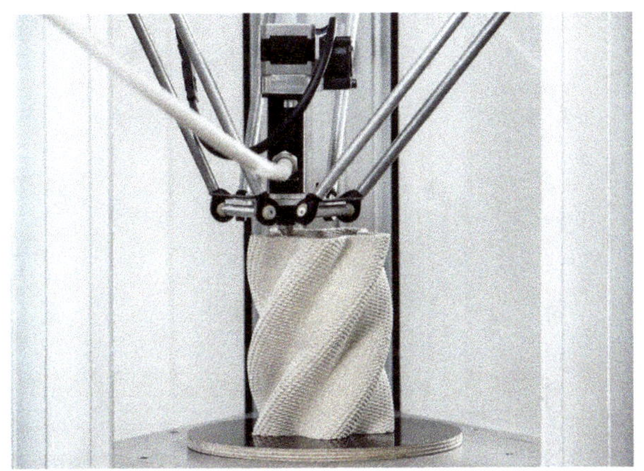

Delta WASP® 2040 Pro printing / WASP®.

WASP® Delta Clay 3D Printers

WASP® Delta printers are characterized by their speed, accuracy, and long-term stability. These 3D printers have robust mechanics that can handle heavy extruders and can print on a stationary plane, which allows for a firm stable foundation.

The Clay Line Printers are designed to be open, enabling interaction with the clay during the printing process. This creates a unique man-machine relationship that opens up countless technical and creative possibilities. These 3D printers work with air pressure, allowing for the easy management of clay flow and extrusion.

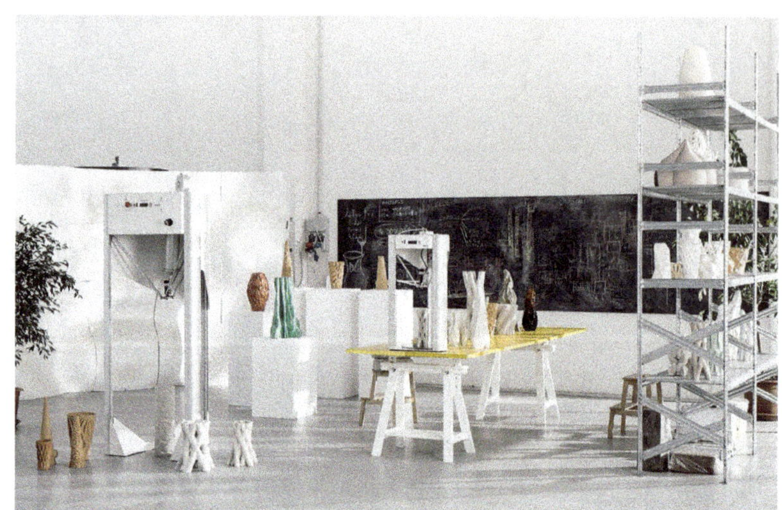

Workshop / WASP® / 2023.

Training and development

WASP® introduced 3D printing into schools in Italy with the help of the Italian Ministry of Education and Research. WASP® operators now demonstrate to students and teachers alike how this type of technology can be used in different industries. They have sponsored many 3D printers for schools and other tertiary institutions globally, expanding the idea that the world can be changed, one student at a time.

Training and support are provided to customers through online tutorials and guides. Their blog features numerous articles relating to the WASP® machine developments of other makers and includes large scale projects and collaborations in different industries across the world. These complementary articles were most informative when I commenced my research into the clay 3D printing industry many years ago.

Architecture

WASP® developed a range of extruders designed specifically for ceramic and cement-based materials dedicated to large and small-scale 3D printing. Furthermore, they specialize in developing material pumping systems that allow for more autonomous printing, particularly when it comes to architectural projects.

DIOR Concept Store

On Jumeirah Beach in Dubai, a one-of-a-kind concept store was 3D printed from natural materials in 2021. Combining clay, sand, and raw fibres, the Crane WASP® system even created a cannage (cane webbing) motif on the walls of the store in the form of a key house code for Dior that is featured on many of their products.

This digitally crafted boutique is a fascinating representation of an intricate architectural interplay. The ability to construct and transform buildings and to add individuality and detail to each 3D printed wall space truly offers exciting prospects and innovative methods for future buildings.

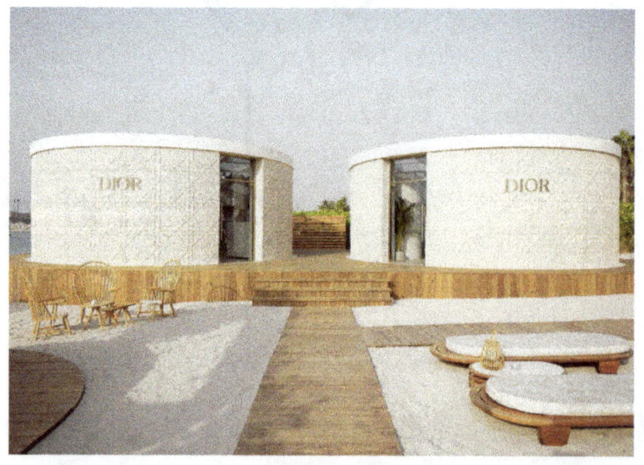

The Dior concept store / Photo by Mohamed Somji / WASP® / 2021.

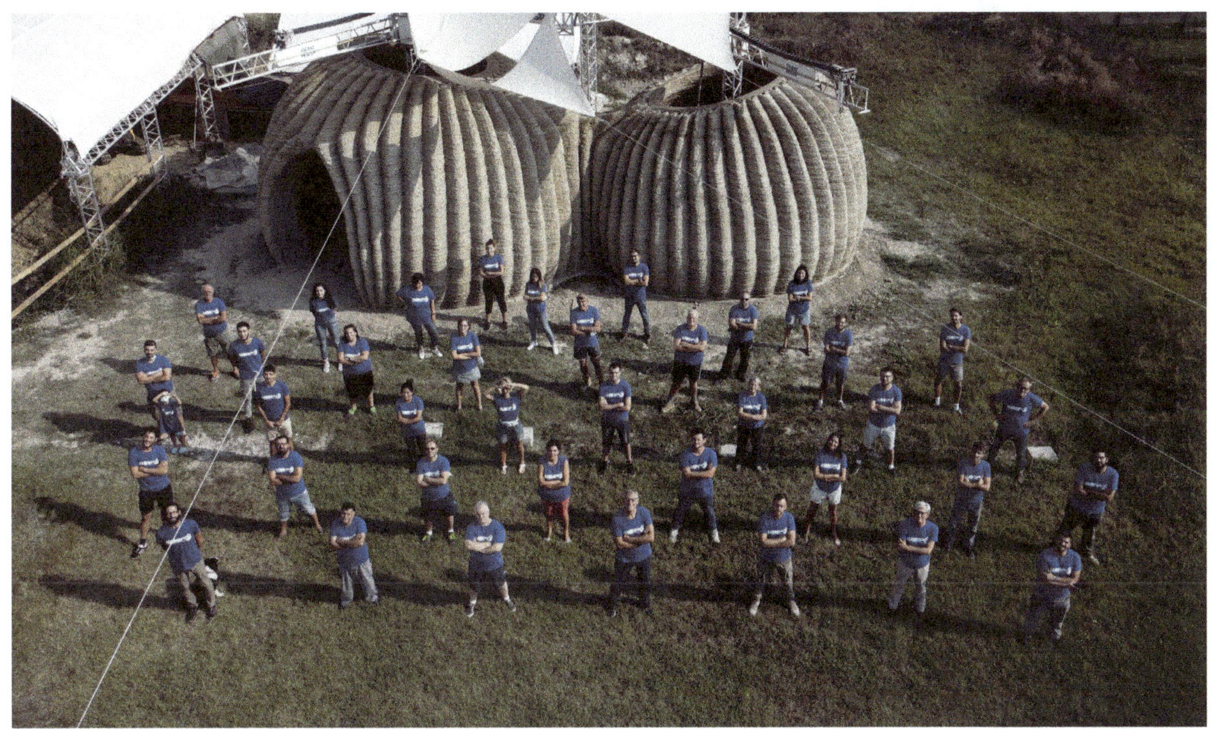

The WASP® team at the TECLA house / WASP® / 2021.

TECLA

TECLA is the first eco-habitat that was built using multiple Crane WASP® printers. Each printer unit has a printing area of 50m^2, making it possible to build independent living modules of any shape in just a few days.

The TECLA house, which has its origins in a combination of technology and clay, is a 3D printed house constructed entirely of recyclable and reusable materials sourced from local soil. It is carbon neutral and adaptable to any climate. The project involves taking shapeless earth and converting it into a fully functional, sustainable home.

TECLA can be constructed within a printing period of 200 hours and involves 7 000 machine codes (G-code), thus creating 350 layers of 12mm each, 150km of extrusion, and 60 cubic metres of natural materials, with the average electrical consumption being lower than six kilowatts.

Today, WASP® continue their research on bio-based materials and recycling, with the focus being on creating objects from natural materials and incorporating the recycling of plastic into granules to produce new items. Massimo Moretti, a philosopher, entrepreneur, and observer of nature, continues to dream of responding to humanity's primary needs through technology. WASP® is his vehicle to develop unique projects that solve real-world problems.

START WITH A PLAN

DO RESEARCH

Clay 3D printing is an intensive process, involving many moving parts. This is not a skill that can be mastered overnight.

Clay as an artistic medium can be rather unpredictable, and a good understanding of how it can be shaped into a solid form is paramount. Clay 3D printing is an investment in terms of both time and money. But don't be afraid to try, try, and try again, because trial and error is a multifaceted component on the path to success!

What type of clay do you want to work with and why? Different types of clays are fired at different temperatures, which will influence the cost of and the time taken to produce a finished clay printed product. The different types of clays are covered in more detail in Chapter 7.

Clay 3D printers have evolved quite rapidly over the past few years, with their capabilities continually being improved upon.

If you are looking at material testing with clay and other extrusion pastes, it is important to ask the printer supplier what will and won't work with their types of printers. Learn about how the different clay 3D printers operate. How does the machine extrude clay? Is it a mechanical stepper motor that pushes the clay out or do you need air pressure? Both types of printers have merit, and looking at your setup and what space you have available for the printer is also important.

Remember that just because a printer is cheap and it creates beautiful, printed forms, does not mean it is durable and will last for years. In my experience, printers and parts that come on the market at a low cost are usually too good to be true, especially if your printer is to be used daily.

If you are fortunate enough to live close to someone who already owns a clay 3D printer, don't hesitate to reach out to them. Ask whether they could demonstrate the operation of their machine and explain the processes that they follow. Consider the undertaking as a whole – not just the printing process. I remember the first time I saw a clay 3D printer in action - it was absolutely fascinating to watch, and my eyes were glued to the print. When I finally took my eyes off the scene, I knew I was hooked!

Clay consistency testing along with the pottery process is not for the faint hearted, especially if it is a new skill that you want to develop. With an industry that is growing larger each day, thankfully, help is never far away. This means that you can cut the time you usually spend trying to find a solution on your own by reaching out to other 3D makers who could help you.

Closely look at the different types of equipment that you may need. Just because you initially think you need a particular tool does not mean that it is a necessity. As I've said before, clay 3D printing demands a financial investment, and cutting costs that are not essential is important because although clay material is not expensive, everything else is.

Do not hesitate to take advantage of all the insights you can gain from 3D makers in this exciting field of work. Like all acquired skills, you will need to develop and nurture them. Having peers to share your work with will help you grow as a 3D maker.

It is important to remember that there is an entire world of knowledge at your fingertips! Take advantage of the insightful "Additional Research" in Chapter 14. Here you will find a variety of sources to inspire you such as online workshops, talks, books, and articles from industry experts and artists from across the world.

Along with this book, these learning avenues will help prepare you for the real journey that lies ahead. And yes, if this sounds as if I am trying to motivate you to embark on a clay 3D printing challenge, well then, I am!

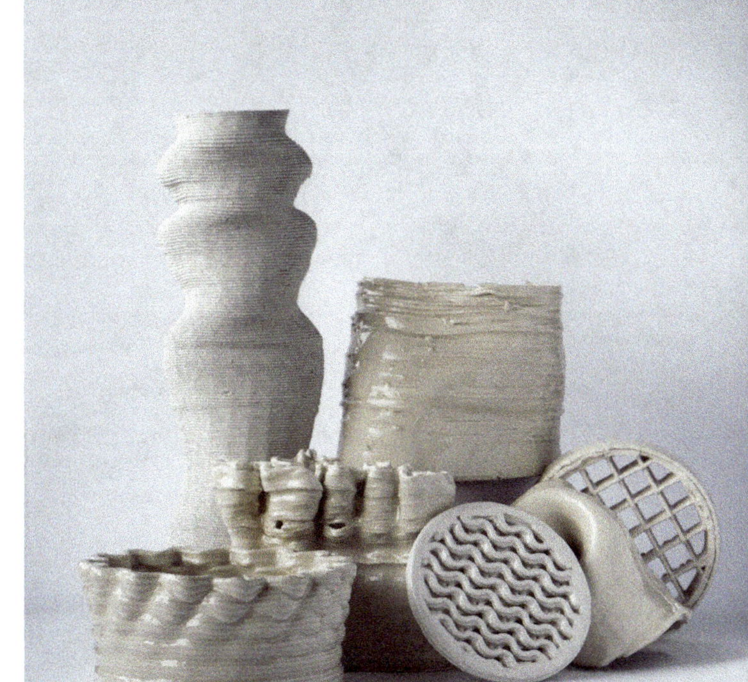

The first successfully kiln fired clay 3D prints by Dino Kartoudes, an architect from South Africa / 2023.

ACTION PLAN

The question that I am most frequently asked is - How does one start? Initially, it may seem quite overwhelming.

When I started on my new clay journey a few years ago, I had confidence in my skills as a potter, but teaching myself 3D design and the transfer from making hand-made pottery to operating a machine was quite complex. I found myself like a deer in the headlights, trying to figure out what to do first. That is why having an action plan and doing the relevant research will help to motivate your progress forward.

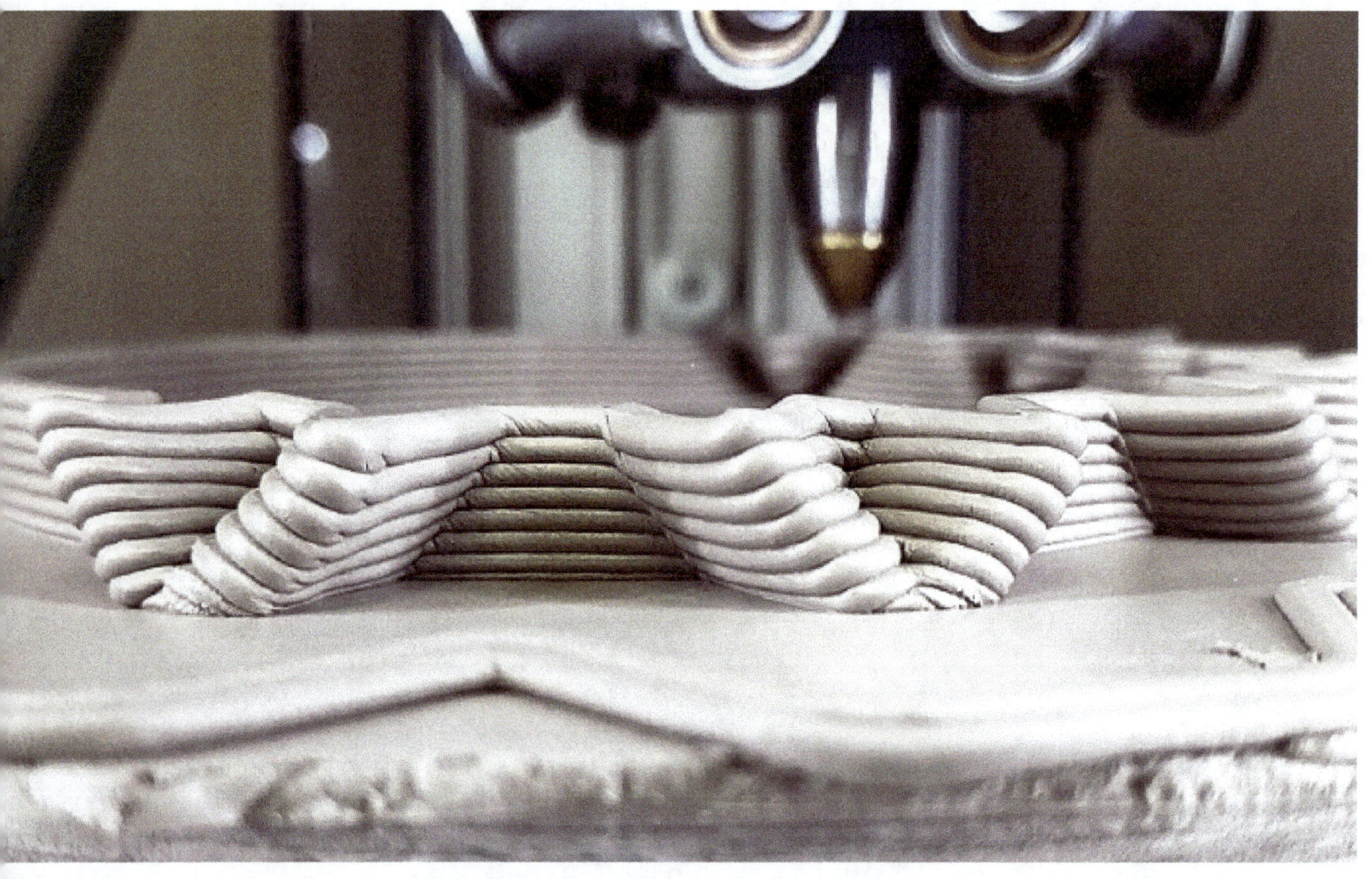

If you are already a 3D maker, consider first signing up for a pottery class at a local studio. Learning from an established potter will be worth your while. To move straight into printing with clay with absolutely no knowledge of the intricacies of the material will only waste valuable time. Clay can be tricky and gaining first-hand experience will empower you with the skills to start you on the right footing.

By joining a class, you would be given the opportunity of playing with the clay, of feeling how it moves between your fingers and seeing for yourself how it cracks when it is dry. Create a form, do some decorating, and play around with different shapes as you create them by hand. Follow the entire action of firing these in the kiln to assess the development of your work at the different stages of the pottery process.

Firing your first creations in a tried and tested kiln will also result in a higher quality finished product that you can appreciate for years to come.

Do not buy pottery tools and materials before understanding which are essential in your work process. As a potter (long before I did any clay printing), I had a total of seven tools in my studio that I could not do without. The rest just took up space, staring out at me from my shelves.

If you are already a potter, you will need to learn how to 3D design using a CAD software. The tools and functions incorporated in this type of software are specifically designed for ease of use and for helping you design in an efficient way.

Free online tutorials are widely available and you don't need to spend a cent. Streamline your work and keep notes from each tutorial. These are helpful when creating something on your own because you do not constantly have to go back and forth through previous tutorials when searching for specific tools or instructions. You will learn plenty about form and function in this way, which will certainly accelerate your learning curve.

Alternatively, explore some of the software available such as Potterware or the WASP® App. These are designed to be used by individuals who do not have a background in 3D design and CAD software and will be discussed in more detail in Chapter 6.

Using these applications will help you to figure out the style of design you are drawn to, and what forms you would like to ultimately create.

Starting from scratch, with no experience in either pottery or 3D design, means that you will just need to put in a little more work to master the skill. Don't be overwhelmed by all the information, take it one step at a time and you will get there.

As mentioned, buying a clay printer can be expensive. You should keep it in mind that such a hobby should be of lasting interest, and not one to fade within a few months.

Once you start printing, explore familiar forms of pottery such as vases, mugs, and bowls. These are often the best on which to test your clay consistency since you already know and understand the purpose behind the shape you are trying to create. By no means should this limit your imagination as to what you could print. The intricate ability of the clay printer affords you the opportunity to experiment with shapes, lines, and forms, and gives you the freedom to pursue new perspectives.

WHAT ARE THE BENEFITS?

Initially, a financial investment will be necessary and a compilation of the expected pros and cons list would be a good strategy.

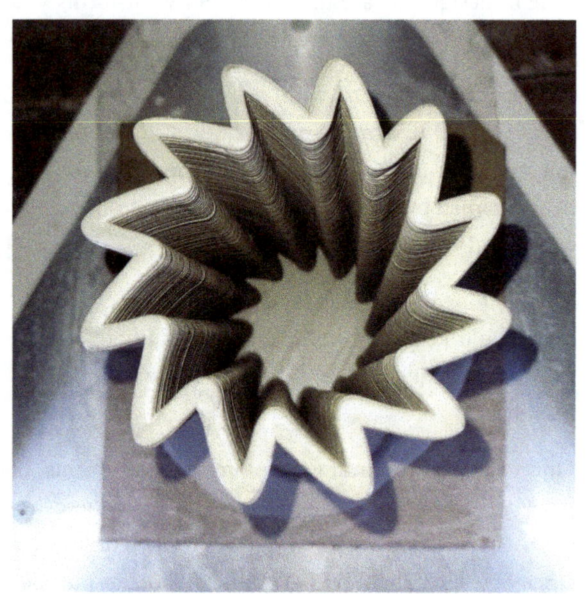

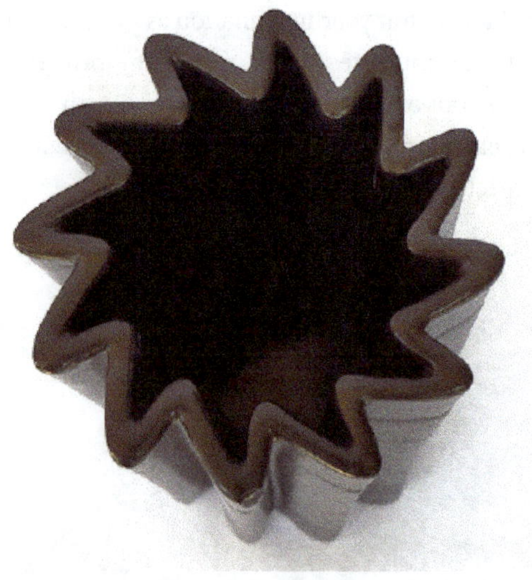

Cost effectiveness

A manufactured clay 3D printer can be expensive to buy for a small-time maker; add on the costs of the pottery decorating and firing processes. So, where can you save on your initial costs? The answer is with your material.

Many FDM (fused deposition modelling) 3D printers use filaments such as PLA, ABS and Nylon, just to mention a few. Once these materials are heated, melted, and printed with, they cannot be used again. Clay, however, can be recycled repeatedly, thereby cutting the cost of buying new materials each time you want to print. So, being able to re-use the material you already have from prints that have failed is a huge advantage.

In the early stages of clay 3D printing, you will find that the correct clay consistency that works for you may require repeated testing. Ultimately, you will waste a lot less clay if you recycle it. Recycled clay, if done well, is usually just as perfect as it was when you first bought it.

A clay 3D printed vase with a mahogany glaze finish / Hendrien Horn / 2022.

Print on demand

This is possibly one of the greatest benefits of clay 3D printing, because you print only what you need. In the past, mass production would have played a huge role in the creation of new prototypes and objects.

Bulk stock orders for outside distributors might have been required for production cycle runs which often meant that extra costs would then have been incurred by the business itself. Production costs would not necessarily have contributed to the baseline income and bulk orders could easily have taken up valuable storage space, adding to costs.

Having the tools and materials to design and produce only what is needed makes sense as the negative impact of mass production on the environment is also an important factor to consider.

Rapid prototyping

No longer is there a need for massive machinery and equipment to make multiple copies of one product before the realisation hits that some kind of an adaptation must be made to the set product.

Traditional manufacturing processes are changing with the advent of real time prototyping. Testing processes are sped up exponentially when one can change the design of the object at any time during the 3D printing process. Should a print fail, the 3D design can be altered in accordance with the improved changes in real time, and then be re-printed.

It is an exciting way to work and a real time process with which I have become very comfortable. Should my prints be in the test phase of my work process, my computer is always at hand for a quick adjustment or change to a 3D design. This saves time when I am experimenting with different design concepts which would otherwise have presented a very costly and time-consuming process.

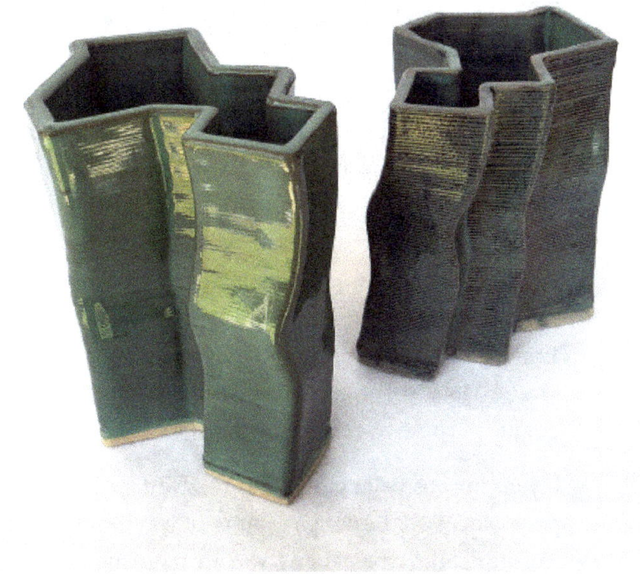

Geometric 3D printed vases / Hendrien Horn / 2022.

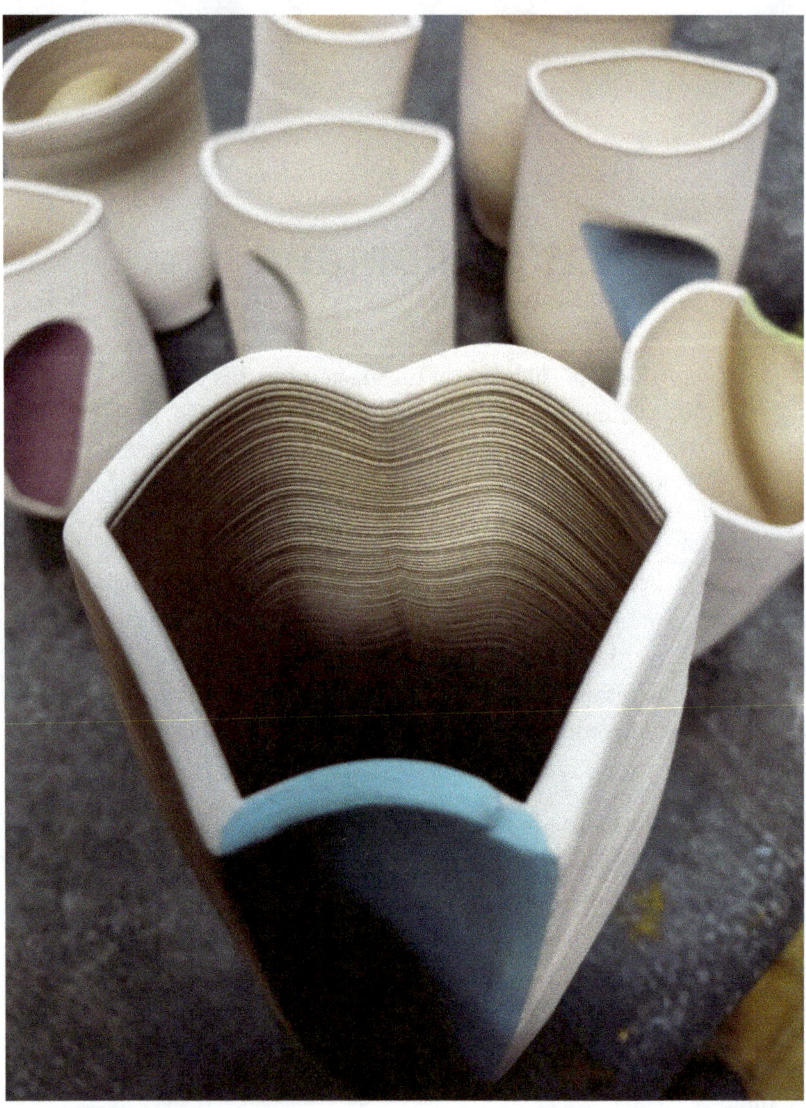

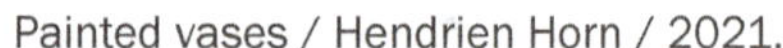

Painted vases / Hendrien Horn / 2021.

Customising your world

Have you ever looked at a particular object or product and thought that you could design it better? A small design flaw or imperfection could be the significant factor to determine whether you choose to spend money on an item or not. 3D making provides the tools to create your dream design and shape it into existence. You could in fact enjoy a product that speaks to your exact style and specifications, all the while serving a unique purpose or desired outcome!

If your purpose is to build a business with your clay 3D prints, focus on the design features of your product that will attract the type of buyer you are targeting.

For example, the clay prints that I create are contemporary artworks that serve a decorative purpose. I target art collectors and galleries who can appreciate my work as stand-alone pieces.

Functional designs could attract a larger market because beautiful pottery works are always in great demand and serve both the practical and aesthetic preferences of the buyer. Consider your projected outcome and design with that in mind.

FIGURE OUT YOUR "WHY?"

Envisioning the different opportunities that clay making can offer you will help determine the type of equipment, machinery, and skill level you wish to acquire.

Business or Hobby?

Do you want to turn your 3D printed objects into a profitable business, or would you rather enjoy tinkering in your spare time? A profitable business may initially require a greater financial investment. This includes the purchase of a high-quality clay 3D printer with a good track record and that can be operated on a daily basis.

These types of machines come with; instructions, a support team, in-house and online workshops, as well as training days you can attend - resources that will make it easier for you, if, like me, you have no interest in building your own printer.

To date, many companies have produced different continuous material flow systems, allowing the makers to produce prints at a faster rate. Such sophisticated systems are not a necessity for the small-time maker as their focus may not include mass production.

If you are thinking of engaging in clay 3D printing as a hobby, creating a business plan and planning a cost projection may not be required.

Perhaps you merely want to experiment and explore clay printed designs, enriching your life for the fun of it. Time and demand may therefore not necessarily be factored into your decision making, giving you the freedom to tinker at your own pace.

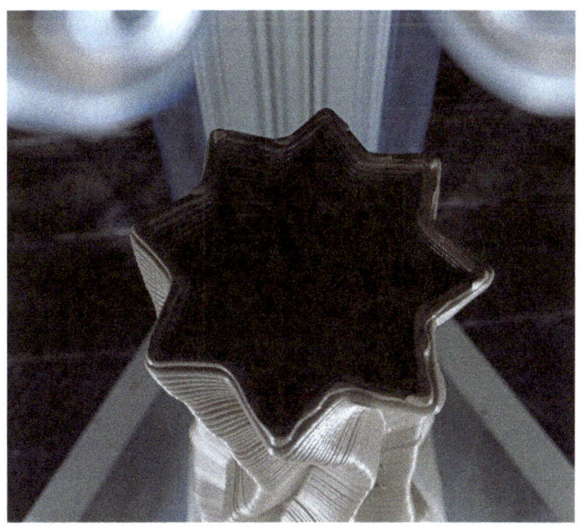

Star shaped spiral vessel with terracotta clay / Hendrien Horn / 2024.

As an Artist

Innovations in different types of technologies have opened the door to developing new ways of creating art. In clay 3D printing, the exploration of shape, form and materials used can be an exciting path. Becoming a successful artist in any medium can be difficult because you open your work up to criticism, which can, at times, be a hard pill to swallow. Not everyone will understand and appreciate your technique and the time it took to create your artwork, but once you find people who appreciate your work, it makes all the difference.

Essentially, you are trying to show your point of view by way of the materials and processes that you choose. Think outside the box. Yes, a printer can extrude clay, but what can you add to the clay that gives it an edge? For example, when experimenting with different clay colours, how does the clay printer extrude the coloured clay according to how it has been stacked in the clay container?

How, apart from just the 3D design, can you manipulate the clay during the printing process? Do you, for example, need to include physical supports to prevent the structure from warping, or should you apply heat to ensure that the clay walls do not collapse?

How do you want to decorate the work? There is a large variety of decorating techniques in pottery for both the beginner and more advanced potters. That is why it is often said that pottery is a science. Experimenting with additives and glazes is a story all together on its own, and you should not shy away from exploring these options!

The art world can be a difficult one to navigate at times, and networking is a very important component if you want to be successful in this industry. Many galleries are eager to hear your story. A pretty work is just that - pretty. Think about how that work of art will speak to your audience and the message that you want to convey.

As an artist, you should remember that you are also running a business. Most artists have multiple streams of income such as hosting workshops and paid apprenticeships. Establishing yourself as an artist may take time initially, so be sure to explore alternative ways of paying the bills.

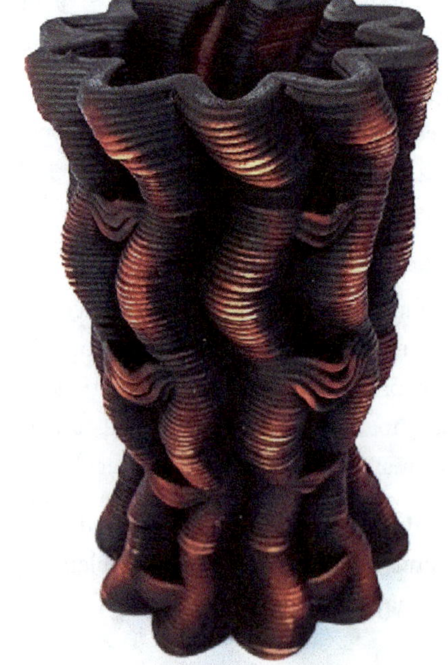

Fossil 1 / Earthenware clay 3D print / 12.5cm (h) / Hendrien Horn / 2023.

Top view of 3D printed clay vessels / Hendrien Horn / 2021.

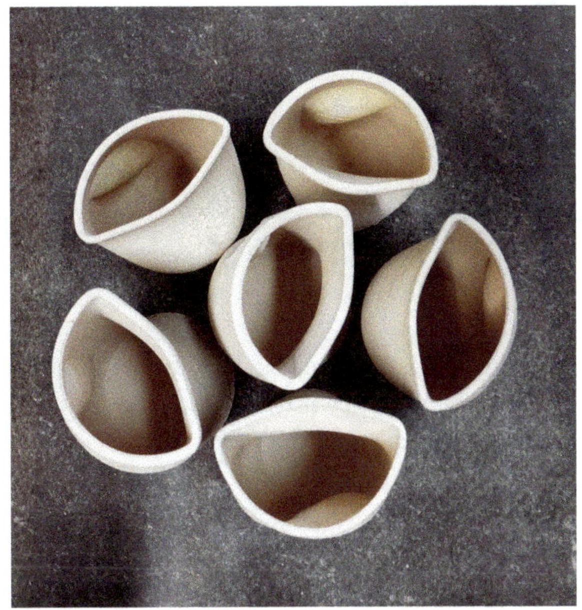

Product Design

Since its inception, 3D printing has changed the way products are made. Now having the ability to custom design, makers can create for people who see the world as they do. This capacity to fabricate on the go drives one to think on your toes and makes it a very exciting industry to be part of.

Many different types of clay can be used in product designs because they can easily be sculpted and moulded by hand. Fashioning a design from scratch and having the opportunity to touch a physical representation of an idea in its finished state are indeed great moments. Experiencing your 3D printed creations first hand, in essence for me, is what designing 3D custom products is all about.

What makes 3D printing so unique is that you can conceptualise, design, and print all in your own time. Experimentation gives you, the maker, the opportunity to unlock ideas that you may not have thought possible before. It is an interesting process to follow, with new ways of creating continually being improved upon.

Companies are starting to use clay materials more and more in the process of designing new products. The versatility of the material allows for faster modifications of an object or product, streamlining the production process and saving on large scale manufacturing costs. No longer is it a requirement to have products mass manufactured, only to find that there are inconsistencies and problems with the design.

With the finished products being market ready in a shorter space of time, 3D printing offers more opportunities for profitability for such companies.

Owing to the advantages of rapid prototyping, a problem can be solved in real time. Adjustments, testing, and improvements offer the inventors and makers the opportunity to explore new innovations as they design and create products to incentivise people to buy. Examples of industries that are currently using clay for prototyping include the automotive and aerospace industries, construction, jewellery, ceramic, as well as animation studios.

I would not disregard functional objects such as crockery. Bespoke pieces are in great demand, with potters and makers constantly looking at new ways to reimagine these. Let's take mugs, for example. They come in all sizes, with the shape varying to some degree, but never really straying from the tried and tested design that we all know and trust. A mug must be functional and be able to withstand everyday use. As a potter, I tend to find the basic form too repetitive, and I often long for someone to design a mug that just blows me away!

"Why fix something that isn't broken?" you may say. I guess my brain is constantly looking for an element of surprise. I no longer find myself making many functional pieces because my passion leans more towards the contemporary art space. That, however, does not mean I can't appreciate someone else's creation, which could turn an old design on its head.

As an Architect

With a universal need for practical and low-cost housing, there has been an upward trend towards exploring 3D printing on a larger scale. With advancements in environmentally friendly designs, the focus on locally resourced adobe materials to 3D print houses is a small but growing industry. Such materials have been specifically created for large-scale construction and are often used in enormous robotic arms and printers.

The exploration of parametric design using multiple software applications and how this can influence, and shape architectural design is exciting to witness. Clay 3D printers are often used to test the stability of new construction ideas on a smaller scale. These prints provide the backbone for proving concepts that include building components and parts and for bringing about new innovative designs in architecture.

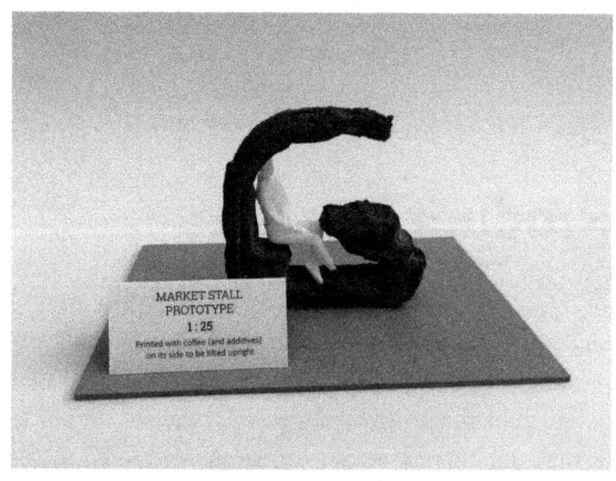

Photo by Marié Snyman.

Marié Snyman, a South African architect, used a small-scale clay 3D printer to explore the different opportunities that 3D printing could provide in the construction industry in her Master's thesis, entitled "Exploring opportunities for 3D printing in emerging contexts"/ 2022.

Mould Making

This technique has accelerated the creation process for many makers who wish to make multiple objects without printing each one individually. Once a completed clay 3D print has been fired, it can be cast in plaster or silicone moulds. These moulds can then be used many times over to produce the same object in a material of choice.

Slip casting in pottery is the practice of pouring a mixture of clay and water into a plaster mould. Plaster is porous, and the water in the clay mixture that fills the mould is absorbed into the plaster walls of the mould as the clay starts to dry. It is then left to stand for a few minutes before the remaining clay mixture is poured out again. What is left is a shell of clay on the inside of the mould, forming the walls of the casted object, for example a vase. The object is only taken out once its clay walls are dry enough not to warp to the touch.

Many potters and craftsmen buy moulds made according to their designs because they are not necessarily interested in creating the moulds themselves. Look at what people, companies and industries could benefit from through the use of moulds. The ability to 3D design and print is a huge advantage that extends to many industries.

Materials Testing

With the advancement of 3D printing, there has been an increase in hobbyists and makers testing and 3D printing a variety of materials. Firstly, you need to do your homework to see which printers can accommodate which type of materials. For example, using a specially formulated concrete material, which will solidify at a faster rate, is not a suitable material to test on just any machine.

Often clay 3D printers are preferred for materials testing because plastic 3D printers require heat to melt the thin filament material, whereas the clay 3D printers do not need any heat. The extruded material is pre-prepared and mixed to the preferred consistency before being housed in a container from which the material may be extruded in both small and large quantities.

Considerations when buying a printer equipped for materials testing should include the following: the physical substances that the existing printer can print with, the nozzle sizes required, the air pressure or mechanical system that might work the best, and the methods for cleaning the printer system after use.

A popular material is a wood slurry, which may contain small wood fibres. This type of material would usually require a larger nozzle size to avoid clogging during the printing process.

Extruding with a thicker, heavier material will also need a strong force to push it through the extruder system. This may not necessarily suit an air pressure system but rather a mechanical one. Once a print has been completed, the extruder system needs to be dismantled for a thorough cleaning. I cannot stress enough the importance of keeping the print head clean! Materials that have solidified on account of ineffectual cleaning can cause huge frustration, but with proper routine cleaning, that can easily be avoided.

You are by no means restricted in your answer as to "Why?". Remember, you can always adapt your vision/plans and change your mind as to the nature of the work you wish to undertake. The field of clay 3D printing offers a variety of opportunities, and this is where your own research into current approaches and practices could be of benefit to your creative process.

Clay moulds / Rhoda and Madeleine Henning Pottery Studio / 2023.

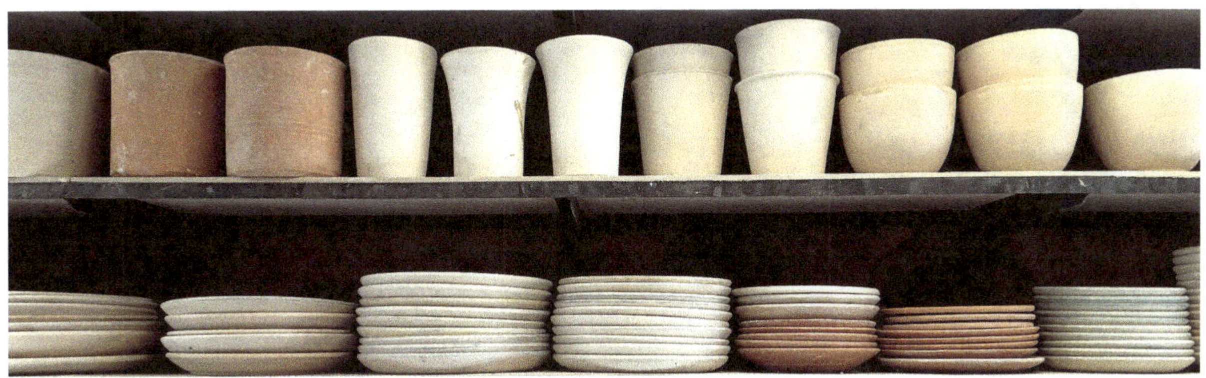

THE IMPORTANCE OF FAILURE

I read an article once that noted how potters are some of the best equipped people when it comes to dealing with failure. The reasoning behind the argument is that the pottery process can really test one's resilience.

Potters advance through the rigorous testing of their materials. If just one small thing goes wrong, there can be catastrophic consequences, such as an explosion in the kiln or a crack that can quickly turn into an unwanted canyon. You constantly need to learn from your mistakes and realise that inherently it is what the process demands of you.

To step into this type of mindset takes determination and a willingness to keep the end game in mind despite what goes wrong.

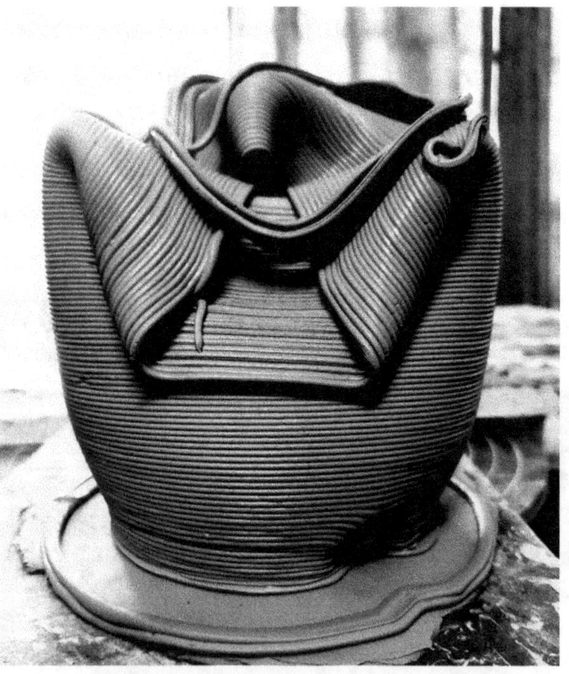

The reality is that from the beginning, failure will have a permanent presence in your clay making process. It is a rite of passage for all clay makers. With each clay print that fails, you will gain a better understanding of what makes a perfect print, so remember to take notes. I have an entire book dedicated to scribbling down nozzle sizes, layer heights and speeds.

As time passes, your individual routine for creating prints will become second nature, and you won't need to record every single step. You will come to know which angles work with each nozzle size and what consistency your clay needs to reach for each form type. Printing will become easier and all the hours you spent trying to find solutions to problems will start to pay off.

Make a resolution to celebrate your failures and learn from them. One day, you will look back on all your efforts with a sense of pride and accomplishment.

A failed 3D print that collapsed beautifully / Hendrien Horn / 2021.

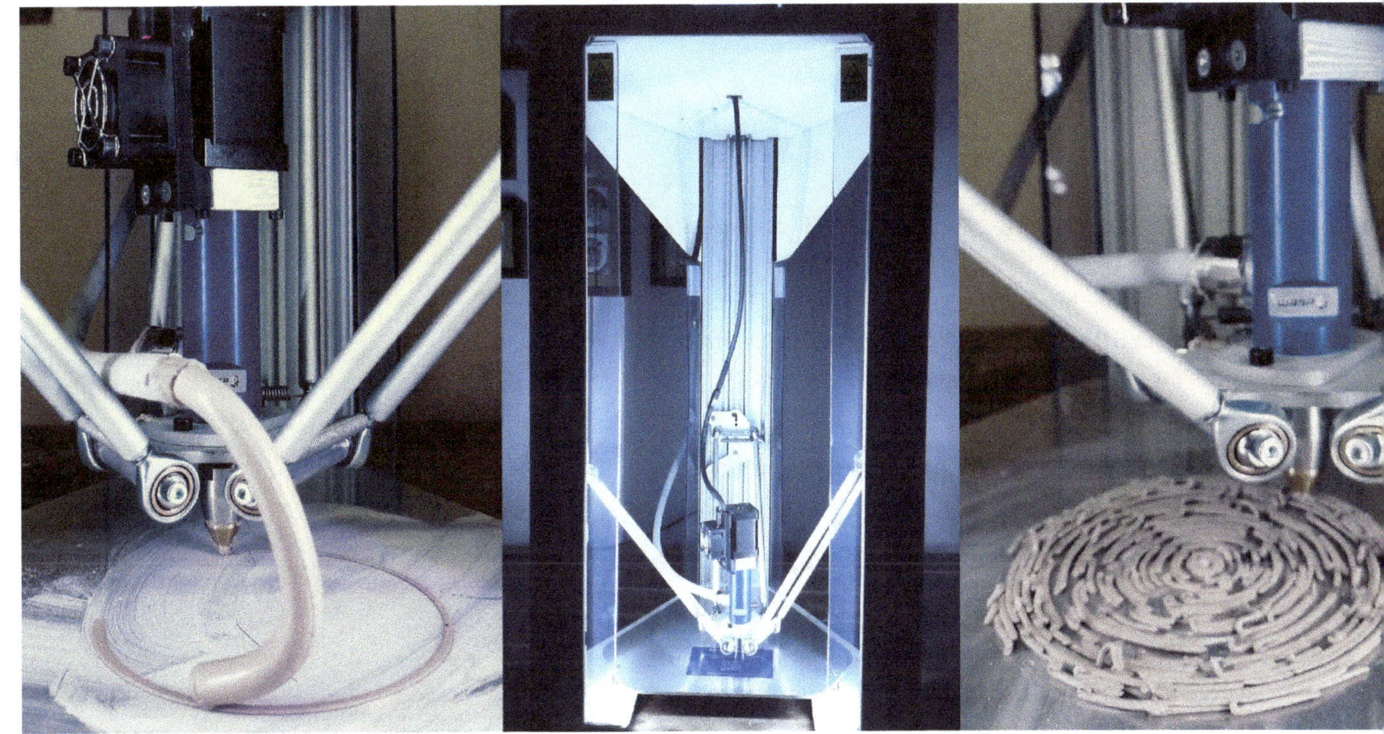

Testing / Hendrien Horn / 2021.

MY PERSONAL JOURNEY

The undertaking of teaching myself how to use the clay 3D printer was much the same as when I started pottery all those years ago.

I started out by printing basic shapes, such as the cylinder. This allowed me to gain a better understanding of layer heights and how to judge clay consistency. Too wet... and the clay would fall in - too dry... and the air pressure would not be enough to push the clay through the pipe and extruder mechanism. It was a constant advanced planning procedure of figuring out how to prepare the clay for optimal results.

This is very much an individual process that you must work through because, a clay consistency that works for one person may not necessarily work for someone else. During this testing stage, there were quite a few moments when I had to step away from the printer and take a long deep breath.

As a potter with little knowledge of the intricacies of the machinery, I felt completely intimidated by the clay 3D printer. I was terrified that I might break my machine, and this fear of imagined horrors initially hindered my progress.

One day I asked myself the question, "How can I make this printer look less intimidating". The answer came swiftly and took me completely by surprise. I had to rummage through my old wrapping collection containing various odds and ends until I found the small pack of stick-on googly eyes. I took a set and stuck them on my printer. When I finally took a step back, the printer was looking back at me with beady eyes and I burst out laughing, instantly feeling more at ease.

From there I relaxed a little and started printing more complex shapes. Testing how far the angles of the clay form could be pushed before collapsing became a challenge that I gladly accepted. Finding my stride, I finally felt as if I was in control of the process.

A few months later, and my printer journey was intercepted by something of a disaster. The cover of one set of wires hooked onto a moving part of the printer and was ripped off completely. This was in no way the fault of the 3D printer, rather I had not done the setup procedure correctly and the exposed wires were all bent in the wrong direction.

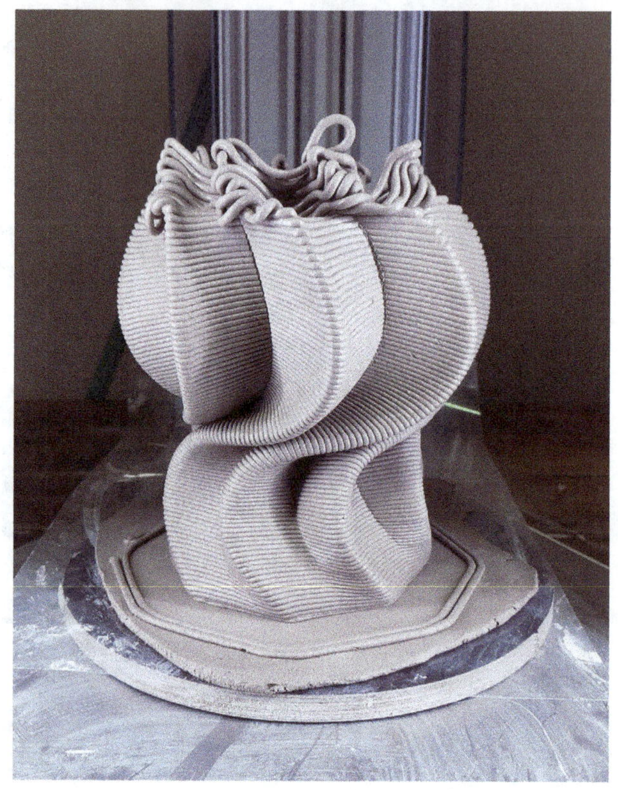

Testing / Hendrien Horn / 2021.

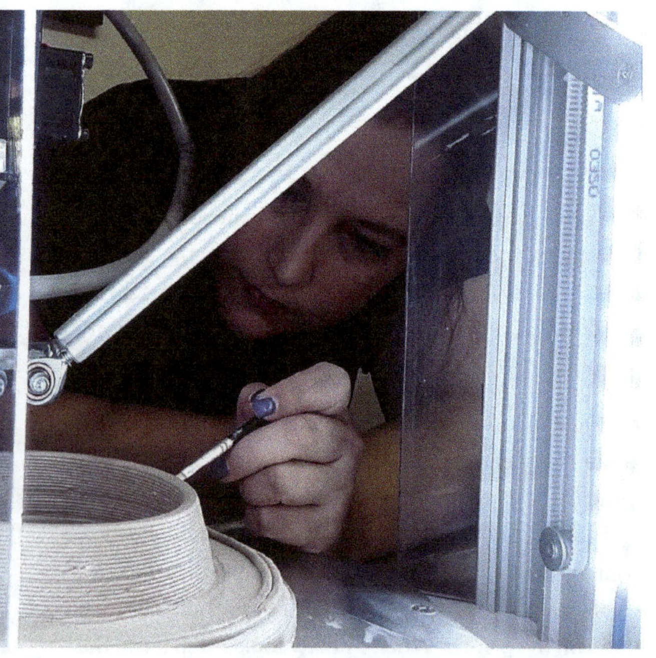

Hendrien Horn / 2021.

To be honest, I went into a complete state of shock and could see my clay printing career flash before my very eyes - a little dramatic, even for me. I had no idea what the wires were supposed to look like in their original state.

With the realisation that the WASP® head office in Italy was approximately 12 700 km away from my studio in South Africa (I checked), I had to deal with this problem on my own and promptly emailed WASP® for help.

Once the dust had settled a little, I recall receiving an email from the WASP® support team, with the liaison person stating, "Honestly, it is something that has never happened before". This comment kept bouncing around in my head, because if she had known me, she would have realised that this was exactly the type of incident that I could imagine happening to me.

The support team really tried their best to help. I still have a video of an Italian gentleman showing me how to delicately move and position the wires into their original position. I sometimes wonder what was going through his mind whilst he filmed himself. I can laugh about it now and understand that what happened with the machine was a freak accident. At the time, however, I felt like a complete idiot.

The above illustrates one of the biggest reasons to ensure that you have technical support for your machine. If something does go wrong, you should at least have access to people who can assist you because they know the exact mechanical make-up of the machine and how to fix it.

After this eventful incident, I started to celebrate my failures. After my machine broke, I treated myself to a celebratory lunch (It was a Monday!).

If you find yourself in a space where you have absolutely no idea of what you are doing, don't start hyperventilating. All prospective clay makers go through that same experience, if not worse! Remember to take a step back when in doubt and to get into the habit of reaching out for help should you get stuck.

As an artist, I intentionally design my clay works to move during my printing process, creating what I like to call "instances of warped states". By strategically designing these instances, I introduce variability into my printed pieces. As a result, not one of my created works is identical, even though they are printed using the same 3D design. Larger nozzle sizes and layer heights work well for this type of printing, allowing for artistic intentionality in the unpredictability of the print.

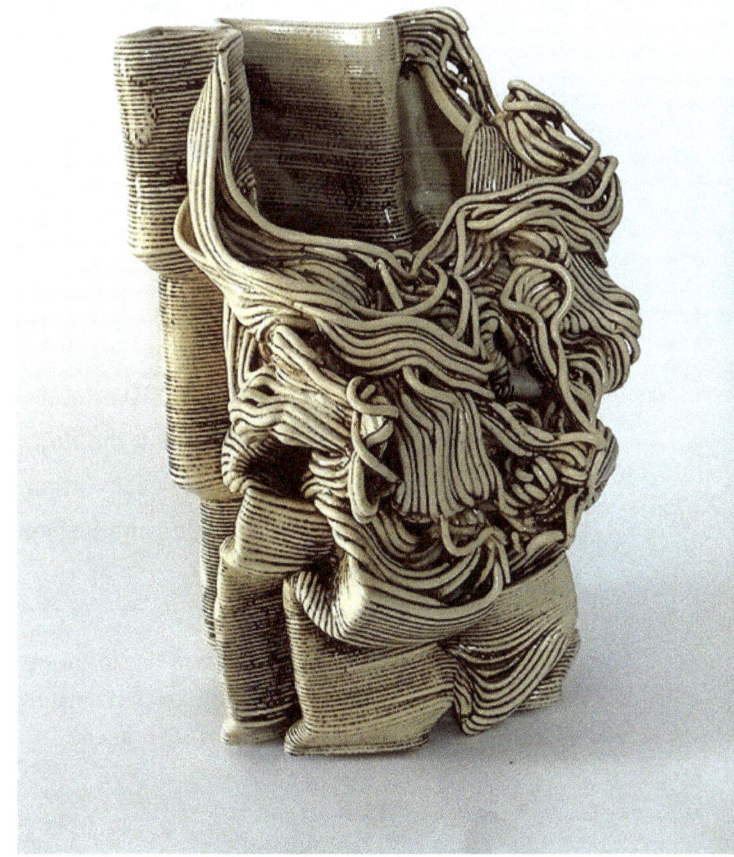

Fossil 25 / Hendrien Horn / 2022.

3D PRINTER BUILDS

DELTA & CARTESIAN 3D PRINTERS

Understanding the basics of how a clay 3D printer operates with all its moving parts will ultimately help you make the decision as to what type of clay 3D printer to buy.

When I was shopping around for clay 3D printers, I read quite a few articles that pitted the delta and cartesian printers against each other. These articles had my head spinning and left me wondering which direction to take.

At the time, clay 3D printers were just starting to emerge in the mass market, with these publications were mainly addressing the use of filament (FDM) 3D printers.

The delta printer is focused on height and uses three arms that are fixed to the platform. As they move around, the changing angles of a complex print can easily be created, with smooth changes in the layer heights. The print bed is stationary, and the natural print shape of the printer is a circle.

The cartesian printer, on the other hand, is more focused on surface volume. With a square or rectangular print bed, some of the print beds are stationary, especially for heavier print builds, whilst others have the capability to move downwards as each extrusion layer is printed on top of the other.

Vases printed with the cartesian 3D printer from Stone Flower / 2018.

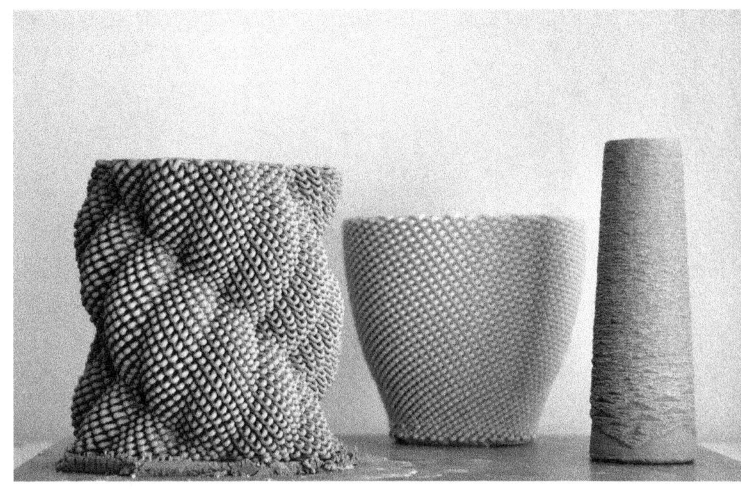

I had some lingering questions about the cartesian clay 3D printers and how they differ from the delta printers - so I enlisted the help of Anatoly Berezkin of Stone Flower.

My assumption that movement could be limited with the one-armed cartesian as opposed to the three-armed delta printer, was quickly disproved. Anatoly showed me some of his earlier prints that had been executed with his Stone Flower 3.0 clay 3D printer in 2018. These widely recognisable printed forms exhibited intricately designed patterns that could easily be navigated by his cartesian 3D printer. Thus, both the cartesian and the delta printers can easily 3D print sharp angles which may require rapid movements from the 3D printer.

As a potter, I could also not understand how a moving print bed designed for some of the cartesian printers could be a particularly good design idea for printing with clay. Surely the print would just collapse if the machine made a sudden jerking movement, or what if the print bed was not stable enough to maintain its level position?

Anatoly explained that linear guides are used to help move the cartesian print bed up and down seamlessly along the stable printer bracket. These ensure that the print bed does not shift or tilt and help with the slow progressive movement between the printing layers. The larger cartesian printers used for heavy print builds and materials are primarily created with a stationary print bed or have the ability to print on a sturdy surface or floor.

Cartesian printers usually have the clay housed in a container above the extruder mechanism which allows for a shorter path for the clay to travel during the printing process. My delta printer has a pipe emerging from the clay container and is separate from the extruder mechanism. This path may appear to offer a longer distance for the clay to travel. However, by using air pressure, the movement of the clay can be easily managed.

Many of the extruders designed for both types of printers can retract the clay in the extruder by means of the built-in auger. This is a splendid capability to have if your printed objects require a gap between two points in your design. This was one of the features that I sought in a clay 3D printer when I first started my research.

Ensure that you take the time to research the printer or printer kit that you want to purchase. Ask questions if you do not fully understand the process. We are not all mechanical engineers, but you need to have a basic understanding of the mechanics of the 3D printer you wish to buy.

When it comes to choosing between the delta and cartesian clay printers, there are not that many differences in terms of the technological capabilities. You will, however, need to consider the print types you want to create and whether the type of printer you intend to purchase can perform at the standard that you require.

FLSUN V400 FDM 3D printer / Delta printer / 2022.

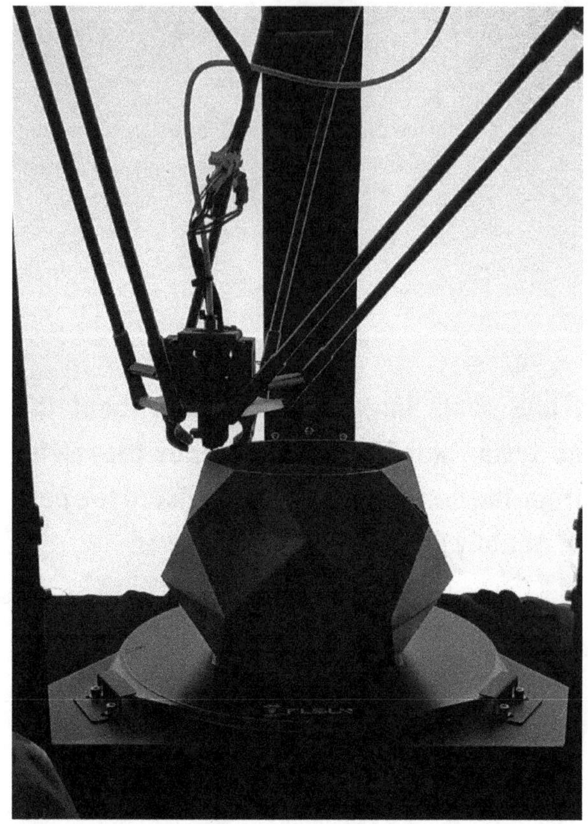

CLAY & FDM 3D PRINTERS

Apart from the materials used, there are several differences between the clay and FDM printer.

Fused deposition modelling (FDM), also known as fused filament fabrication (FFF) 3D printers, work by extruding melted thermoplastic filaments through a heated nozzle. Thermoplastics melt rather than burn when heated and are widely used in 3D printing by hobbyists and makers.

A clay 3D printer does not have a heating element, known as a hotend - this is used in FDM printers to melt the filament so that it can easily move through the extruder. The clay, which has water in it (making a paste) does not need to be heated before it moves through the extruder mechanism, and then finally through the nozzle.

Clay printers do not have a heated bed at the base where the print starts. A heated bed for filament printing produces better results in that it prevents uneven cooling and poor adhesion between the layers. Should there be a heated bed on the clay printer, it would cause uneven drying in the clay body and result in warping and cracks.

FDM printers do not use compressed air as is the case with some clay printers. Instead, they use only electricity to heat and melt the filament for extrusion.

The cost of clay is a lot lower than that of FDM filaments. As discussed before, clay as a material can be recycled repeatedly, whereas the thermoplastic filaments cannot.

Another advantage of printing with clay is that it dries slowly, allowing for modifications to be made by hand. This is not something that can be performed with a completed plastic print, as it dries quickly and must be sanded down to produce a smooth finish.

A clay 3D printer cannot be left without constant supervision. The FDM printer, on the other hand, allows for the maker to start the print and to leave it to print away, and for checking on it only every now and then. As a beginner, you may find that you spend much time working with your clay 3D printer on perfecting the correct parameters for the respective designs. However, the designing and setting up stages will eventually become second nature as you master the technology.

BUILD OR BUY?

I am not an engineer, and I knew right from the start that if I wanted to build a printer, someone else would have to do it for me. Essentially, you need to figure out where you want to focus your efforts and where your passion lies.

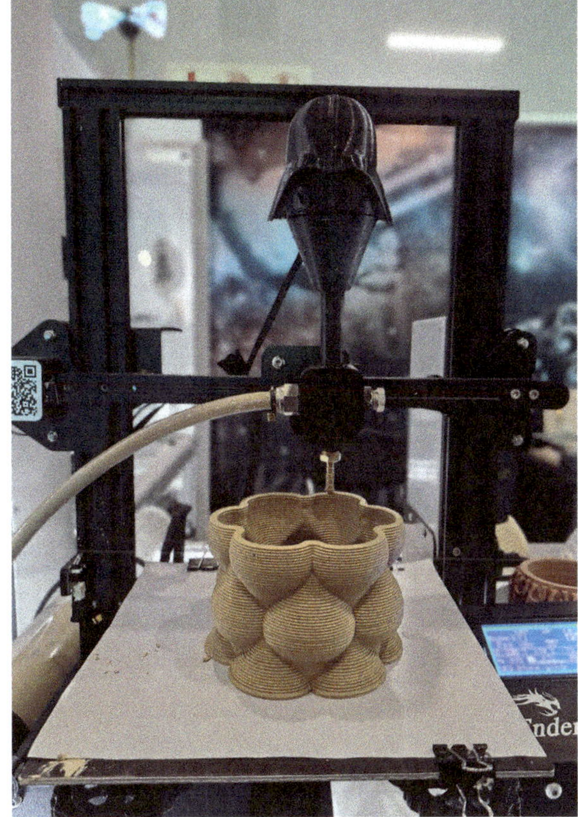

An FDM 3D printer that has been converted into a clay 3D printer / An early prototype of a cartesian printer by DRIP AM© / 2023.

Budget

The clay 3D printers on the market today vary in size, shape, ability, and cost. Most have a steep price tag, merely because they are built as industrial grade machines that can achieve precision prints at high speeds. Such printers are essentially an investment built for repeated use over long periods of time.

The cheaper options are not necessarily built for excessive and continuous use. Do not let a perceived bargain sway you into thinking you are necessarily getting a good deal. Low quality and cheap parts are exactly as is stated on the label. When it comes to equipment, you get what you pay for.

Do not get me wrong, if you are unsure if this is just a hobby or a full-time venture, invest only as much as you can afford. If you want a machine that is durable and made of strong parts, is easier to clean and creates intricate designs, make sure to do your research and find out from others who already own the printer you are, perhaps, considering buying.

If you have the skills to build your own clay 3D printer, you will probably find yourself buying the parts and kits from different supply companies anyway. Don't be afraid to use this exciting technology and equipment because it will help you to build a machine that is long lasting and that can produce quality prints.

Be sure to ask questions about the capabilities of the kits on the market. Some may look great on the screen, but the quality of the materials used to build a specific part may be of a lower grade.

Many makers who have built their own 3D printers have often modified their plastic filament printers. Just remember that the bracket on which you mount any equipment or clay must be strong enough to hold the weight. Clay is heavy and clay containers braced on top of plastic brackets are not always very stable and may move and buckle during the printing process.

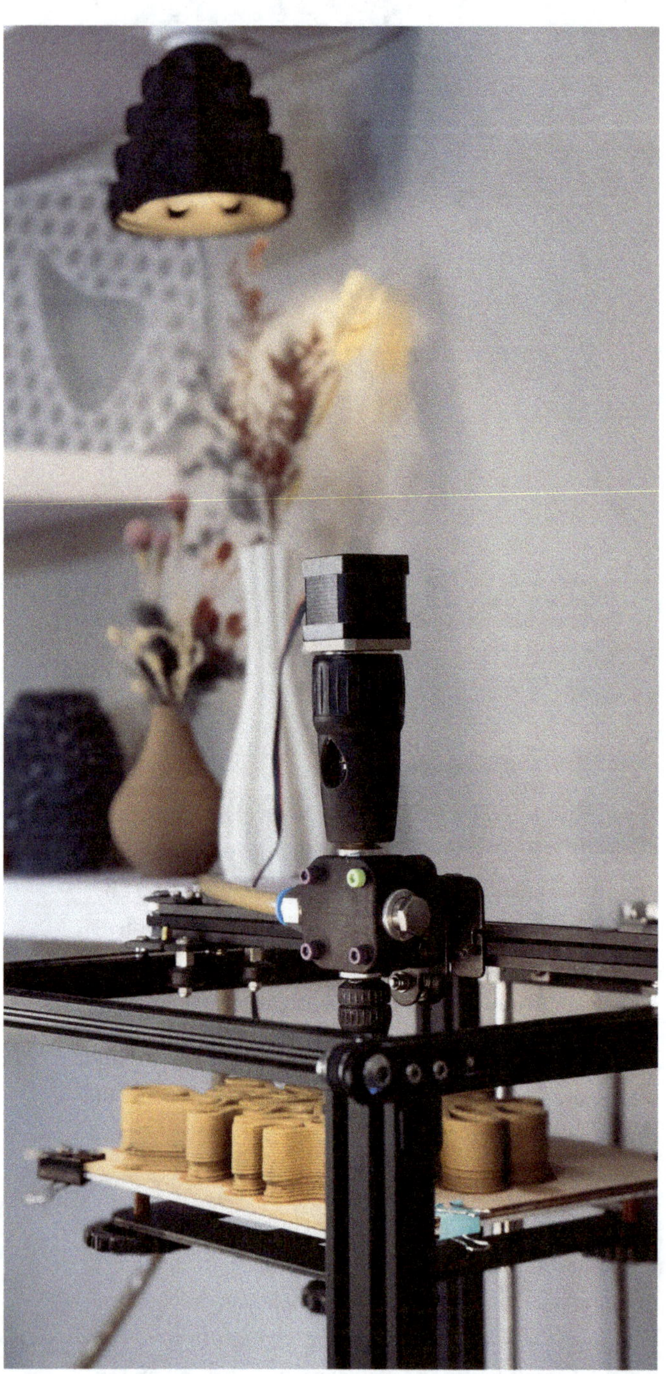

Photo by DRIP AM© / 2024.

3D Printer Size

Educate and evaluate the build volume of the printer you wish to buy. Initially, you will not be able to determine your clay shrinkage rate but be aware that this will have an impact on the final size of your prints. This refers to how much the clay shrinks due to the loss of water when it is dried and kiln fired. My shrinkage rate of approximately 17% is quite high, but that is because I use a lot of water in my clay and use stoneware clay that shrinks even more after being subjected to high firing temperatures. This percentage can usually vary between 10-20% depending on the type of clay and your kiln firing procedures. An example of how to calculate this percentage is discussed further in Chapter 9.

Some printers can stand on the floor while others need to be set on a table. Ensure that if a table is used, it is strong enough to support the entire weight of the machine and that the legs are stable enough not to buckle or vibrate under moving mechanical parts.

At times, you may need space to move around the printer as you work. Ensure that the space is adequate so that you can view the prints from any angle.

As mentioned previously, the delta printers focus more on height, whereas the cartesian printers focus more on surface volume and can produce wider prints. There is no point in buying a massive clay printer if you do not have access to a kiln that can fire a large-scale print. It is advisable to do some research on kilns and studios that have the capacity to fire items. Their costing structures and time constraints will have an impact on your budget.

Studio charges vary with some only invoicing firing costs relative to the weight of the finished clay body and with others looking at how much space your print will take up in the kiln.

Technical Support

Buy a machine or parts from a well-established supplier, ensuring that you have technical support. Having some expertise in your corner to help is never a bad idea – to know exactly how a specific machine works, and where to look if a problem needs fixing. They can also help you with specialised training and development, ensuring that you can make optimal use of the machine's capabilities.

Modifying a plastic 3D printer to print with clay may be a cheaper strategy, but you will need to remember that if it breaks or presents problems, the responsibility will fall entirely on you to find further support. If you have no technical knowledge, this could definitely slow down your working process.

You will need to figure out your working technique and incorporate that into your build. Clay printing is not a difficult concept in theory; however, all the other moving parts can make printer builds tricky at times.

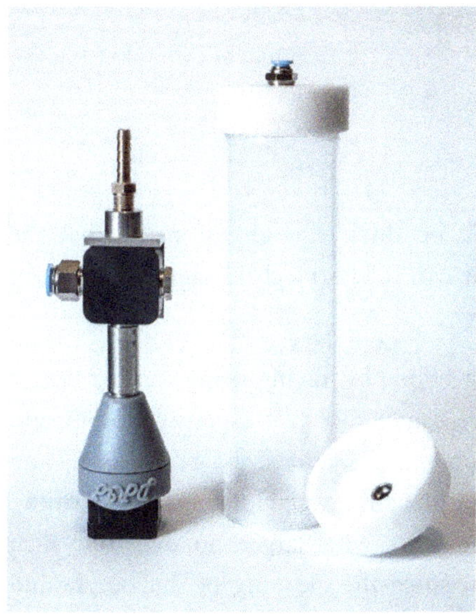

Extruder and clay container prototype that uses air pressure by DRIP AM© / 2023.

Mechanical Extrusion or Compressed Air?

There is no correct or wrong choice here. It comes down to personal preference as both options are easily available for purchase on the global market. I enjoy the fact that I can easily adjust the flow of my clay with the aid of the air pressure regulator. The choice of having an air compressor presents an additional cost so it is important to ensure that you buy the correct size.

For example, I require an air compressor that does not exceed eight bars. As such, a small silent one is a good investment. Noise pollution is reduced, and it allows for more focused attention to the task at hand. Some clay prints can take hours to finish, and you need to be considerate of the people in your immediate surroundings and the environment. One of the cons is that you need to monitor your air pressure during the print run, but I have found that this does not hinder my clay print-making process at all.

If you want to build your own printer, consider the clay container options already available to you. These should have safety features already built in such as a safety valve should you accidently set your air pressure too high.

The mechanical system allows your material to be deposited in a continuous flow, with layer heights and flow remaining constant, unless adjusted on the printer itself. With these types of ram extruders, make sure to check the printer's capabilities.

Can the clay printer retract its clay if it needs to move from one position to another? You may think this is not an important feature, but if you are printing an object that has multiple starting points, such as a three-legged vase, the retraction of clay by the printer will be necessary if you want a precision print that does not extrude clay where there should be gaps in the design.

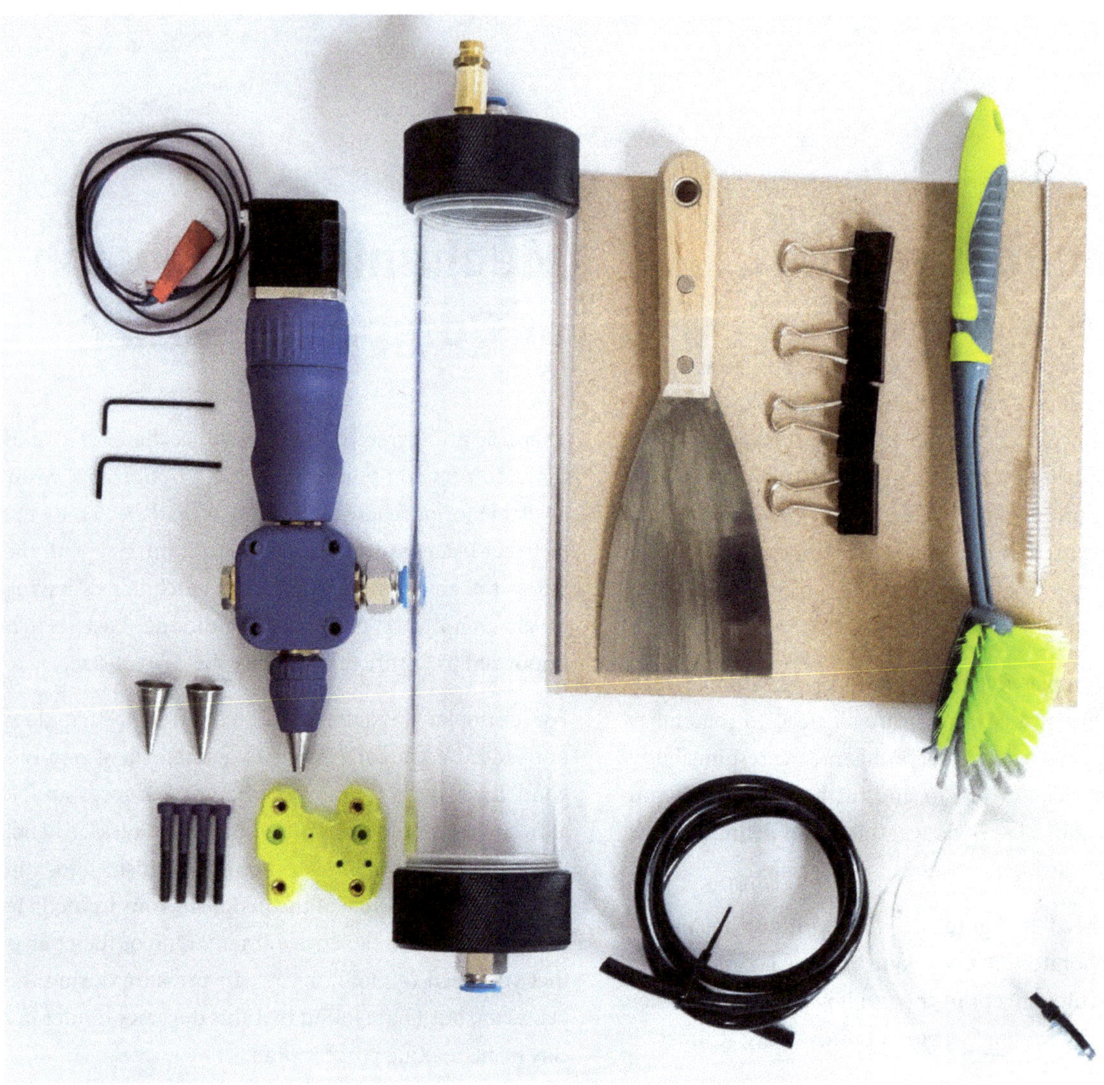

Photo by DRIP AM©/ 2024.

Extras

When you buy a new clay 3D printing machine, all the extras are already included and constitute the overall cost. Building a clay 3D printer requires that you do some research into what extra equipment will work best for you.

For an air compressor setup, you will need connectors and piping for the air to travel from the compressor to your printer. Debate where your compressor will be placed relative to your printer and make sure that the air pipe is long enough. My pipe size is twelve millimetres wide, which means that my connectors to and from the printer must also be the same size.

The pipe must be thick enough to ensure that the compressed air can safely travel through it to prevent it from bursting.

One cannot go wrong by having many varying nozzle sizes. These are usually not that expensive to buy and come in various shapes and sizes. Brass, steel, and plastic ones are usually available at hardware stores. As a beginner, start with larger nozzle sizes, such as 2mm/3mm, since the cleaning of the nozzle and observing how the clay moves through it will be easier. From there moving to the smaller sizes such as the 1mm/ 0.5mm nozzle will then be much easier.

THE OUTLINE

1
Design a CAD 3D Model
2
Export as an STL file
3
Create the G-code
4
3D Printing Process
5
Pottery Process

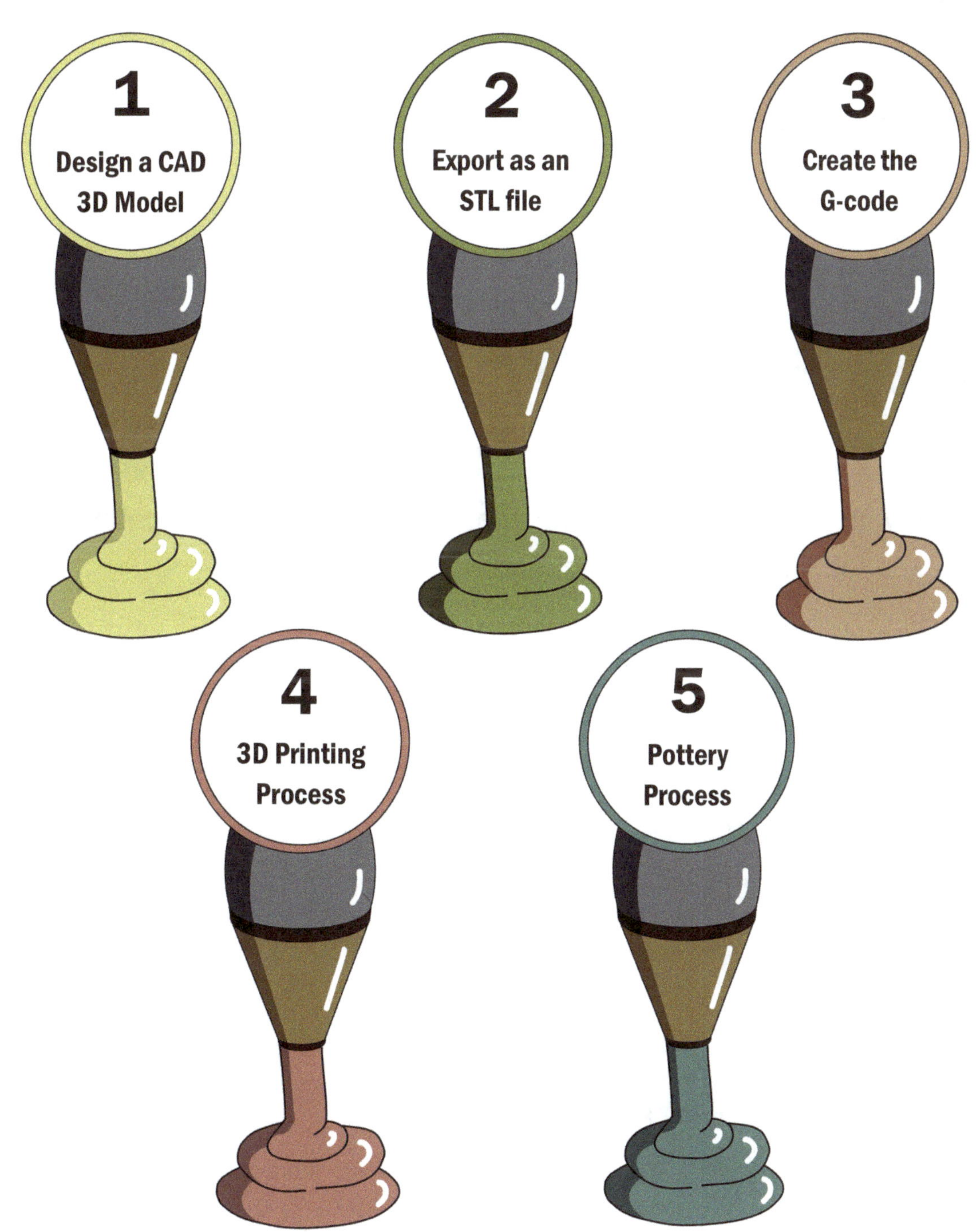

3D DESIGN (CAD)

WHAT IS 3D CAD?

3D CAD is a computer-controlled process where computer aided design (CAD) software is used to digitally fabricate designs. Digital fabrication is a widely used manufacturing technique.

You can modify and apply changes to a 3D design much faster digitally than revising a physical drawing or constructing an object repeatedly. The collaboration of makers across many different industries and countries is simplified as file types can be shared online, ensuring the design process is more cost effective and in real time.

CAD design software exists to produce optimal designs. You don't need to be skilled at drawing to work with the software. As long as the basics within the specific programme you are working on can be learnt, you will eventually be able to build on that exponentially. Think of it as a very advanced sketching tool that assists in digitally creating complex 3D forms.

Examples of CAD software currently available:
Autodesk® 123D, Autodesk® Fusion 360, Tinkercad®, Blender®, Rhino3D®, SketchUp©, Solidworks®.

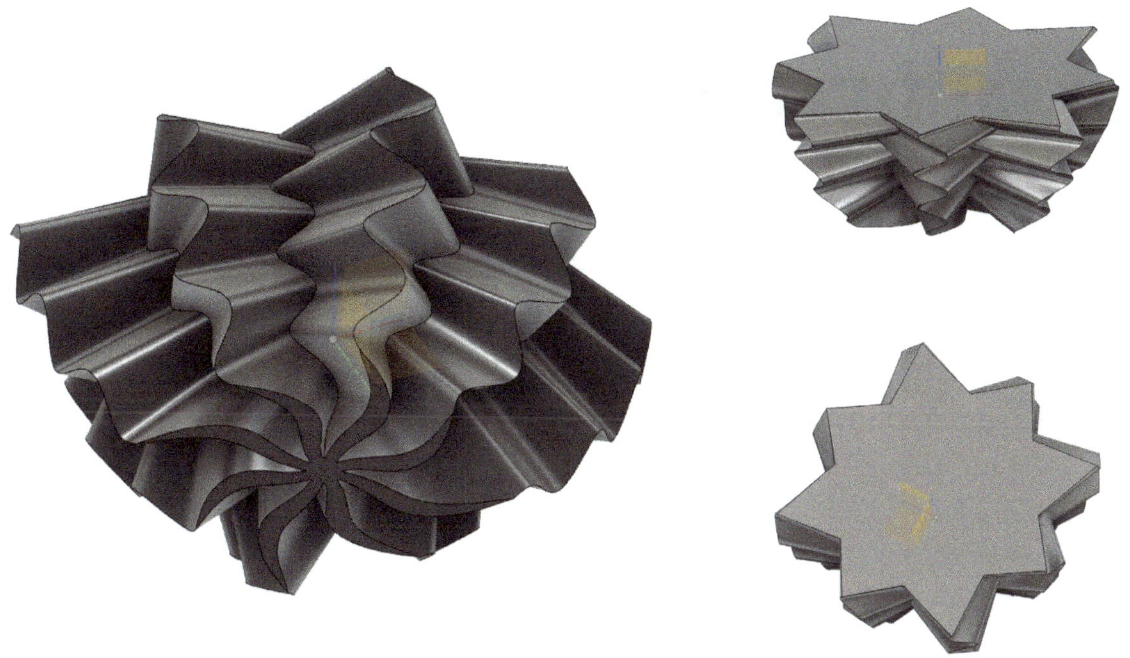

The different angles of a 3D design created in Autodesk® Fusion 360 / 2023.

With online tutorials being readily and freely available, teaching yourself the software has never been easier. You can learn at your own pace, concentrating on the tools within a particular software that you want to develop.

To start with, I would suggest finding a well-established online creator that has a cohesive teaching style that suits you. Build your skillset from the ground up, learning the basics of the software whilst concentrating on the shapes that you understand. In this way, when you are ready to design your own objects, you have a foundational understanding of where to start and how to 3D design in a cohesive way.

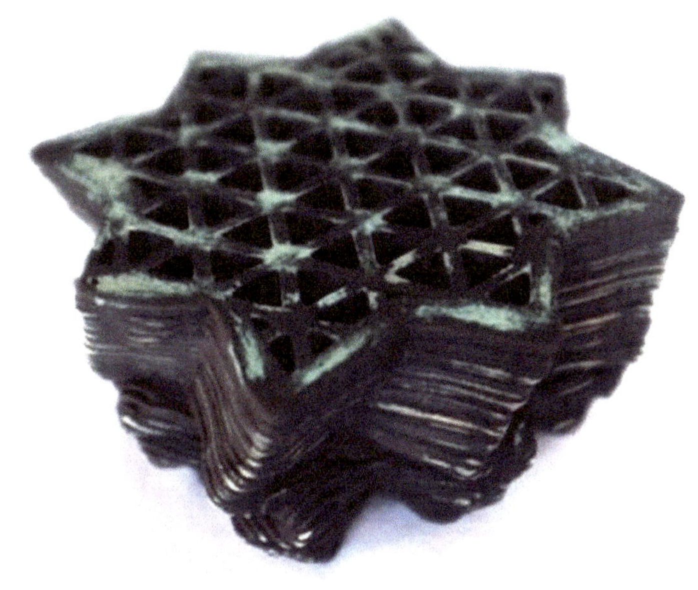

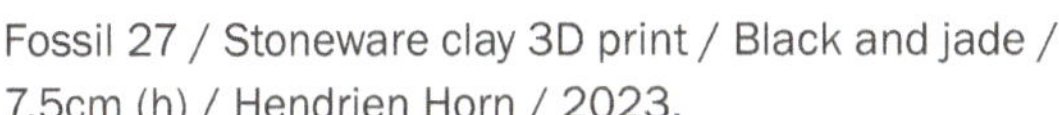

Fossil 27 / Stoneware clay 3D print / Black and jade / 7.5cm (h) / Hendrien Horn / 2023.

3D MODELLING SOFTWARE FOR CLAY

For many makers, learning 3D design using the traditional CAD software can be daunting. There are, however, software programmes that are specifically designed just for clay 3D printing, making it a little easier for the clay maker who wants to venture into clay 3D printing.

Potterware

Developed by Ronald Rael, Virginia San Fratello, Barrak Darweesh, Constantina Tsiara and Alexander Curth.

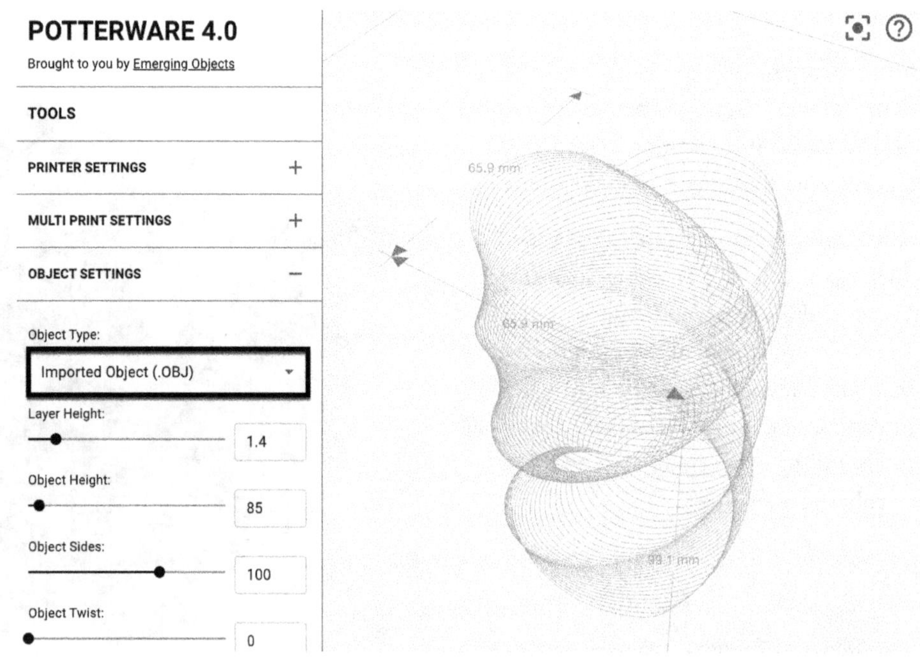

Potterware 4.0 Interface.

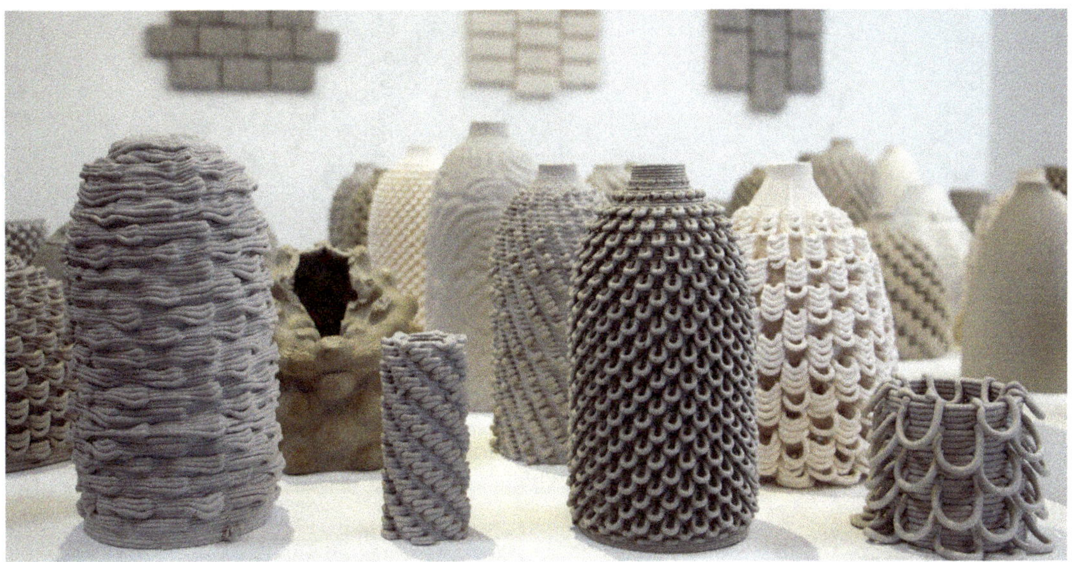

g.code clay / Potterware was used to design these clay 3D prints / Emerging Objects.

This software was the first of its kind to be made available to the public for downloading in 2019. It is a browser-based application created by Emerging Objects, a company that provides innovative 3D printing solutions in the architectural industry and was founded by Ronald Rael.

The focus of the software is to give you the opportunity to 3D design and sculpt vessels and functional pottery, ready for 3D printing. It is an intuitive design application that allows you to manipulate the shape of a vessel with easy-to-use sliders and menus. With the ability to warp, twist, adjust, contort, and swivel the design, you can add extra design characteristics to make your vessel uniquely yours.

A unique feature of the Potterware software is the image map function. You can wrap an image around your object which can be used to create the surface pattern. You need to consider nozzle size and layer heights, ensuring your design is not too complex as the print resolution of clay 3D printers is not as high as that for filament printers. With that said, this can allow makers to explore different patterns and ideas that would ultimately result in new and innovative clay prints.

The software also gives the maker the ability to print multiple copies of a design in a single print. This can be very useful in reducing the printing time if you are creating small scale identical clay 3D prints.

For first time makers, there is an online forum for information and to access many easy-to-follow tutorials. Potterware is compatible with the Potterbot, LUTUM® and WASP® Delta 3D printers and is used by many educational institutions worldwide.

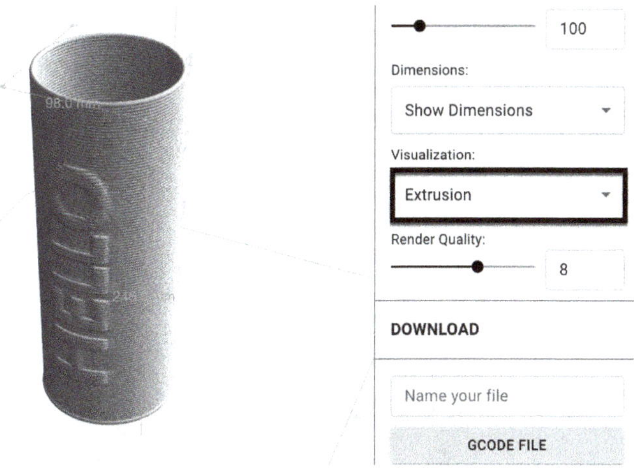

The Image Map function in Potterware 4.0.

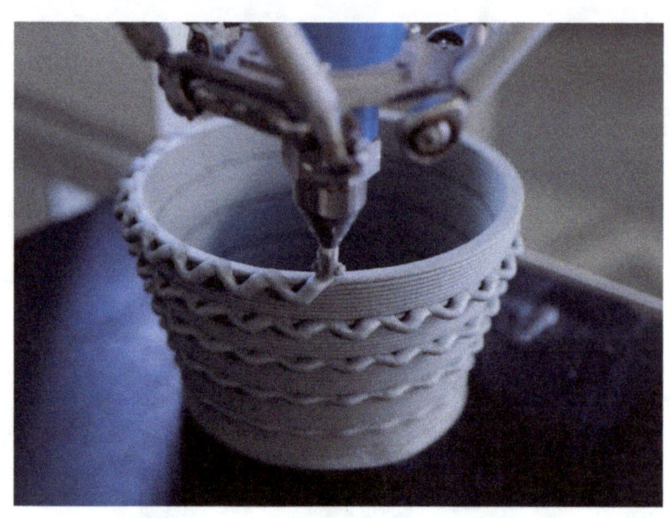

Clay vessel created with the WASP® App / WASP® / 2023.

WASP® App

WASP® App is a new slicing and parametric 3D modelling software that is compatible only with WASP® Delta printers, allowing for complete control in conjunction with their technology. This type of software ensures that customers have access to the best information and experience in that it offers a user-friendly approach to 3D modelling. Experimentation in terms of the Delta Clay 3D Printer capabilities and creative potential for works is strongly encouraged.

WASP® created their first software, called Vase Generator, which was developed by Tommaso Casucci in 2014. Since then, the WASP® team has worked extensively on this type of technology, capitalising on the 3D modelling experience that they acquired over time.

WASP® App can be used to manipulate the parameters of shape, size, texture, and the slicing settings of a vessel. The WASP® team is also working to incorporate different design objects, facades, tiles, and vases for modification - including how to queue different G-codes in the same file. These new features are designed to work in conjunction with their WASP® 40100 Clay Production System.

The software is freely available online and users are encouraged to give feedback on their experiences with it. Anticipating future expansions, including the integration of large-scale 3D architectural prints using the Crane WASP®, the possibilities of this type of technology are growing exponentially.

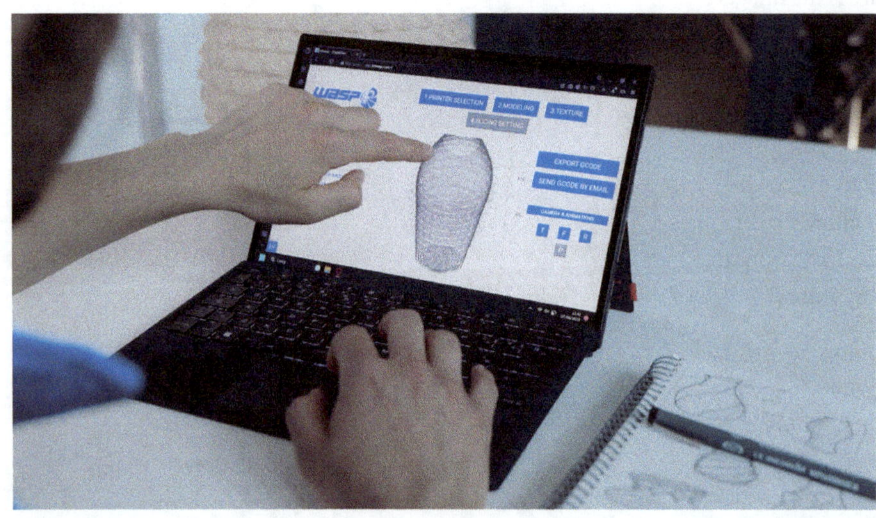

WASP® App / WASP® / 2023.

GRASSHOPPER®

Grasshopper® is a very useful software tool that 3D makers can use within the Rhino3D® software. To gain a better understanding of why this software's popularity is growing and how it differs from other AutoCAD software, I asked Professor Cuevas to explain it to me, since he co-authored a book about it!

Diego Garcia Cuevas

Diego Garcia Cuevas is the co-founder of Controlmad®, a Rhino3D® Fab Studio, which focuses on advanced architecture, design and engineering in Madrid, Spain. This design centre hosts workshops and training in parametric and computational design using both Rhino3D® and Grasshopper®. He emphasised that their focus encompasses several technologies, namely, CNC (Computer Numerical Control) milling, 3D printing in different materials, as well as robotics. He combines these technologies and teaches at several universities worldwide.

Initially, Professor Cuevas discovered the Rhino3D® software in 2007, when he was working for Dominique Perrault, a world-renowned architect in Paris. At the time, he was using AutoCAD software, much like the ones I introduced you to earlier in this book. Noting how fast Rhino3D® software was and wanting to explore this further, he subsequently went on to do his Master's degree in Biodigital Architecture in Barcelona, experimenting with different technologies, using Rhino3D®, and with Grasshopper® (released in 2008, as an add-on plug-in).

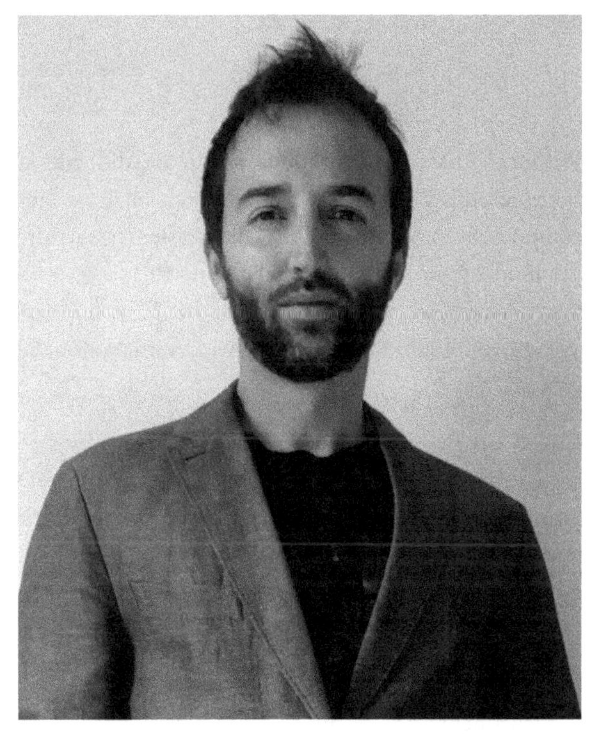

Diego Garcia Cuevas / 2020.

Rhino3D® is a CAD modeller, similar to AutoCAD or others where the maker must use sketch and modelling tools to design and model their 3D object in the workspace.

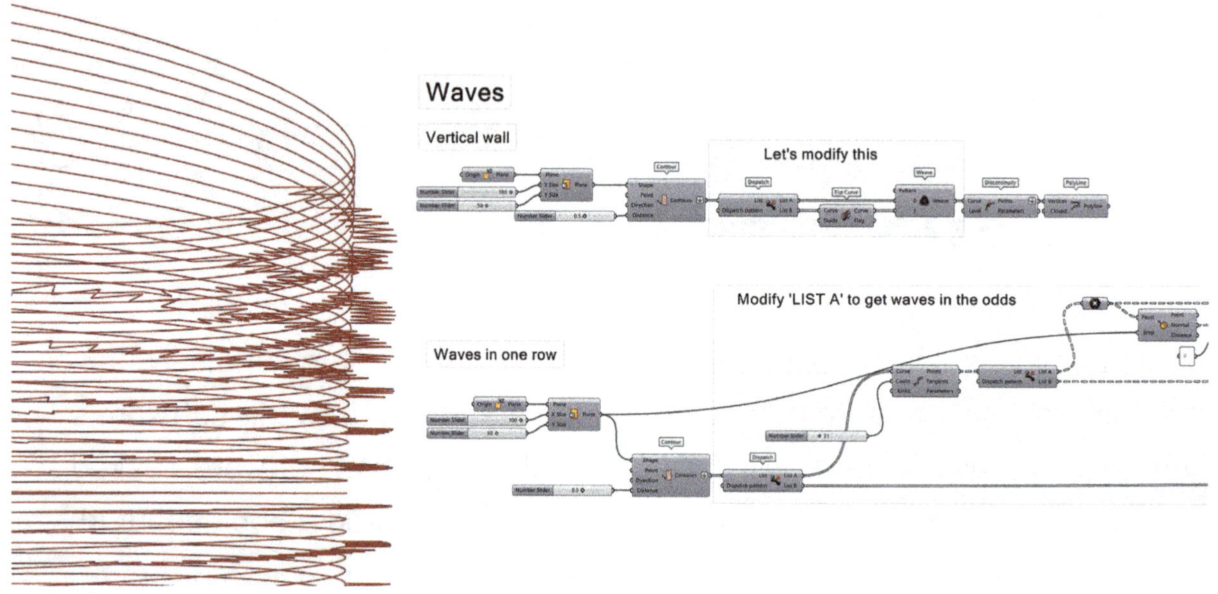

G-code with Grasshopper®.

With an AutoCAD workflow, it can be difficult at times to adjust and make changes to an intricate and complicated design. Sometimes, it is easier to start the 3D model from scratch, rather than struggling to fix a small mistake, and this is where the Grasshopper® software built into Rhino3D® can help to streamline the process.

Grasshopper® is fully integrated and works side by side with Rhino3D®. It is a wonderful tool to use in 3D designs that have complex geometries. For example, if you want to create 1 000 circles, each with a different radius according to one point, you can easily insert the code, giving the instructions for the software to do so - instead of creating each circle individually.

If adjustments are required, all that is needed is to change the relevant parameter that is easily visible in the Grasshopper® software window. Once done, the design in the Rhino3D® software will change the 3D design accordingly across all the parameters of the design.

Grasshopper® software focuses on nurbs, which are points connected by curves that give the mathematical representation of the surfaces in your design, such as the x, y and z co-ordinates. These curves form paths for the 3D printer to follow during the printing process.

Where this technical application becomes useful is where normal slicers are unable to create a curve moving in a vertical upward and downward continuous motion - slicing software is often designed to print well, without skipping any coil layers and printing in a continuous loop. Grasshopper® offers the capacity to create a curved path while following the pre-determined co-ordinates during the printing process.

Grasshopper® falls into a category between computer aided design and coding. It replaces the code written in the text with nodes. Nodes are components that perform specific functions and are essentially codes connected to one another. Anyone who has explored a coding language, for example, Java Script, will know it is not always easy to learn. Grasshopper® enables you to write your own instructions and scripts without all the intricacies of the coded language models and, at times, difficult mathematical equations.

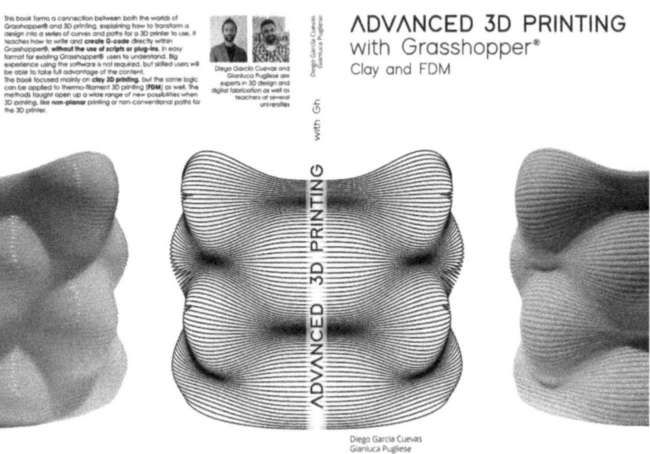

Book Cover: Advanced 3D printing with Grasshopper®: Clay and FDM / by Diego Garcia Cuevas and Gianluca Pugliese / 2020.

His book, "Advanced 3D Printing with Grasshopper® : Clay and FDM", was published in 2020 and was co-authored by Gianluca Pugliese, the founder of LOWPOLY in Madrid; a company focused on researching and developing sustainable materials for large-scale 3D printing.

The book came about through the additional time that became generally available during the Covid-19 pandemic. People started asking more questions and wanted to learn about Grasshopper® and the capabilities of the software. Professor Cuevas did not think the book would be a great success since the demand for this type of design making was such a niche market. However, demand for it has grown substantially over the past few years, with the book selling many thousands of copies on Amazon to date.

Controlmad® was part of a project to design a façade for the Real Madrid Stadium. Working together with the manufacturer of the building materials, they helped the team understand this new process and how to manufacture these types of parametric designs.

Controlmad® are also currently working on other projects that involve the use of concrete and clay. Many of these projects are still under lock and key, which means that this space must be watched!

Professor Cuevas also found that using a pen plotter to show how 2D sketches work without the extrusion of a material helps his students to visualise the 3D printing process based on the Grasshopper® software. It is a great learning tool that is faster and more cost effective than continually loading a 3D printer before creating a model.

Different experiments that are being conducted with their robotic arm, really pique my interest. One is the DrawBot. This robot is programmed to paint on a canvas using a variety of colours. It can be a messy and time-consuming process, with the accuracy of the arm movements still being adapted and improved upon, but something like this has much potential in the industry.

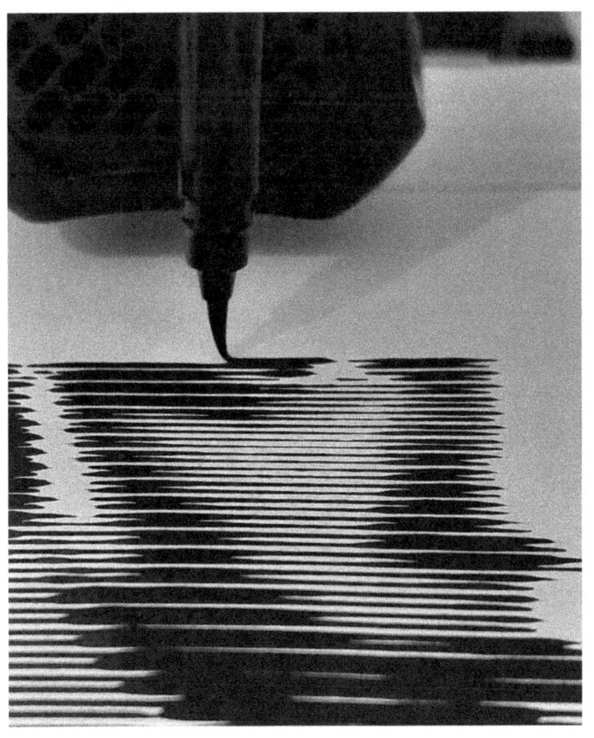

Drawbot / Diego Garcia Cuevas / 2023.

Professor Cuevas made a short video on "Winning the lottery with Grasshopper®", as the software is also very good for data management and numbers. The lottery consisted of 49 numbers, and six correct numbers were needed to be picked from these. He calculated the probability of each number being drawn and calculated that a person has one in an approximately 14-million chance of winning the lottery with all six correct numbers.

To achieve this, he used the statistics from previous winners and input the data into Grasshopper®. With a few added calculations, the software gave him the numbers that he randomly played for one consecutive week. It turned out that he won only four euros, and he jokingly added that "if I had won the lottery, you would probably not be talking to me now." He, however, wanted to prove the point that Grasshopper® can be used in many applications, and that thinking outside the box should be encouraged.

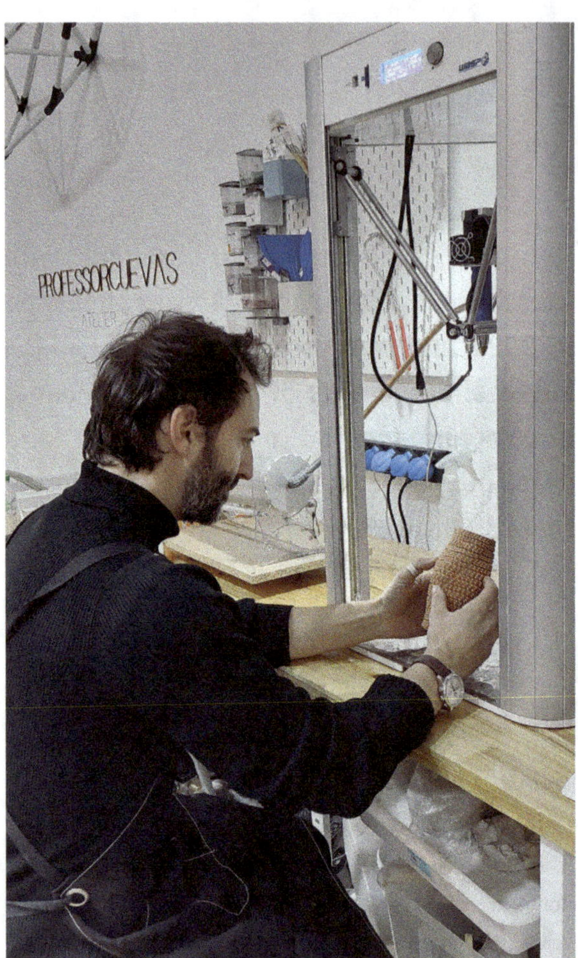

Teaching in his studio / Diego Garcia Cuevas / 2023.

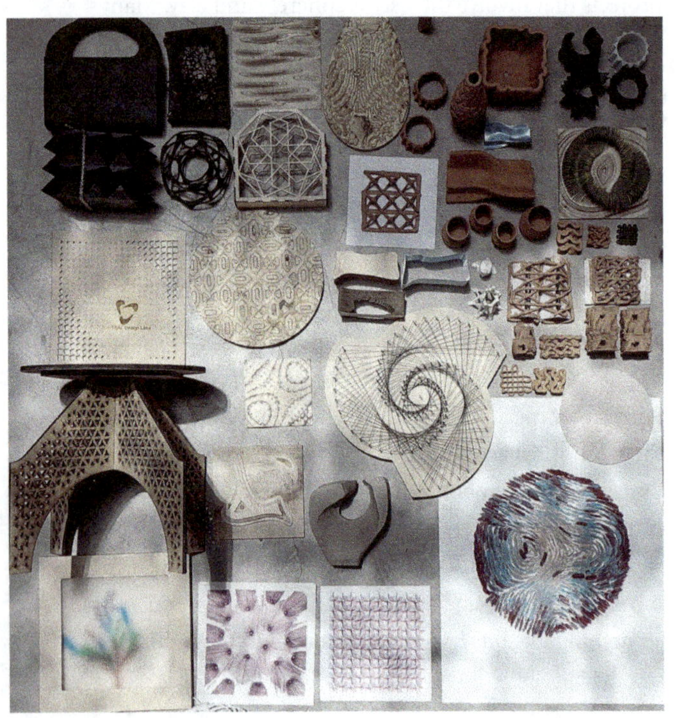

Creative Robotics / Diego Garcia Cuevas / 2023.

When I asked his opinion on the impact of 3D printing on the world, he told me that it is becoming vastly more popular and will become common practice across many industries. Schools across the globe are already adopting some of these practices, as is the case with the exclusive designs with CAD, which will become a part of everyday life. The direction that artificial intelligence will take us, however, is currently a big unknown. How will these technologies create 3D designs in the future and what will they look like? Furthermore, we do not yet know the impact that AI will have on some industries.

"Will two types of artisans emerge, one making an item by hand and another using robotics and ChatGPT? Only time will tell."

– Diego Garcia Cuevas, 2023.

STL FILE

Once you have finished creating your 3D design within your CAD software, you need to export it as an STL file.

Think of a STL file as a 3D drawing file that includes all the parameters of your 3D design. These files are easily transferable between makers, allowing for multiple designers to work on the same 3D design.

Various STL files are freely available online for download. They may simplify the process when you are starting out and want to try tester prints with your clay 3D printer. Ensure your STL files are prints that can be printed with clay. Clay contains water which means that the prints can easily warp if sharp angles are included without the necessary supports. Downloading free STL files also comes with a responsibility to credit the original 3D designer when you create a print using their design.

I would strongly suggest learning how to 3D design your own prints. Only printing other people's designs instead of your own will severely limit your growth and development as a 3D maker once your fresh ideas become more complex.

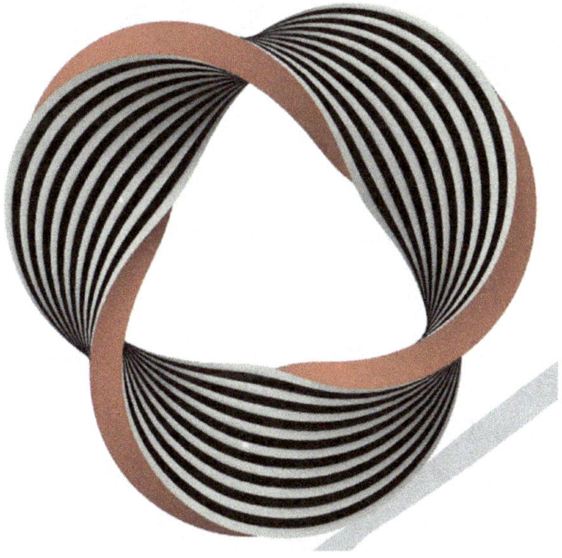

This may not be a printable 3D design for clay, but I found playing around with different shapes and tools within the CAD software helped me to learn faster / Autodesk® Fusion 360 / 2020.

SLICING SOFTWARE

Slicing software provides a visual representation of the path that the 3D printer follows when it executes a print. It indicates for how long the print will run and if there are any sections that may cause problems along the way (e.g. an overhanging area that may collapse during a print).

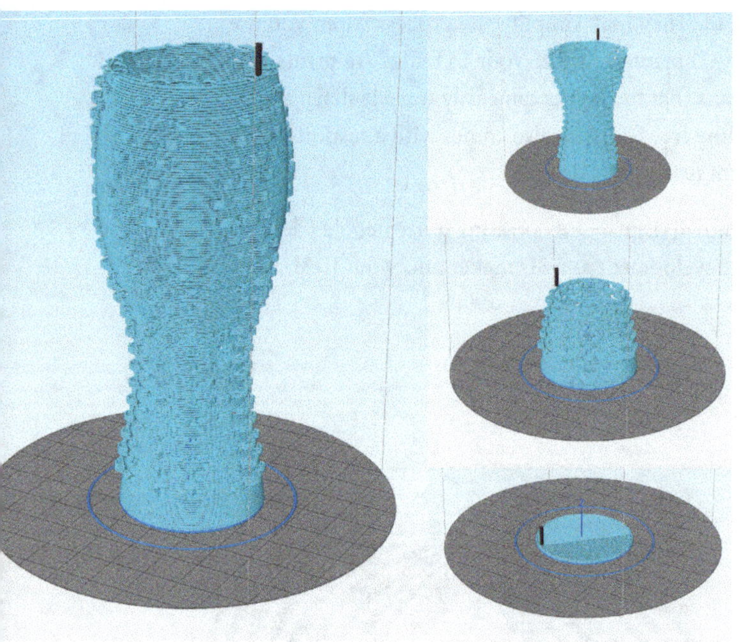

Slicing a vase - each layer height of your print is visually represented / Simplify3D® / 2023.

An STL file must be imported into the slicing software on the computer. The software allows you to change some of the parameters which are important for the printer to know before you can start printing. Some of these include the speed, nozzle size, layer height, whether the clay walls are single or double, the thickness of the solid bottom layers, and whether extra supports are required.

These variables all work together to create the perfect print. As a beginner, you may find yourself spending a lot of time tweaking your settings to make sure your clay 3D print is created to the level of detail that you want to produce.

As mentioned previously, start with a larger nozzle size (2mm/3mm) so that you can see how the clay coils move during the printing process relative to the weight distribution, design features, overhangs, layer heights, and the speed of the clay form. This will also make it easier if you find that your printer nozzle is clogging or if you have not yet settled on a clay consistency that works for you.

Many clay 3D printer manufacturers include pre-set procedures for their printers to relate to some of the above parameters. This can be very helpful for beginners, making the time spent on testing just a little bit less.

Examples of Slicing Software currently available:
Ultimaker Cura®, MakerBot Print©, PrusaSlicer©, Simplify3D®, Slic3r©.

G-CODE

Once all your parameters are set, the slicing software will translate your 3D design's build instructions into G-code (Geometric code). Your G-code must then be exported so that it is ready to be used by your printer.

G-code is a language that a 3D printer can understand. Without G-code, your printer would not be able to print. This code is also used in many different CNC machines, and not only in 3D Printers. These machines play a huge role in the manufacturing industry. Some include robots, laser cutters, waterjet, milling and sheet metal stamping machines.

If it had to be done manually (you are not required to learn this), an example of a G-code command would be -

G28 X0 Y0 Z0

Once a print has been completed, the pre-programmed G-code will give the 3D printer a command to move its print head to the home position (the pre-set start and end position), also known as true zero and represented in the command above.

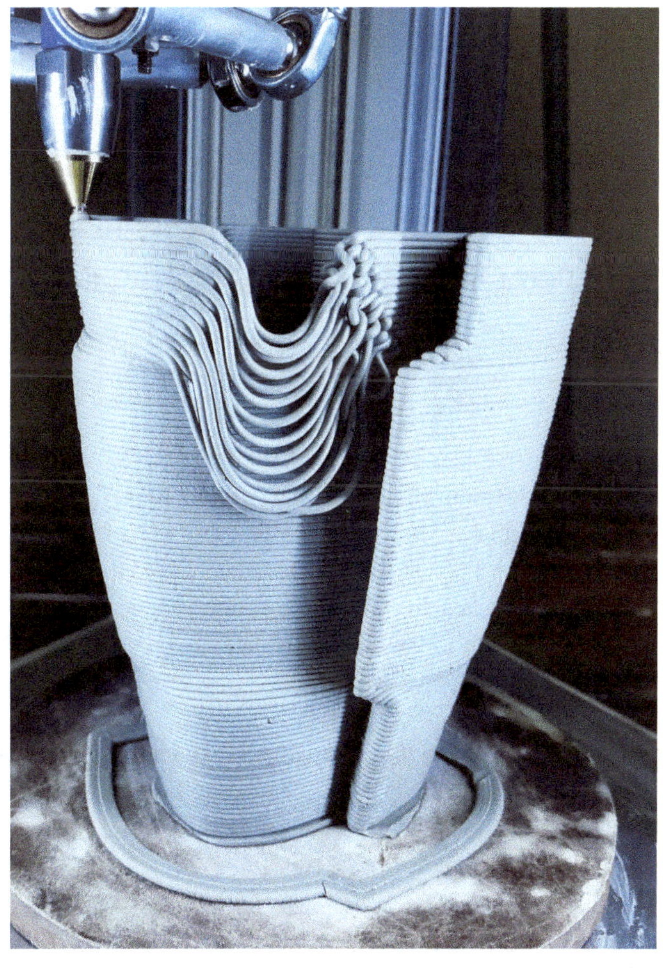

A clay 3D printer following its pre-determined path as instructed by the G-code / Hendrien Horn / 2021.

THINK CLAY

WHAT CLAY TO START WITH

It is important to note that clay needs to be able to move freely through the extruder nozzle of your 3D printer. You cannot have large pieces of coarse clay moving through the extruder mechanism as it may clog and break it.

Most manufactured clays contain grog. Grog is clay that has already been fired once in the kiln and then finely ground up and mixed into other clay. Find a fine-grained clay that contains grog and can be used on a pottery wheel. It should be noted that you can't use clay that has massive clumps of dried material in it when you are working on the pottery wheel as you may cut your hand. This fine material is, however, perfect for a clay 3D printer.

Earthenware (Terracotta) / Stoneware / Porecelain.

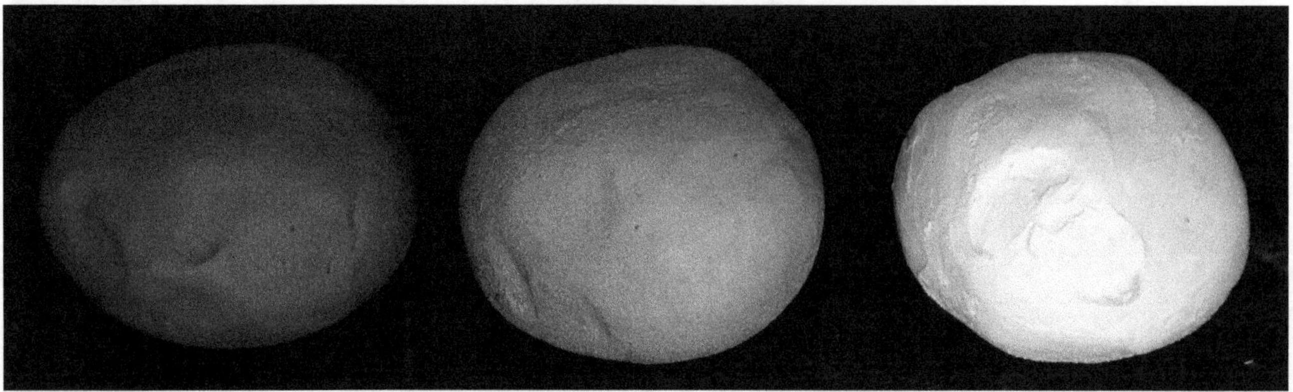

Some of the advantages of grog include the following: it improves the drying performance of the clay, reduces the amount of shrinkage the clay body will experience during both the drying and the firing processes, improves fire abrasion resistance, and reduces thermal expansion (the tendency of a clay body to change shape, volume, and area in response to a change in temperature).

It is important to note the different consistencies of clay. Wet clay can easily be sculpted and shaped, but when it dries out, it becomes brittle and easily breakable.

Earthenware Clay

Earthenware clays are a favourite for making vases and garden planters. It is more porous than stoneware clays, allowing liquid to move slowly through the clay body once fired making it suitable for plants that need to be kept cool and hydrated. They are usually kiln fired at approximately 1 000°C and have a lower shrinkage rate compared to that of the high-fired clays. The completed item usually requires a glaze covering to make it "food safe" and suitable for everyday use (e.g. when making a mug, bowl or plate).

Earthenware clay is a favourite amongst clay sculptors because, as a material, it can at times be more forgiving. Many of the red terracotta clays contain large pieces of grog. Always ensure that the clay is suitable for pottery wheelwork when choosing this type of clay for clay 3D printing.

Porcelain Clay

As a beginner, porcelain clay can be very challenging for 3D printing because it has a very soft texture and can be extremely elastic. The flexibility of the clay can mean that clay printed walls could easily collapse during a print, and at times the clay will buckle under the weight of added clay coil layers. This can be very frustrating when working with a clay 3D printer and clay for the first time.

Once porcelain clay is fired at a temperature of approximately 1 300°C, it can become partially translucent. This is one of the main reasons why many makers enjoy making lighting fixtures with porcelain clay. It is an expensive clay to buy because it contains rare materials such as kaolin. Kaolin helps to give the clay its signature white colour and produces a very delicate clay body, requiring a higher skill level to work with than that of other clays.

Stoneware Clay

If you have never worked with clay before, I would recommend starting with stoneware clay. It is a plastic clay that is kiln fired – at approximately 1 200°C, a higher temperature than earthenware clay. Do note that the clay body shrinkage rate is higher than that of clay that is fired at a lower temperature.

It is often used for both functional and decorative pieces because it can usually withstand heat from both a dishwasher and a microwave and, in some cases, even an oven. Check with your supplier what the limitations of the kiln fired clay are when it is subjected to these intense temperature changes.

CLAY PREPARATION

This is one of the most important steps in your entire process and should not be underestimated. How well your clay moves through the nozzle of your clay 3D printer will depend on the material and preparation.

New Clay

Newly purchased clay should be properly sealed in a plastic bag to ensure that the moisture of the clay is retained. Store-bought clay is usually compressed, which means that there should not be many air bubbles within the clay body. If you are unfamiliar with the clay's consistency, I would suggest breaking it into manageable pieces and wedging the clay into balls the size of your palm. Wedging is the process of removing any air from within the clay by reworking it with your hands. Sometimes wedging is not enough to get all the air bubbles out. Another method is to use a scraper tool to push the air bubbles out – a few at a time. Water can be added to your clay bit by bit to ensure that it does not dry out too much during this process.

Next, you need to focus on the type of printer setup that you have. Does your clay 3D printer use air pressure to push the clay through the extruder nozzle or does it have a mechanical system?

The air pressure systems sometimes require the clay to be of a wetter consistency. In fact, many of the smaller printers allow for only up to eight bars of air pressure. The mechanical extruders can exert a stronger force and therefore a thicker type of clay consistency can be used. If you find that your clay consistency is not wet enough, fully immerse your clay balls in water for a few hours or even overnight.

Since the clay balls have already been compressed through wedging, they will slowly start to absorb some of the water. If the clay is not compressed, you may find that it will start to disintegrate and make muddy water. This method may take some practice; so, use your good judgement. Once the clay consistency "feels" ready, remove the clay balls from the container of water and shake off any excess water.

Adding too much water to the clay could lead to the 3D printed walls not being stable enough to stay upright. They could warp or simply just fall over.

Should you be using an air pressure driven printer and the clay be too dry, the force needed to push it through all the equipment may not be sufficient, resulting in clay not moving through the connector pipe and the extruder.

What works for someone else may not necessarily work for you. Take sufficient time to test your clay mixture by adding water bit by bit to your clay until you are satisfied with its consistency. Remember to record your measurements, including the air pressure reading, if that is relevant. It will soon start to become second nature – just by touching the clay, you will be able to tell whether you need to add more water or not.

Filling the Clay Container

There are three methods that can be used to help fill the clay container with your material. They include the use of a pugmill, a scraper, or for you to stack the clay.

A pugmill is an expensive piece of machinery which can be operated to mix large amounts of clay and water together. It can then be used to deposit the print-ready clay directly into the clay container. For small-time makers this is an expense that is not necessary, unless you are planning to do large print runs daily.

The scraping method is performed by scraping your clay into the clay container, a little at a time. This helps to compress the clay whilst ensuring that no air bubbles are trapped. This can be a time-consuming process, but for small amounts of clay, it gives amazing results.

The stacking method is my favourite because my clay container can hold up to five kilograms of clay, and is, therefore, not really suited to the scraping method. I stack the clay balls neatly, taking the time to compress each clay ball as I go. This ensures that there are no air pockets trapped in between the clay layers within the container.

If you are doing clay consistency testing, do not fill your entire container with clay. To save time rather do small clay batches. You will immediately be able to see if the clay moves through the extruder at a rate that you want.

Recycled Clay

Recycling your clay can be a time-consuming process but you will find that the amount of clay left over from prints would be a huge expense if not recycled.

Once you have collected enough offcuts and shards of clay, set them aside to dry out completely. I have found that spreading the pieces out on a table covered with the same plastic bag that the clay came in and leaving them to stand in the sun is the fastest way to dry them out. You can also set your table of spread pieces of clay in a dry and well-ventilated area, if finding a sunny spot is a challenge.

Once the clay is fully dry, place the pieces in a bucket and add water. Because they are fully dried out, they will slowly start to disintegrate and form a paste in the bucket. This should be left to completely dissolve of its own accord. If the clay is not fully dried out before you add water to it, it can leave chunky pieces within the clay paste which you will need to break apart.

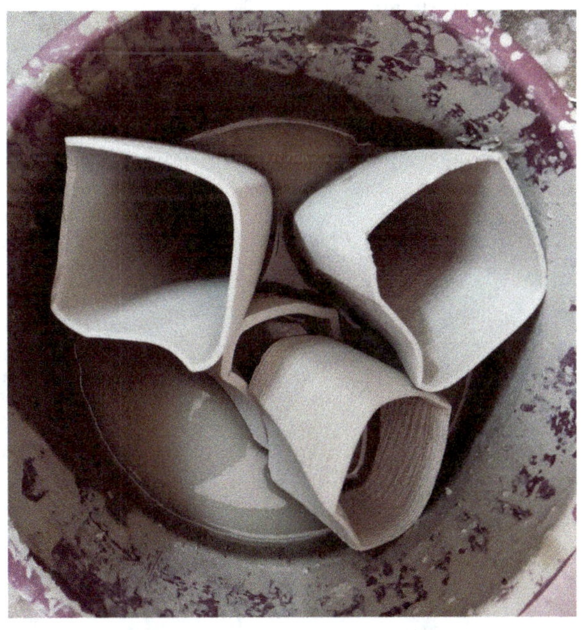

Recycling dry clay 3D prints by placing them in a bucket of water.

Initially, I would take the newly formed clay paste as is and let it dry out enough, ready to be wedged. However, experience has taught me that recycled clay can often contain small unwanted pieces of fluff and hair. There is a large German Shepherd dog and a black cat that occasionally enjoy popping in to say 'hello' at my studio! This is why I run my clay through a sieve with a mesh count of 80. The mesh count is determined by how many openings there is in one square inch of a sieve screen.

This ensures that any unwelcome particles get caught by the mesh and do not end up in the clay that moves through my printer nozzle. Unwanted pieces of fluff and pet hair will cause blockages and halt your print runs. Having sieved the clay paste, I let it dry out enough for it to be wedged. This usually takes a day or two, depending on how hot, humid, or dry the air is. Clay dries much faster when the air is warm and dry than it does when the air is cold and humid.

You will know that the clay is ready to use if it does not stick to your hands as you wedge it. From there, I follow the same process that I would for any new clay.

Air Bubbles

Air bubbles in the prepared clay can cause gaps in the layers of your printed forms. I usually do not spend sleepless nights over these gaps because my nozzle size and layer heights tend to be on the larger size. This means that when a printer completes one full rotation of the print, and there may be one small gap, the next time the printer does another rotation, the clay coil should close the air bubble gap, with the weight of the new clay coil.

When you are working with a very small nozzle, air bubble gaps may be a bit more obvious and could lead to an uneven distribution of weight in your clay coils. Most of the time these tiny imperfections can easily be dealt with, but only once your print is dry enough to be smoothed or shaped.

An air bubble that was trapped in the clay pierced through the wall of the clay during the 3D printing process / Hendrien Horn / 2021.

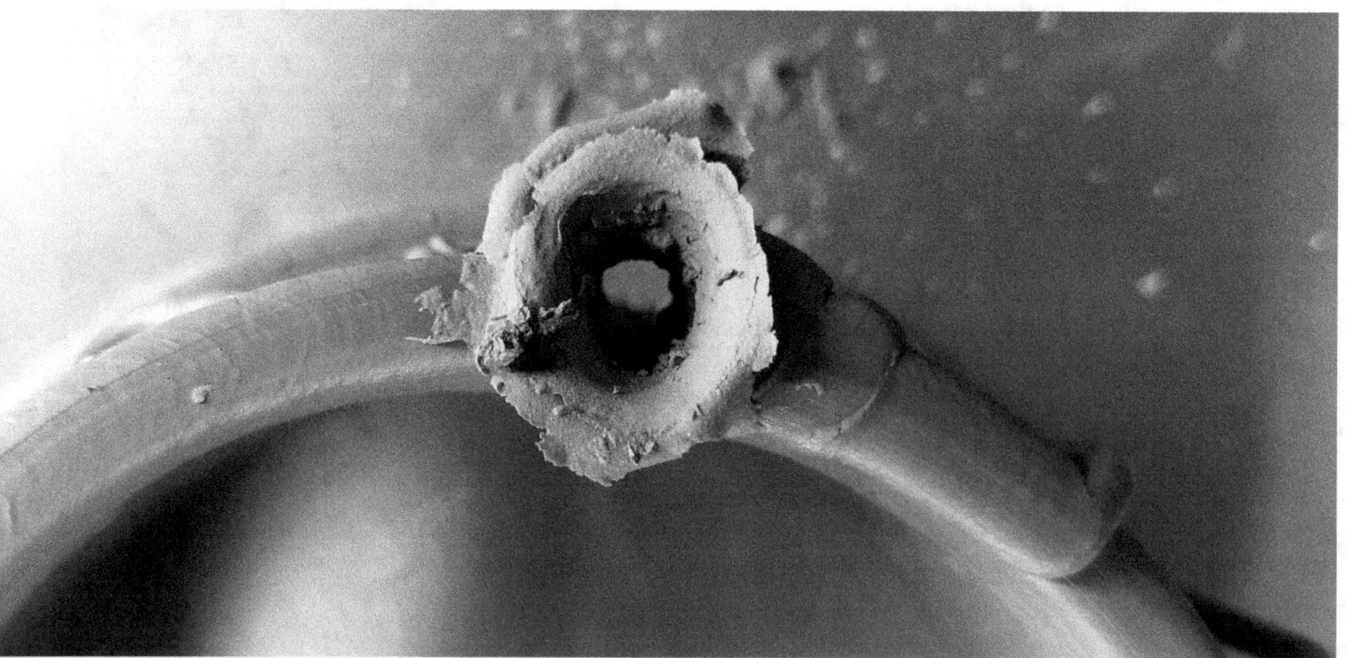

CLAY 3D PRINTING

THE 3D PRINTING PROCESS

Please keep in mind that not all clay 3D printers look alike and operate in the same way. Remember to check your printer manual and follow the instructions, as directed. The 3D printing process used as an example in this chapter employed a Delta Wasp 2040 Pro Clay 3D Printer that uses air pressure to extrude the clay.

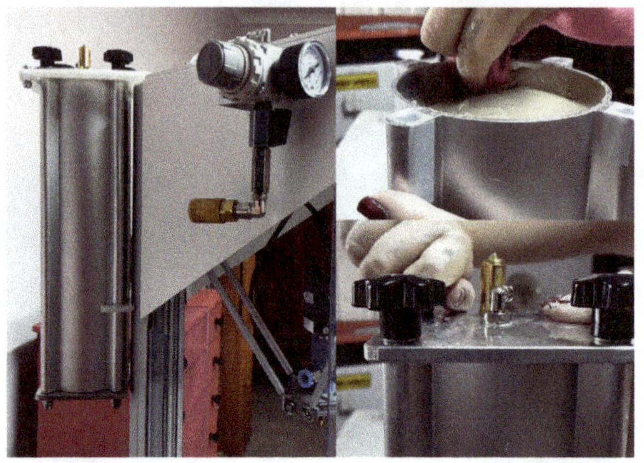

Step 1

Pack your prepared clay into the container, insert the stopper and seal it properly. Attach the filled clay container to your clay 3D printer.

Step 2

Connect the piping from the air compressor to the printer and clay container.

Connect the piping from the clay container to the extruder mechanism.

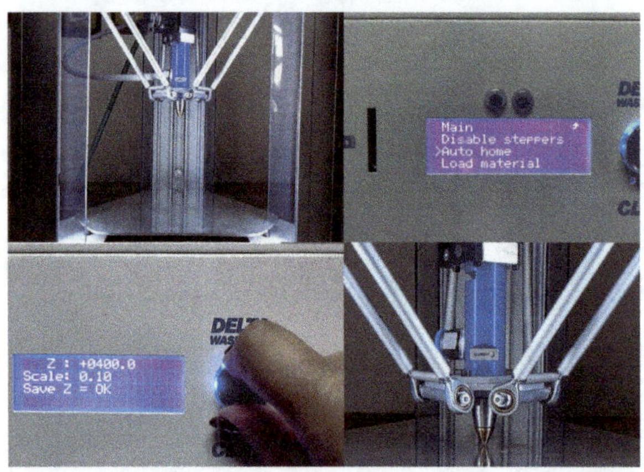

Step 3

Switch the clay 3D printer on and load the G-code.

Set the printer to its home position (start and end position).

Set the start print height. How far above the print bed you will start your print will depend on your nozzle size and layer height (for this, you will need to experiment to see what works best for you).

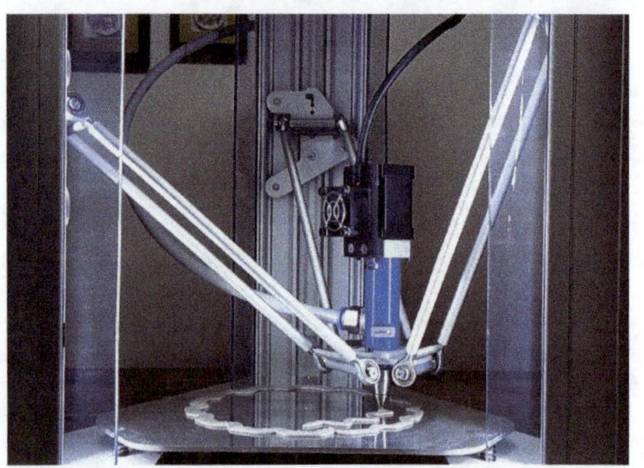

Step 4

Switch on the air compressor. Air will start to fill the clay container, pushing the stopper down and forcing the clay to move through the pipe and into the extruder mechanism.

Activate the extruder. Regulate the amount of clay extruded per second by using the air regulator on the printer. Make sure your printer is in the home position and start a test print, stopping the print only once you are satisfied with all of the adjusted settings.

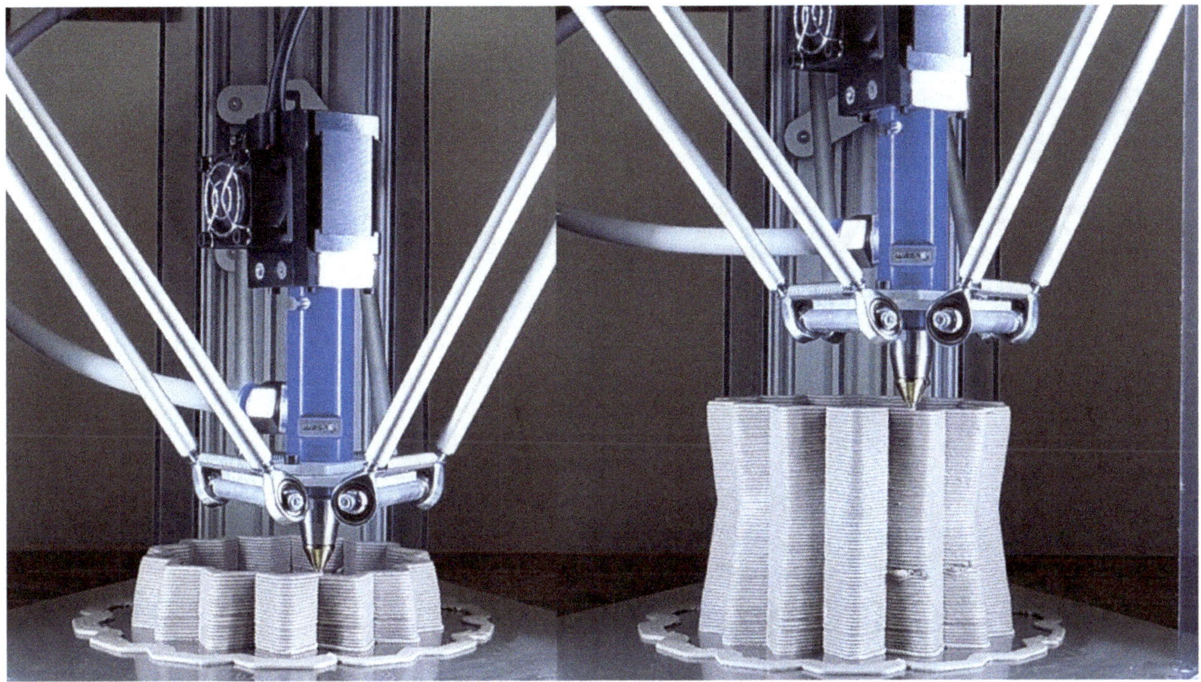

Step 5

When you are ready and happy with all the settings and air pressure, start your clay 3D print. The printer will follow the pre-coded path that has been set by the G-code, building up the layered clay coils. Your printer should allow you to make changes to the speed and flow during the print.

Once your 3D print is completed, the extruder will move back into the set home position. At this time ensure that you stop the flow of air pressure. Always remember to switch off the clay 3D printer and the air compressor, to decompress the clay container, to clean the extruder and to remove clay from the container and piping.

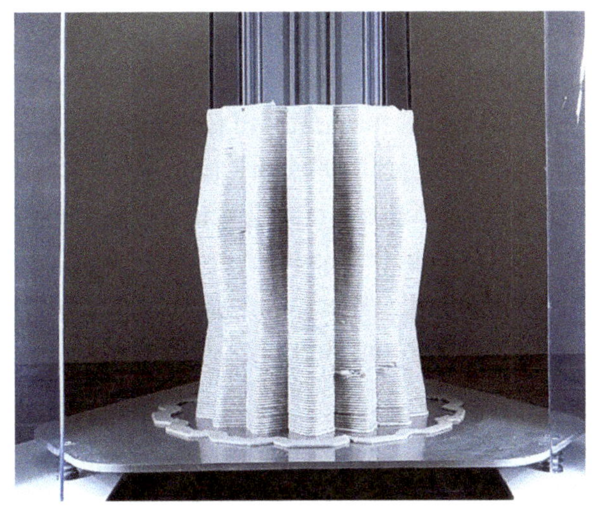

If you do not clean your extruder and piping before the clay dries, you could risk damage to your equipment. Clay can stay in the container for a day or two (depending on your clay consistency) before it starts to dry out; however, your extruder should be cleaned daily.

PRINTING PREFERENCES

As a clay maker you will need to figure out how you want to develop your technique and optimise your workflow.

Print the bottom or use a clay slab?

Whether to clay 3D print the bottom of your object or to hand make a clay slab, ultimately comes down to your personal preference. Some clay makers prefer to print the bottom layers of the clay print and if required, to smooth it out later. Others prefer to roll out a clay slab to the same thickness as the clay walls that will be printed, and then to place it on the bat and print the clay directly onto it.

When printing straight onto a clay slab, the trick is to make sure that the first printed clay layers stick to the slab properly so that there are no gaps for air to travel through. Use a paintbrush or sturdy tool to help close and flatten areas that may seem to be problematic. Many clay 3D printers have the ability to be paused mid-print to allow for adjustments to be made.

If the clay walls are not attached properly to the slab, cracking, or the detachment of the entire bottom of your printed object could occur in the various stages of the pottery process. Sometimes, cracks will only be revealed once the object has been kiln fired.

To help overcome this problem, you should wait until the print is leather hard, which means that it will not warp if you touch it. Use a spray bottle filled with water and evenly spray the work until it is covered. Then place the object in a plastic bag, making sure that the clay does not touch the sides of the bag. This will create a damp environment within the plastic bag as it starts to regulate the temperature, helping the clay body to absorb the water and giving it time to dry slowly and evenly.

When 3D printing the bottom of an object, remember that clay shrinks when it dries. As such, two to three bottom layers for a small single walled print will work well. The thicker your clay walls, the more bottom clay layers should be added. This is an easily adjustable feature in your slicing software that should be noted when you set up your G-code.

Printing on a Bat

Clay is a material that should not be overworked and prodded whilst the final product is drying. Any small adjustments or movements in the clay while it is drying could lead to the warping or collapsing of the walls of your printed object.

Printing on a bat allows you to do multiple prints in one print run. A bat is a thin slab of wood or plaster tile that is used to support a clay form whilst building and/or sculpting it. Once a print has been completed, you can easily remove the bat holding your printed object without touching the clay body and place another bat on the print bed ready for the next print.

The bats absorb the water from the drying clay object and therefore assist in evenly drying the clay print. You should not print on a surface where the water cannot be absorbed through the bottom (e.g. plastic), therefore printing directly onto the bed of the clay printer is not advised, unless it is for a quick test print.

When starting out, you might want to experiment in printing different shapes. Should a print fail, the bat can be easily removed and cleaned, thus preparing the printer for a new start.

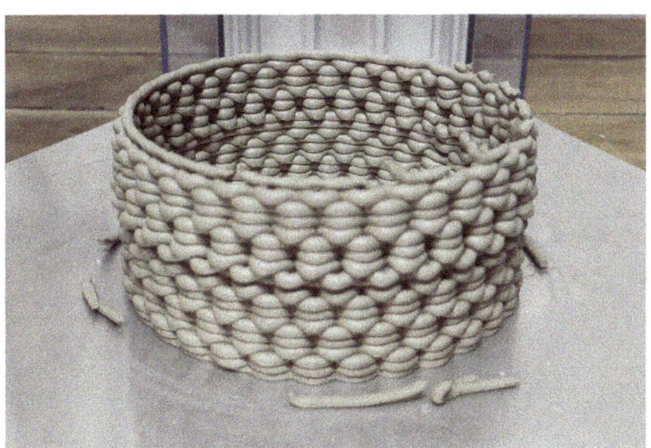

A test print checking layer height and speed settings.

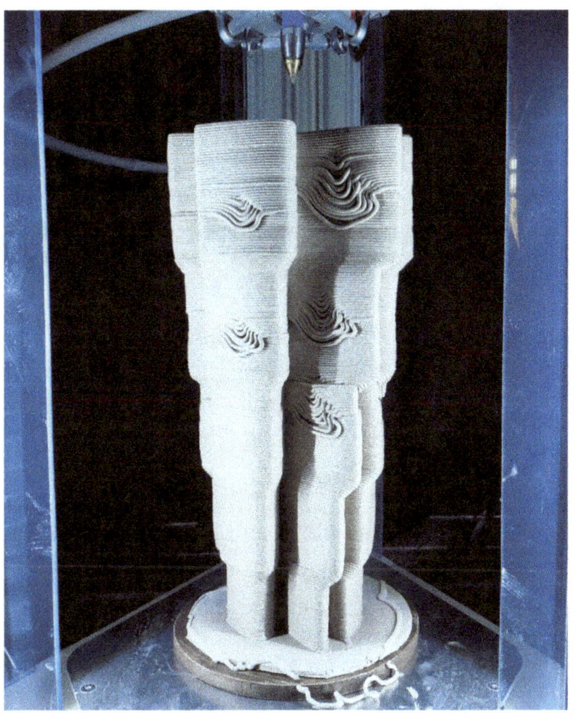

A clay form that has been 3D printed on a wooden bat with a clay slab forming the bottom of the print / Hendrien Horn / 2021.

Test Print

It is advisable to do a test print to see if the layer height is correct in relation to the starting point. I suggest that you always do a few rotations to test the consistency of the clay and to ensure that the clay is flowing through the nozzle without any obstruction.

If the flow is set too high, the clay could over extrude, causing bulging clay coil layers that are not level. If the flow is set too low, it could result in a very thin clay wall. You are looking for the perfect amount of clay in relation to flow, speed of the printer, and the coil layer height. Once that balance has been found, write down all the measurements and stop the print. Restart your print with the tested measurements, ensuring that all the settings are correct.

The test print assists in speeding up the printing process because you won't be wasting time by realising a few minutes into a print that you are not happy with the results!

Gravity, Coil Layer Heights and Nozzle Size

Sometimes your finished clay print may not exactly resemble your initial 3D design. One reason for this is that your print will move according to the weight distribution of the coiled clay body. If the top coil layers are heavier than the bottom layers, you may get bulging or warping of the clay walls of your finished object.

Slicing software allows for the inclusion of double walls within your print. If the angles in the design are very sharp, you may have to play around with this feature to find a suitable solution, such as including extra supports that can be sculpted and cut away from your finished printed object.

Another reason for imperfect prints is linked to the nozzle size and coil layer heights of your print. Ultimately, the more intricate and detailed the design, the better it will be to print that object with a smaller nozzle size and a thinner coil layer height.

For example, if you want to print a design that has direction changes occurring every 1mm, you should look at using a nozzle size of 0.5mm and a layer height of between 0.5mm and 0.8mm. The slicing software will consider the coil layer height and nozzle size, eliminating design features that do not fit within the given parameters. This may mean that you could lose intentional design details when your object is printed. This is where test prints will help in your decision-making when it comes to your 3D design choices.

The clay was too wet, with the bottom part of the print unable to support the weight of the top clay coil layers.

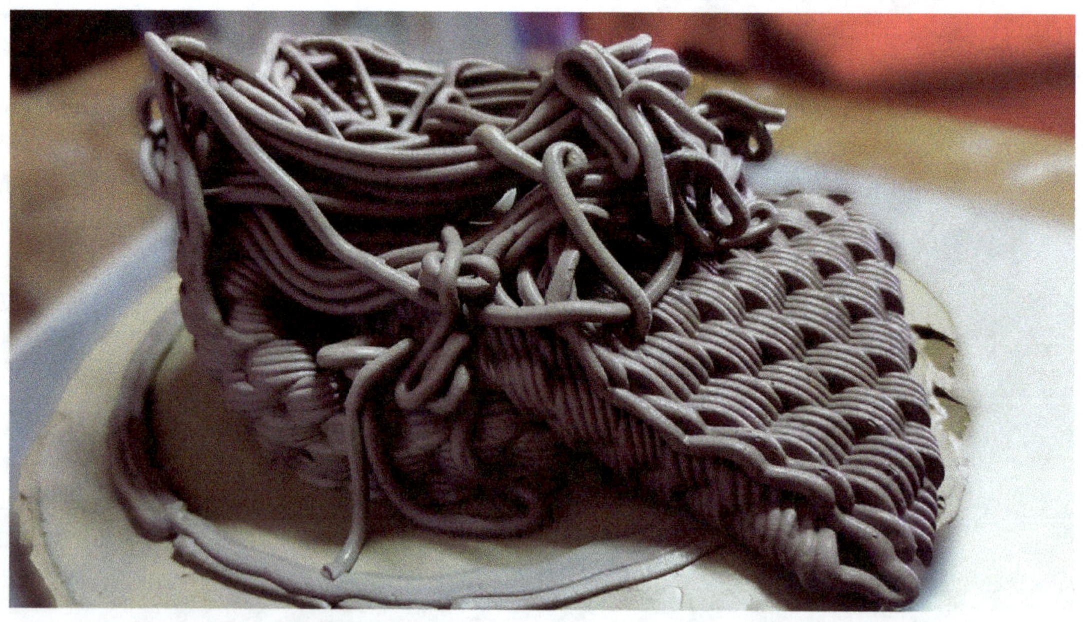

POTTERY

Pottery is the art of making objects out of naturally found or synthetic clay and hardening it at high temperatures using either fire or an electric kiln. Widely used in crockery and sculpture throughout the centuries, the art of pottery has fascinated many people because of the ability of the material to be manipulated and decorated in a large variety of ways.

Clay 3D printing is a tool that can be used to create pottery, much like when the electric pottery wheel was introduced in the early 1900's. Working with clay, however, does require a maker to have knowledge about the material and firing procedures which I refer to as the pottery process. Clay is a fragile material when it is dry and must be kiln fired at high temperatures to make it hard and durable.

Understanding the basic procedures of the pottery process will be paramount to building and developing your skills as a clay maker. Many potters spend years trying to perfect their sculpting and decorating techniques, building up their knowledge over time, and I would like to encourage you to do the same.

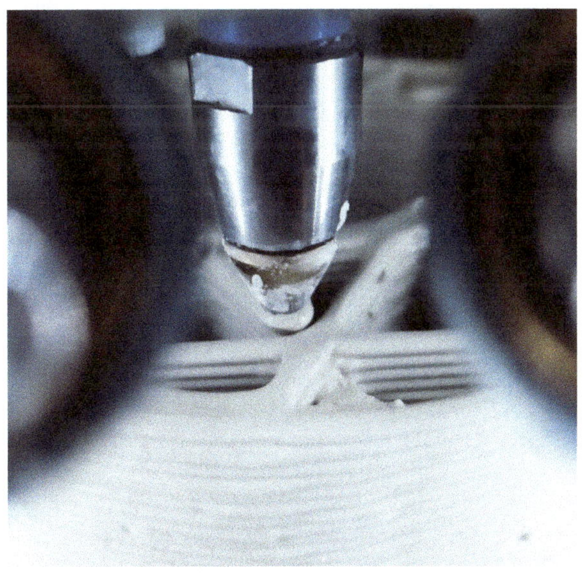

Closeup of the nozzle after the printer has been paused / Hendrien Horn / 2024.

THE POTTERY PROCESS

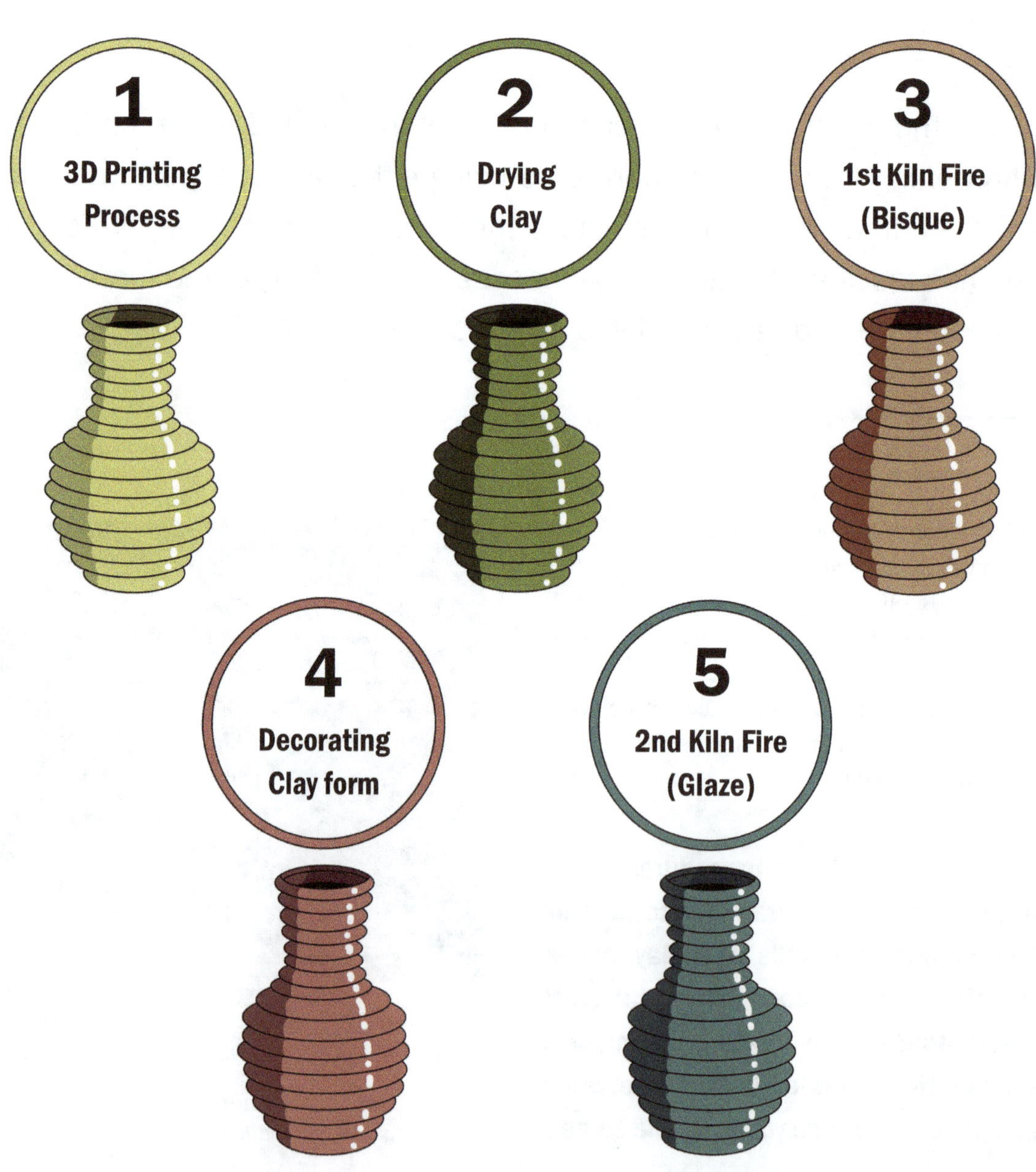

POTTERY 'LINGO'

It is important to know some of the jargon ('lingo') as you continue your pottery journey. The sequencing of the terms below is in the order in which they are related to the pottery process – from start to finish.

Leather Hard

Leather hard is the stage when the clay body has dried half-way through and does not warp to the touch. At this stage you can start smoothing or carving your clay form.

If you want to create holes within the clay body, you need to remember that the bottom part of the clay design must be able to support the top. If it is top-heavy, the bottom clay body may warp during the kiln firing. Therefore, the testing of the wall thickness of your printed object will be of paramount importance.

Greenware

This refers to pottery that has been shaped and is drying. If some parts of the print walls are thicker than others, you must make sure that enough time has been given for drying. If not, parts may detach and break apart in the kiln firing.

Bone Dry

Bone dry is when your clay object is completely dry. The clay at this stage is at its most fragile and should be handled with extreme care. Only once bone dry, can it be bisque fired in the kiln.

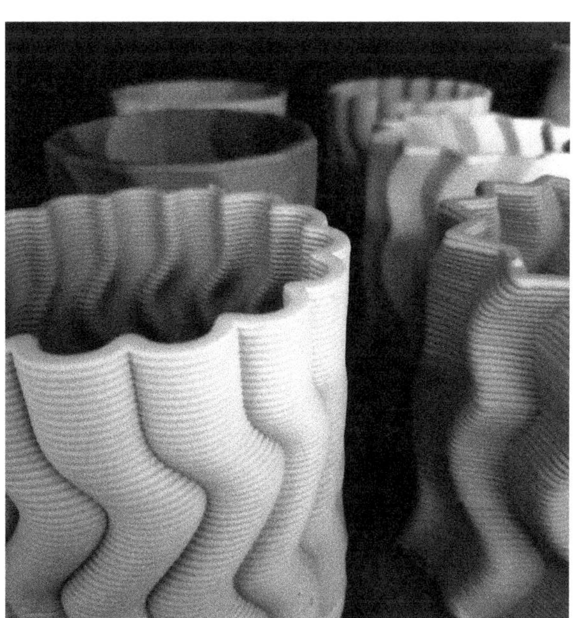

Greenware vases.

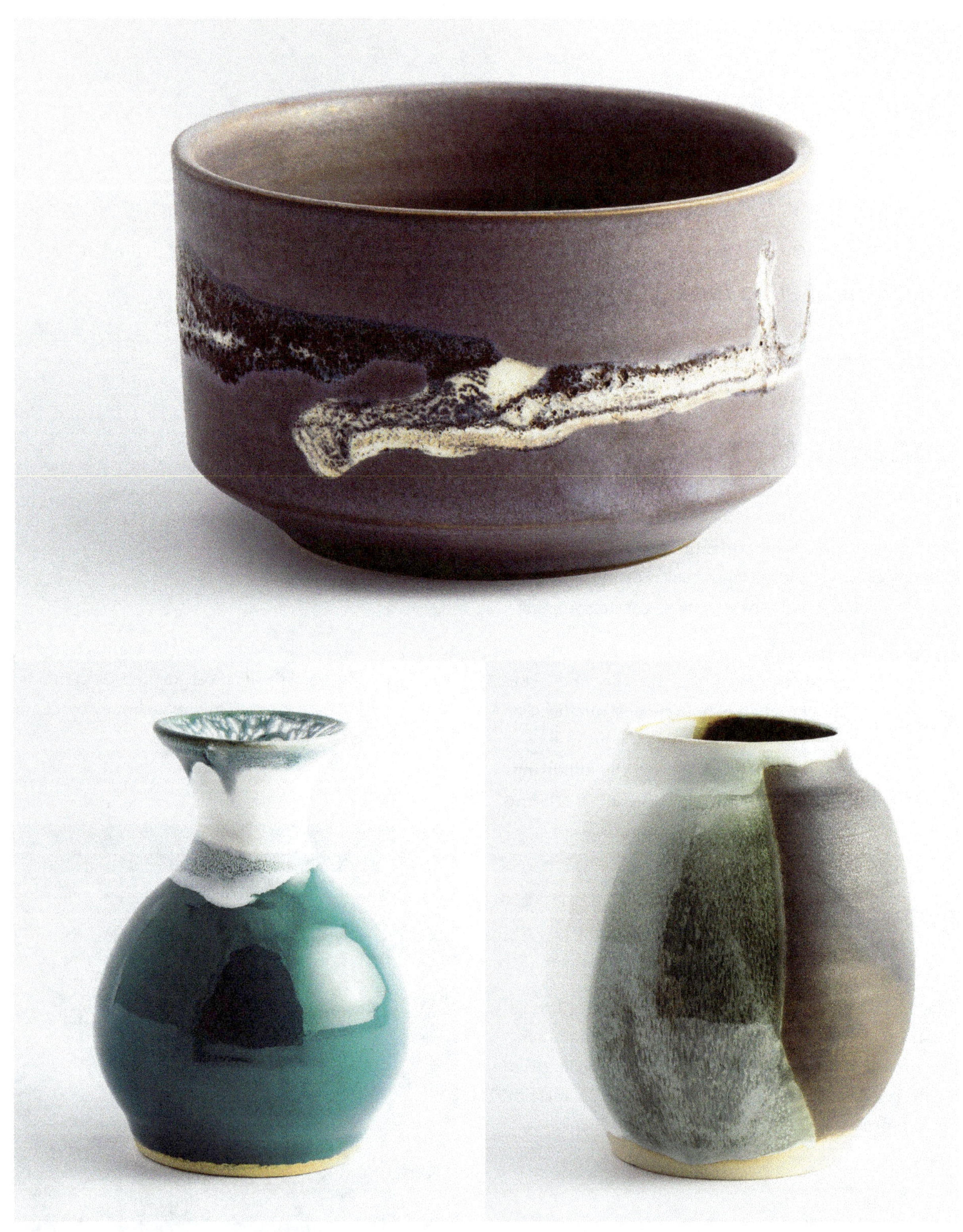

Before clay 3D printing, I enjoyed creating vessels on my pottery wheel / Edgy Clayware© / 2017.

Bisque Firing

When a clay object is kiln fired for the first time at approximately 1 000°C, it is bisque fired. When it is taken out of the kiln, it is extremely hard and rigid.

As a beginner, it can sometimes be confusing to determine whether an object is in the greenware stage or if it has been bisque fired. This is because the colouring can look the same - especially in the case of clays that are white or beige in colour.

I like to think of the clay as having a memory because once out of the kiln, the clay body "remembers" everything you have done – whether right or wrong. If you have perhaps moved your object while it was still wet, it might have warped. Or, if the clay was stretched or knocked before firing, there might be a crack or breakage once it emerges from the kiln. It is important to remember all the steps as to how you handled the clay material so that when something does go wrong at a later stage in the process, you can recall your actions and rectify them in the future.

Some methods used to check if your clay has been bisque fired include;

Knocking on it gently with your knuckles - if it makes a low "bong" sound, then it is still unfired.

Rub your fingers over the clay body, if a lot of clay dust comes off, then it has not been bisque fired.

Put a drop of water on the clay body, if it is absorbed immediately then it is still unfired. Keep in mind that earthenware clays are porous and do absorb water once bisque fired, however, they absorb the water at a slower rate than unfired clay.

Rock Hard

Rock hard is the state of any bisque-fired object. Once the object is out of the kiln, it is strong and firm in its shape.

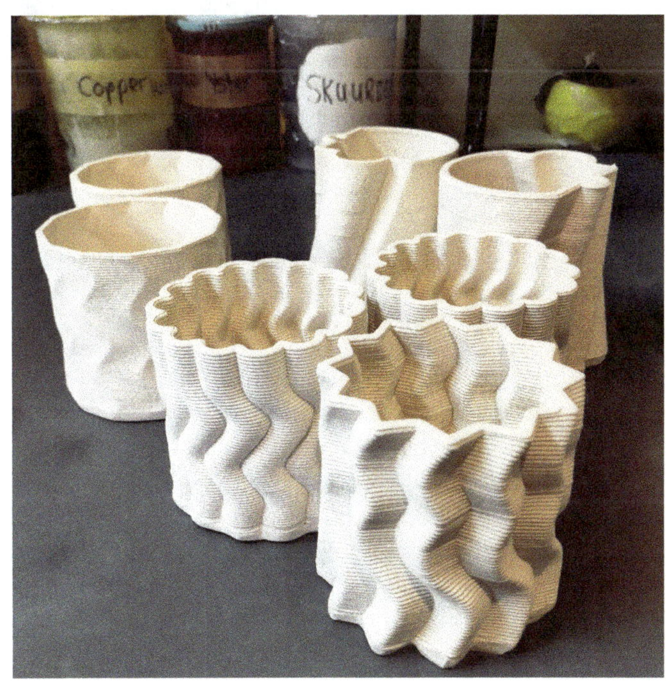

Bisque fired vases that are rock hard.

Dry Foot

This refers to the bottom of the clay body that touches the kiln shelf. After dipping the object in a glaze, you will need to ensure that all the glaze on the foot is neatly wiped away. Not cleaning the glaze off will result in the clay object sticking to the kiln. If you are unsure of how your glazes will run in the kiln, wipe off the bottom and about 1cm of glaze up around the side of the object before firing it.

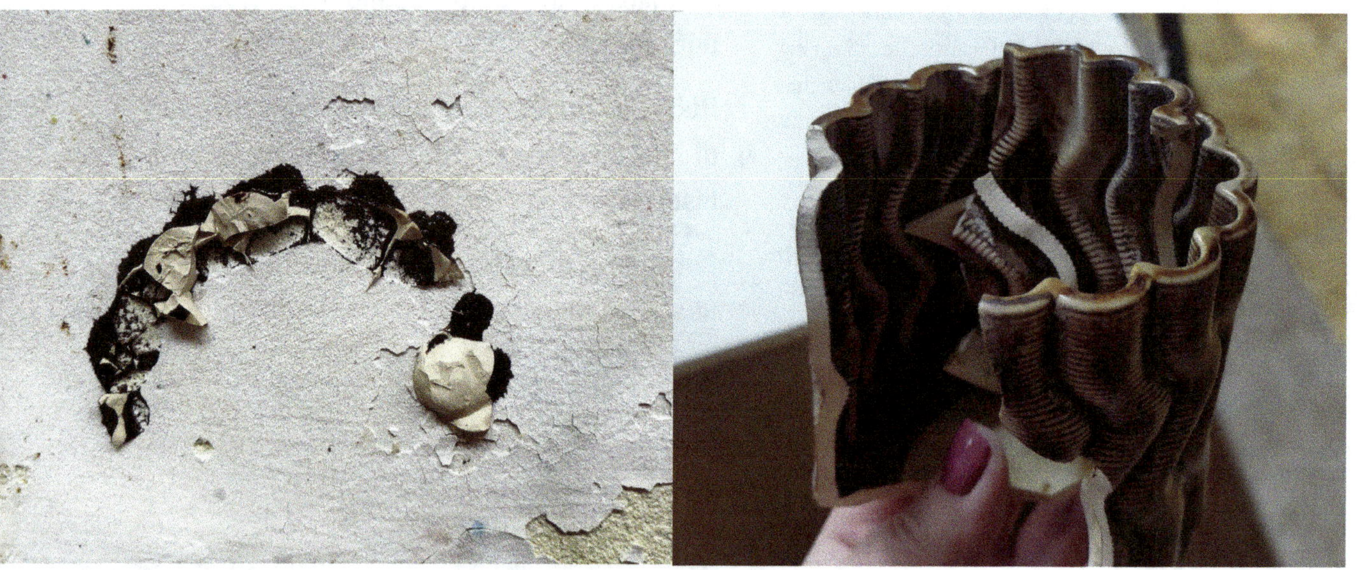

Glaze that was applied too thick and not cleaned off the foot of the vase enough caused the glaze to run, resulting in the vessel sticking to the kiln rack.

Glaze firing

Once the glaze coating has been applied, the piece must be left to stand and dry before it can be fired again. Keep a record of your glazes, listing what went right or wrong and how thick or thin the glaze was when you applied it. This data will assist in creating a better understanding of how the different glazes work and react in the kiln firing.

If you are a first-time potter, your glaze kiln results may vary. To get a smooth finish without running glaze lines takes practice. With that said, many people like the fact that the glaze is not always perfect because it gives it a human touch. The kiln can sometimes leave you with surprises – both good and bad. It is best to embrace the process and to keep trying until you are happy with the outcome.

DECORATING MATERIALS

When decorating any pottery object that is to be fired in a kiln, special materials need to be used that can withstand the high temperatures. These can produce beautiful results.

Underglazes

In liquid form, underglazes are commonly used for painting detailed designs on clay bodies. They can be painted on pottery during any stage of the pottery process, namely at the leather hard, greenware, bisque or glazing stages. If you choose to paint on top of your glaze, you must remember that glaze melts and is inclined to run during the kiln firing. This means that the design painted on the glaze may warp and react with the glaze colour, producing varying results.

Painting with underglazes differs from other types of paints, such as acrylics or oils. When the underglaze is applied to the clay body, it dries almost instantly. Think of it as painting on a dry sponge; the water will be sucked into the sponge quickly, leaving only the pigment powder on top.

A thick coating may create pin holes which are small air bubbles that may only appear once fired. If the underglaze is thinly applied, it can resemble watercolour paints which could also be very beautiful.

Underglazes can also be used in powder form. Underglaze powders are often used to change the colour of clay (e.g. with clay slips used in the casting of moulds). This can be very expensive as large amounts of powder need to be mixed into the clay to create bright colours.

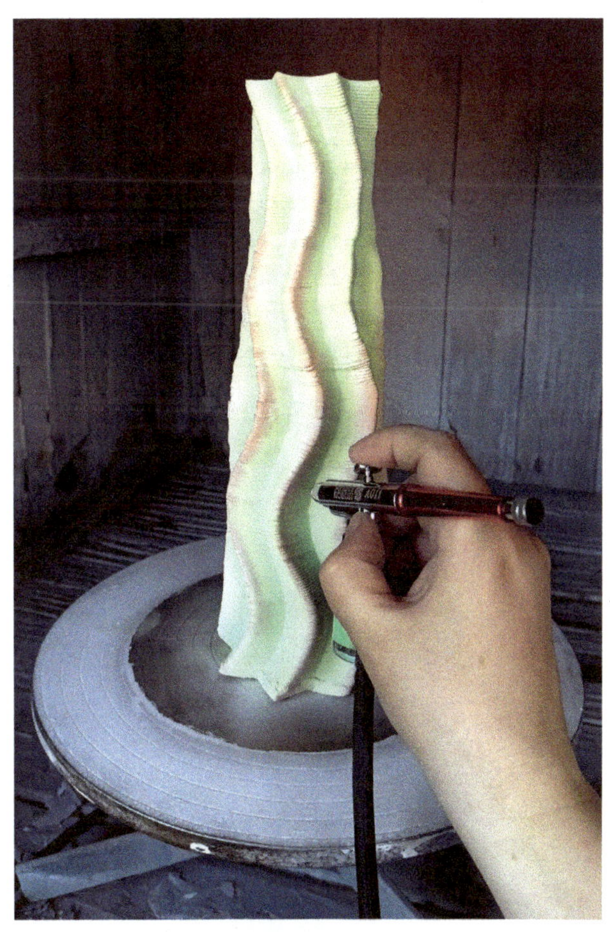

Using an airbrush to apply underglaze colour to a bisque fired clay 3D print / Hendrien Horn / 2023.

Oxides

Oxides are powdered metals that can be made into a liquid form and applied to pottery to create varying decorative effects. It is always advisable to wear gloves when working with these materials because they can easily stain your hands. It is also important to ask your supplier whether these materials are ethically sourced.

For example, the global demand for cobalt (produces the colour blue when kiln fired) has gone up over the years and because of this, illegal mining of these metals occurs across the African continent. Companies may often not even be aware of the sources of these materials. This can result in a market primarily flooded with stolen products.

Iron, manganese, chromium, nickel and copper are some of the other oxides that are also commonly used by potters and makers. Oxides produce varying colours when painted under or on top of glazes. The application techniques of oxides vary and must be understood fully before use. Oxides are toxic in large quantities. If you want to create an object that is "food safe", you need to ensure that the oxide is painted beneath the glaze. Knowing when and how your decorating materials can be used is an important element in the pottery process.

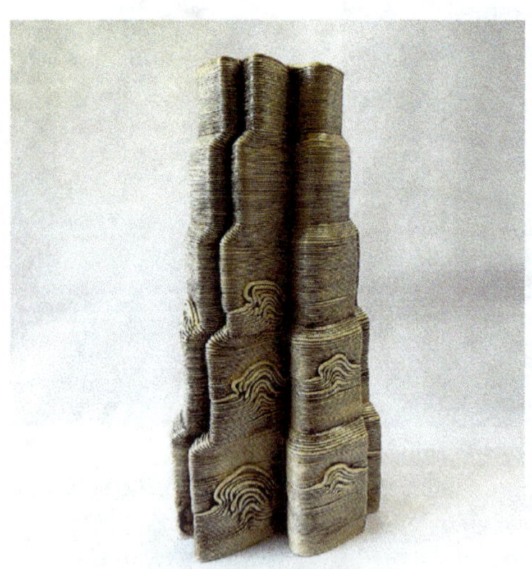

Wax Resist

It is a special liquid that is painted onto a clay object. Once dry, it repels other liquids, which makes it a favourite choice by many potters for a variety of decorating techniques. It is mostly painted on the bottom of clay objects, thus creating a dry foot before they are dipped into a glaze solution. Glaze will not be absorbed where the wax resist has been applied. It is important to note that if the glaze is applied too thick, the wax will not prevent the melting glaze from running in the kiln firing because it will be fired away fairly quickly during the firing process.

Decals and Transfers

These are stickers that are often made of underglazes or oxides which can easily be applied to either greenware, bisque or glazed clay - depending on the specific firing instructions of each product. Usually, only water and a sponge are used to stick the transfer to the clay form. They are used by makers who want a consistently high level of detail on large production runs of crockery.

This is a great idea when you want to create unique patterns and designs for your clay objects. In some cases, you can make your own transfers, or you can find a supplier that can print your transfer designs for you. The cost of this can sometimes be high because decals are printed by layer - each being of a different colour. The more colours you need, the more expensive the production will be because there might be a minimal number of transfers required by a supplier to undertake a printing run.

Oxide was used to stain the clay / Hendrien Horn / 2022.

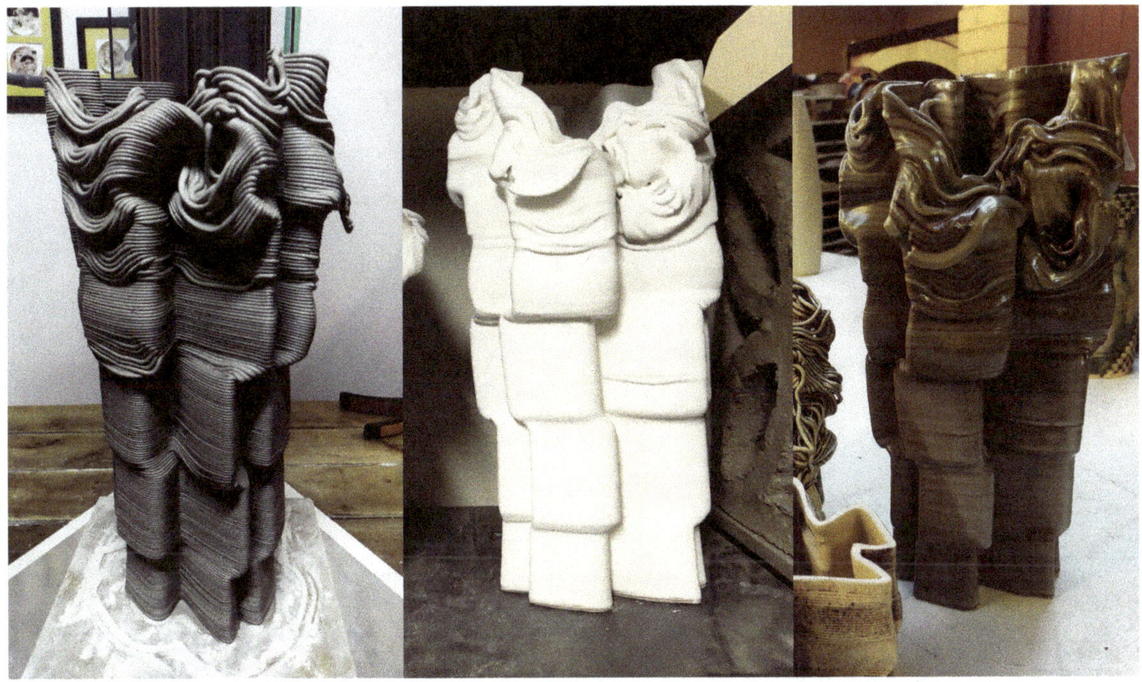

3D printed with underglaze-stained clay / Bisque fired and dipped in a transparent glaze / Glaze kiln fired / Hendrien Horn / 2022.

Glazes

Pottery glazes add an extra coating to the clay object, resulting in a surface finish that can be smooth, glossy, matt or textured, to name but a few. Each glaze comes with specific kiln firing instructions. Some glazes are "food safe" and can be used for crockery, whilst others are not. Ensure to research the glazes that are available for the type of clay you are using. Many potters and makers enjoy making their own glazes and experimenting with the reactions of these in the kiln. Glazes can be applied by dipping the clay object in a glaze, pouring or painting the glaze onto the clay object with a soft-haired paint brush.

Glazes consist of the following materials which make them suitable for firing at high temperatures:

Glass-forming substances, such as silica or boron trioxide;

Stiffening components, such as alumina hydrate, to help the glaze stick to the ceramic surface;

Fluxes, such as manganese oxide, to promote fluidity.

Lustres

Lustres are an overglaze usually painted on top of a fired glazed surface with a very fine paintbrush. They are made of metal particles that are suspended in a liquid. Some of the particles include gold, platinum, and mother of pearl. The fumes from these lustres are toxic; so ensure that you wear a mask and that you have good ventilation in and around your workspace. Many potters will sit outside with a mask on to apply a lustre. Amongst the most expensive materials that you could use, they are mainly used for accents

SHRINKAGE RATE

The shrinkage rate is the percentage that the printed clay object will shrink from the time it is printed to the final stage of the bisque or glaze firing.

It is important to know the shrinkage rate of the clay you are working with, especially if you have been commissioned to create works for others. Different types of clays have different shrinkage rates. The clay that you use for printing contains water and as the water evaporates and the clay hardens, your clay object will start to shrink. The higher the water content of your clay, the higher the shrinkage rate will be.

Also, the higher the firing temperature, the higher the shrinkage rate. For example, stoneware clay has a higher shrinkage rate than earthenware clay, because it is fired at a higher temperature during the final glaze firing. It is also important to note that height and width shrinkage rates for the same clay printed objects can also differ and both should, therefore, be calculated separately.

To get your final shrinkage rate percentage, you will need to do three calculations. Let's look at an example using the measured heights of a printed object at all the stages of the pottery process.

Shrinkage Rate Calculations

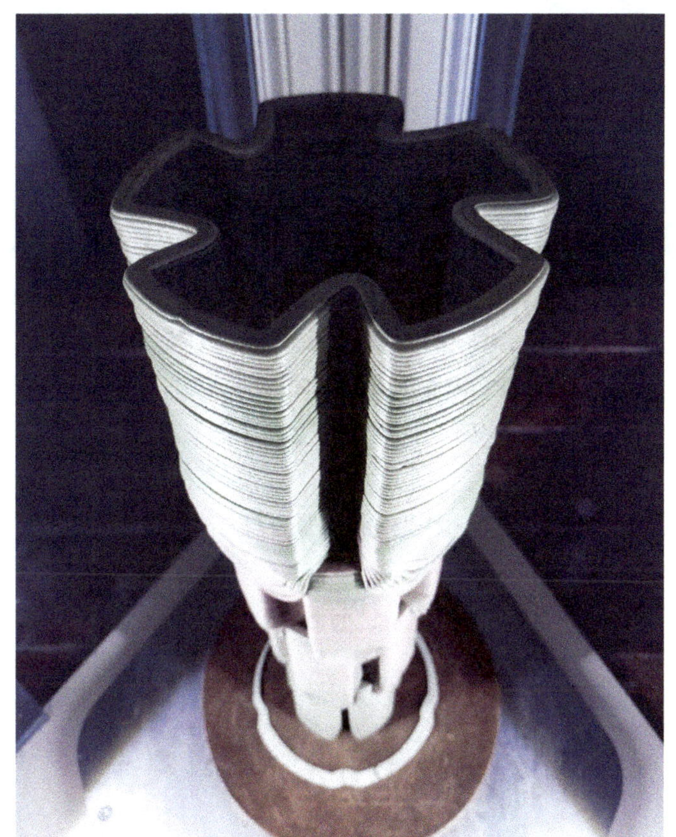

Hendrien Horn / 2022.

PR = PRINTED	**= 38cm**
BD = BONE DRY	**= 34.5cm**
BQ = BISQUE FIRED	**= 33.5cm**
GL = GLAZE FIRED	**= 31.5cm**

The shrinkage rate (PB)

Printed (PR) to Bone Dry (BD)

$$= \frac{(PR - BD)}{PR} \times 100$$

$$= \frac{(38 - 34.5)}{38} \times 100$$

$$= \frac{(3.5)}{38} \times 100$$

$$= 0.092 \times 100$$

$$= 9.2\%$$

The shrinkage rate (BG)

Bone Dry (BD) to Glaze Fired (GL)

$$= \frac{(BD - GL)}{BD} \times 100$$

$$= \frac{(34.5 - 31.5)}{34.5} \times 100$$

$$= \frac{(3)}{34.5} \times 100$$

$$= 0.087 \times 100$$

$$= 8.7\%$$

You may think that by adding the two percentages together you would get your overall shrinkage rate. This would be incorrect, however. The two percentages are based on different starting points and that is why you need to do one final calculation.

Printed (PR) to Bone Dry (BD)

PB = 9.2%

Bone Dry (BD) to Glaze Fired (GL)

BG = 8.7%

Total Shrinkage Rate (TR)

$$= 100 \times (1 - (1 - \frac{(PB)}{100}) \times (1 - \frac{(BG)}{100}))$$

$$= 100 \times (1 - (1 - \frac{(9.2)}{100}) \times (1 - \frac{(8.7)}{100}))$$

$$= 100 \times (1 - (1 - 0.092) \times (1 - 0.087))$$

$$= 100 \times (1 - (0.908) \times (0.913))$$

$$= 100 \times (1 - 0.829)$$

$$= 100 \times (0.171)$$

$$= 17.1\%$$

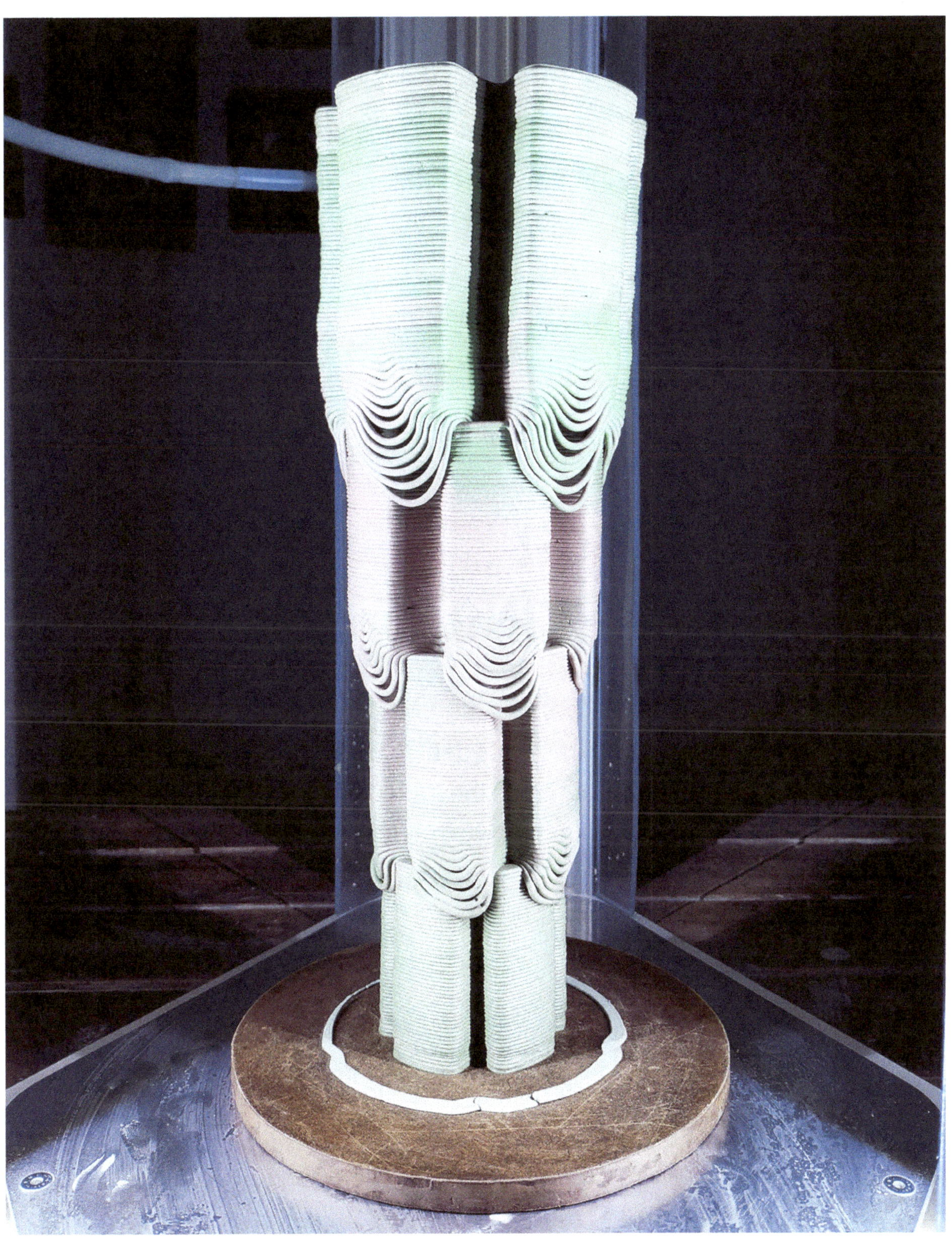

Blooming of a Blossom / Stoneware-stained clay / Hendrien Horn / 2022.

MY TIPS & TRICKS

DESIGNING FOR CLAY 3D PRINTING

Printing with clay differs from printing with other extrusion materials. The water content in the clay can limit your designing and printing capabilities in some ways, and this will need to be taken into consideration when conceptualising a design idea for a clay 3D print.

Print Size

It is important that your intended 3D design and/or its parts are modified to fit onto the print bed of your 3D printer. Designs are easily scalable in both the 3D modelling and slicing software. If your print is too large and falls beyond the printing area parameters, the manufactured clay printers should inform you accordingly on their digital screens. Remember to consider what the shrinkage rate of your clay print will be for the different stages of your pottery process.

Accuracy of Prints

Think about how you want your design to translate into a clay print. Must it be identical to your 3D design or is there room for unpredictable deviations from the envisaged end product? This decision will depend on the type of clay prints you want to make.

Smaller nozzle sizes and layer heights produce more accurate prints. When adopting such an approach, it is important to ensure that your print walls are thick enough not to collapse. If this is the case, think of printing more than one clay wall. Double or even triple walled prints are sometimes a good idea if your printed object is very fragile. Once printed, these clay forms still need to be handled, prepped, and/ sculpted before the kiln firing can make them rock hard. The opportunity for clay breakages is usually at its peak just before the first bisque kiln firing.

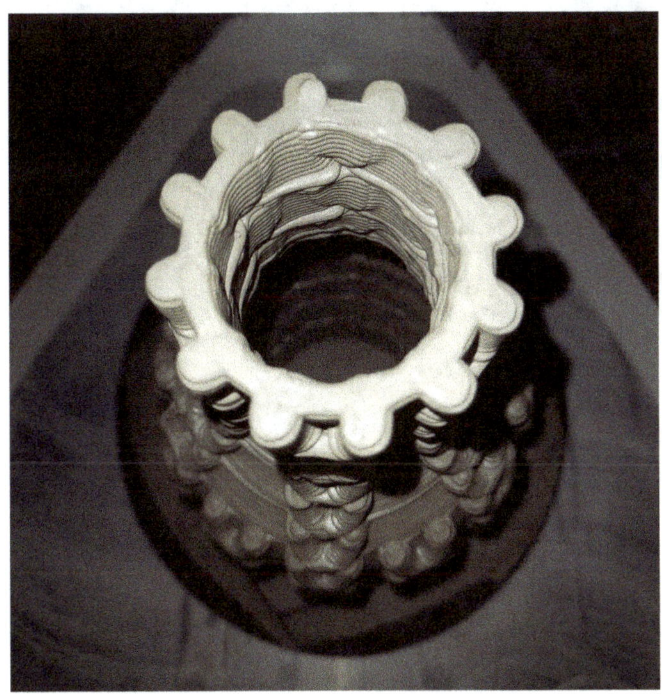

The accuracy of the 3D print was low due to the use of the 3mm nozzle instead of a 2mm / Hendrien Horn / 2021.

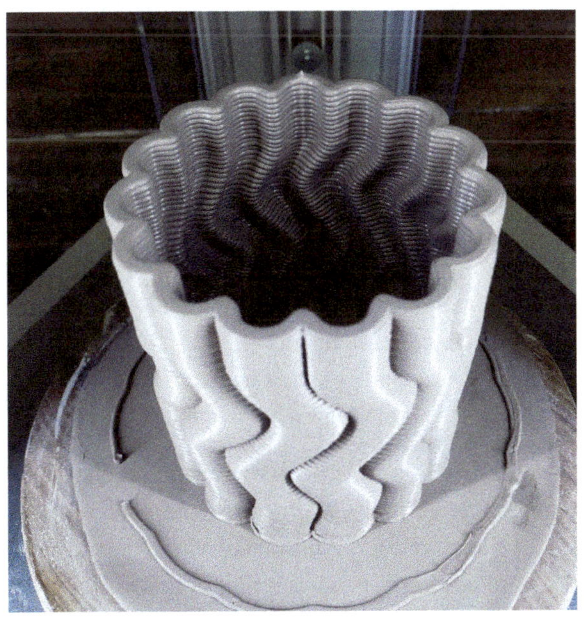

The textured 3D printed forms are often just as beautiful on the inside as on the outside / Hendrien Horn / 2023.

Print Duration

Consider how many hours there are in a day and the amount of time you have available for the printer to complete a print. To some degree, clay printers can be left without supervision, but unlike the plastic 3D printers, they cannot be left to run overnight without at least an eye being kept on the process.

The scale and detail of your designs will play a role here, so be sure to design with intent. High levels of detail can be achieved with a smaller nozzle size, but if the design is large, expect a long printing time. If you want to conduct fast production print runs, make sure that your design is easily printable within a set timeslot so that you will have enough time to produce the intended number of prints per day. This is very important if you want to run a successful business with a streamlined production process.

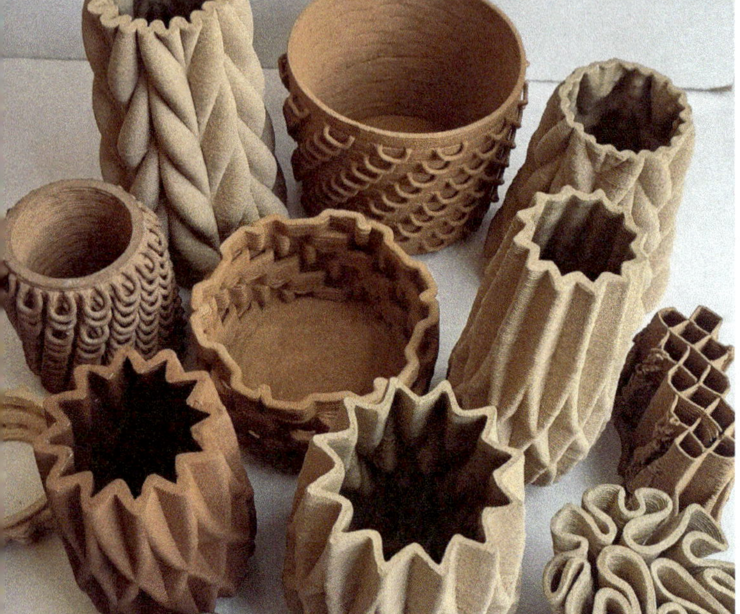

Clay vessels by DRIP AM© / 2024.

I cannot emphasise enough that you should not be rushed in allowing your clay printed objects to dry as part of the pottery process.

Drying Pottery Clay

As discussed previously, if your clay print is not dried all the way through (bone dry) before it is placed in a kiln for bisque firing, it could crack, or parts of the object could break off during the firing.

Consider the day-to-day weather conditions in which you are working. On warmer days it is often drier, which will help the clay to dry faster, whereas, on colder or wetter days the clay will take longer to dry. Weekly weather observations are important when it comes to large production runs that have been paid for by clients and have hard deadlines. Time management is very important and will differ from season to season.

The thickness of your 3D printed clay walls is important because the thicker the walls, the longer it will take for them to dry out. Small prints on a bat can be moved easily and set aside to dry out slowly. If you are printing large objects with very wet clay, I would suggest leaving your finished print exactly where it is on the print bed overnight.

Moving tall printed objects that are still wet could lead to the walls warping or even collapsing as you move the bat. It is crucial to leave the object and allow the clay to settle and dry first.

Otherwise, all those hours of hard work would be wasted on a beautifully finished print that fell over just because you moved it too soon! This happened to me multiple times when I tried to rush the process.

Well-ventilated, cool, and dry conditions will help to speed up the drying process. Placing prints to dry in direct sunlight can cause uneven drying as the outside shell of the body may dry faster than the inside, or even cause large cracks.

It is my practice to avoid placing my works directly in the sunlight because it is very hot and dry in the highveld region of South Africa where I live. More moderate climates might allow for objects to be placed to dry in the sunlight, but first test to see how your clay responds to your environment.

As discussed previously, you can regulate the temperature of your clay print by controlling its own evaporating moisture. Whilst it is drying, cover and seal the print in plastic, being careful not to touch any wet clay with the sides of the plastic sheeting.

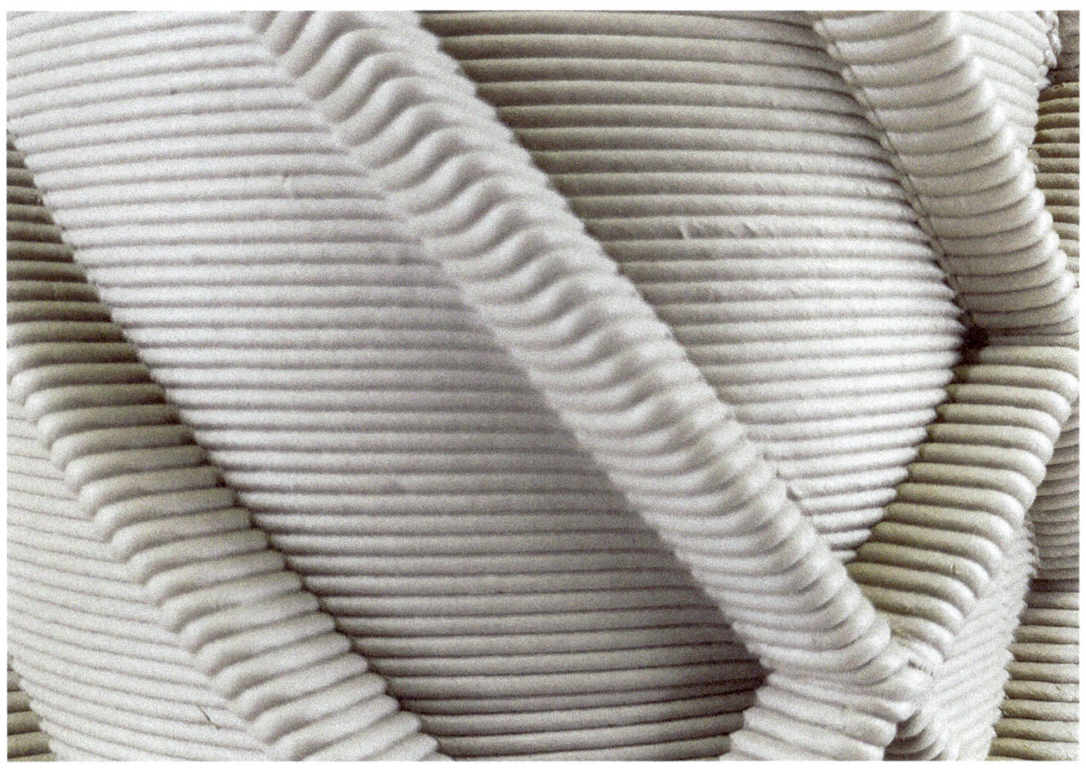

Sharp angles achieved with a 3mm nozzle and a layer height of 1.5mm, with speed set to a low rate per second / Hendrien Horn.

This will even out the temperature across the entire surface of the object and ensure that no part dries faster than another. This is not necessary for smaller prints with quicker drying times. It is mainly for large pieces that have very intricate builds that need to dry very slowly in a regulated moisture-sealed environment.

A technique many clay 3D makers use is to blow regulated hot or cold air onto the clay print whilst it is printing. This process helps to solidify and dry the outer layers faster, helping the clay walls to retain their shape.

It is, however, not a complete solution, and attention to how your clay reacts to heat is important. If hot air is blown directly onto a clay print, the clay layers may form tiny crevasses in the clay as it dries, which may need to be smoothed out at a later stage. Ensuring that heat is evenly distributed around your clay print is very important. Very hot air continuously directed at the print will cause more harm than good because the layers will dry unevenly and may cause unnecessary cracking or warping.

Much practice is required in using this method, which is not, however, necessary for printing shapes that do not require much help to stay upright, or if you are using a thicker clay consistency that is better able to hold its shape.

GLAZE TESTERS

Achieving a perfect glaze colour is like hitting the jackpot every time, and that winning feeling never gets old!

My traditional pottery background trained me to always create glaze mini tester tiles that I would make by rolling out and cutting a slab of clay. With a clay printer however, you can print the same object repeatedly as a quick substitute.

Another reason for using test prints and not mini tester tiles is because the printer creates seams in the clay as it changes direction. Observing how the glaze runs and interacts with these indents in the clay is essential if you do not intend to smooth out your clay layers after a print.

It would be a worthwhile exercise to design and print small testers that have elements of the printing patterns and shapes that you expect to work with. Different glazes have different consistencies and react differently in the kiln according to their application thickness.

Knowing how they work and what finish they will produce is important if you want to decorate many prints in a consistent manner.

Once the finished clay printed testers are leather hard, if required, smooth the areas that you want to glaze. Since the glaze usually thins out in the kiln around any sharp corners, you can accentuate interesting contrasts to your 3D printed object. If you want to avoid this, then you will need to round off the edges of the object using your fingers or a damp sponge before applying the glaze.

Glaze tester tiles / Hendrien Horn / 2018.

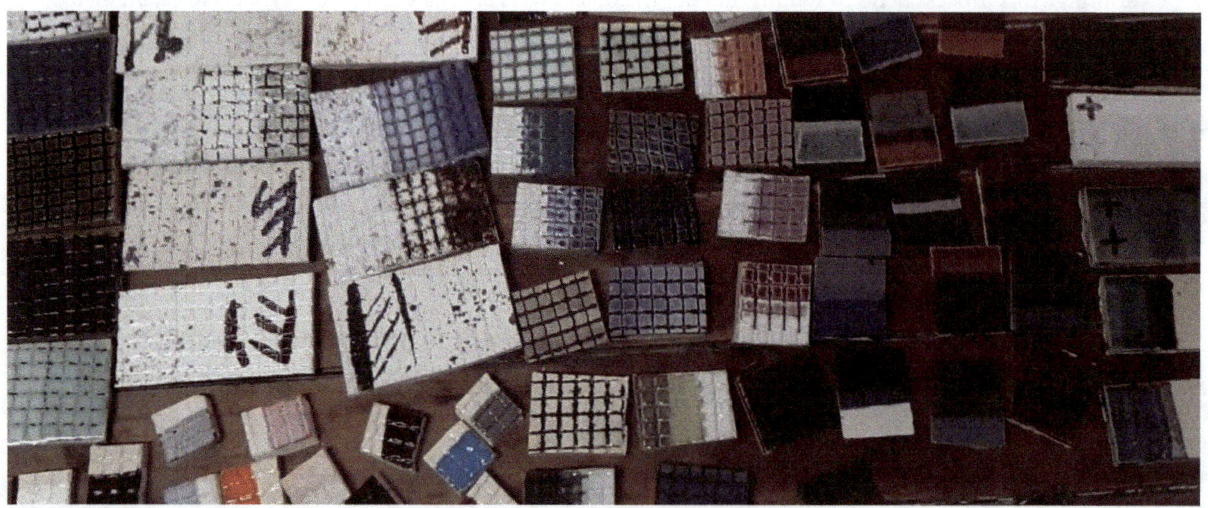

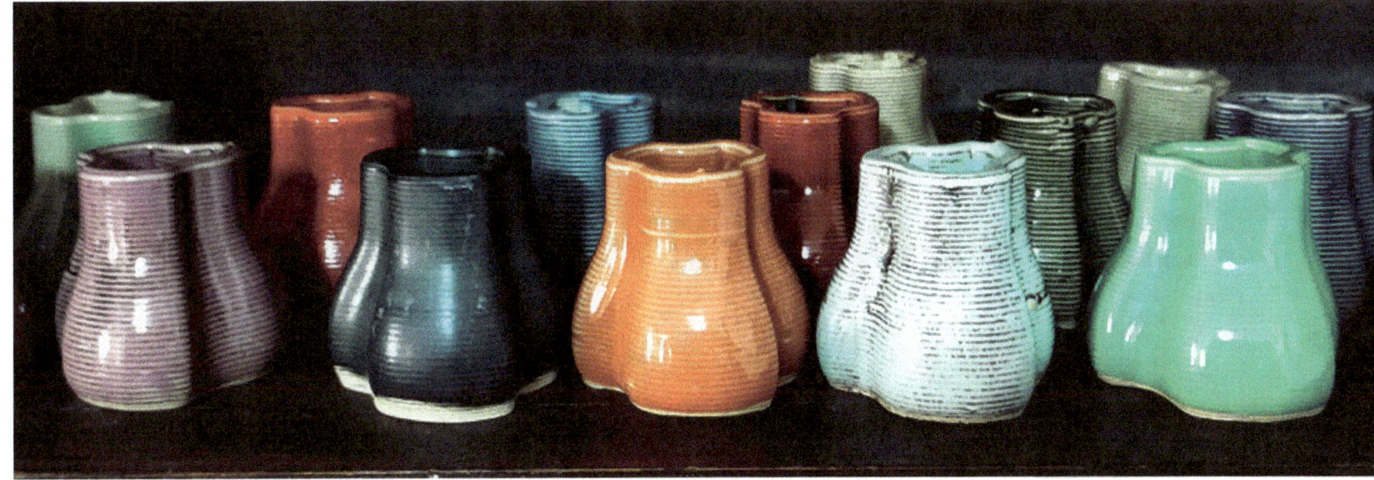

3D printed glaze testers / Hendrien Horn / 2021.

Number your mini testers with a cataloguing system that works for you, and in so doing, making it easier for you to identify each glaze colour at a later stage. Use a sharp pencil and etch the number below the print. The lead from the pencil will fire away in the kiln, leaving you with the engraved number. So, if you ever need to draw or make any markings on your clay piece, use a pencil! I never use a pen as some inks can affect the glaze.

I strongly recommend that you join a communal pottery studio that will allow you to use their glazes for testing prints. Check that their glazes work with your type of clay. Most studios should have their own tester tiles up to show you what their glazes look like once fired with their type of clay. Use these to your advantage by identifying in advance which glazes you prefer.

If you are working towards creating objects for clients, you need to remember that the colours that you like may not necessarily be the colours that someone else would choose. Buying many different glazes can be rather costly, especially if you end up never using them after the testing phase! Ask for samples where possible.

Glaze testing can be a long and tedious process because of all the mixing and cleaning. Therefore, it is advisable to glaze no more than 20 - 25 mini testers at one time. It would be a good idea to enlist the help of the potter to whom the glazes belong. They will be able to inform you about the thickness of each glaze, which is important to know as the dipping times for the glazes could differ.

To test the thickness of a glaze once it has been mixed, dip your finger in the glaze and count to three. If, when you pull your finger out after the count, the glaze is not translucent enough for you to see the lines and partly show the colouring of your skin, then it is too thick. You can always add a splash of water to thin the glaze out slightly, or by emptying just a little of the glaze you need into a separate container. Always ask permission from the potter whose studio it is as to what will work best before you make any changes to the consistency of their glazes.

Remember to record which colour was dipped with each numbered tester. You may think that it could be easy enough to tell the difference, but sometimes the glaze colours are so similar that you may struggle to identify which is which.

The above steps will help you point out which glazes run more than others and how they react to the clay body. Glazing is a science all on its own and to master it will take time and patience.

GLAZE BODY FIT

The glaze body fit is probably one of the biggest challenges that clay makers struggle with because the glaze and clay body both expand and contract during the kiln firing. When the glaze expands at a different rate from the clay, problems often arise.

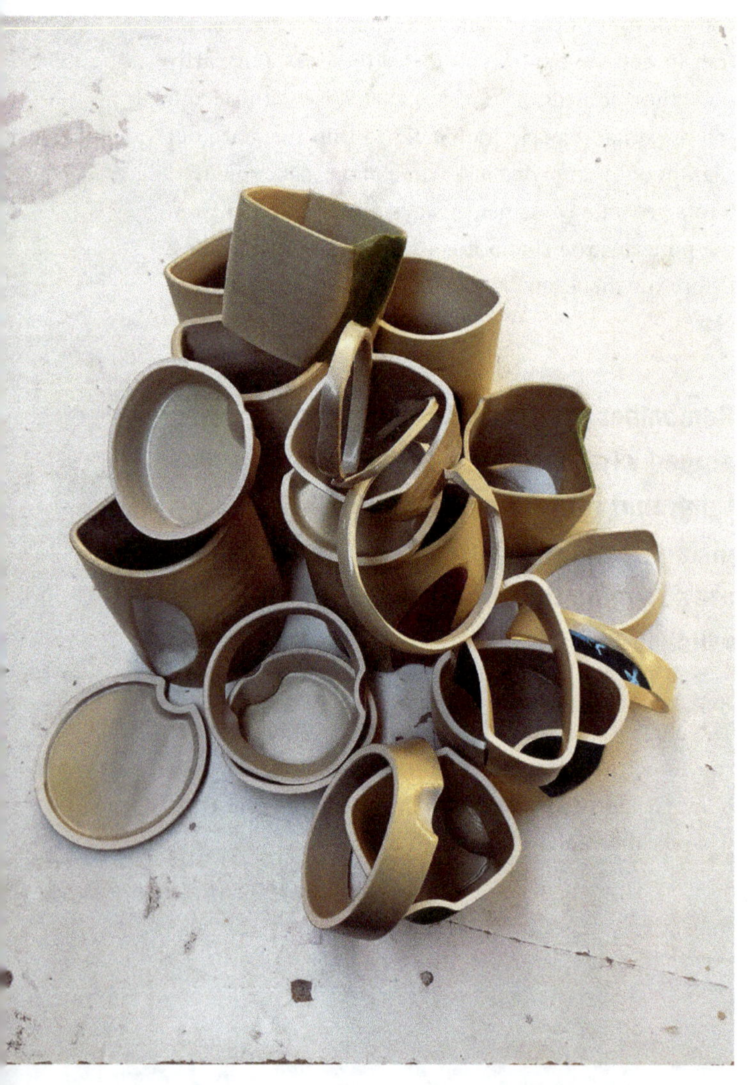

Consider the thickness of the printed walls of your objects. For example, if the clay walls are very thin, then your glaze coating needs to be thin and you may need to water down your glaze. If the clay walls are thick, a regular glaze coating will suffice. Repeated testing of the glaze thickness and its application will help you figure out the perfect consistency.

If your finished glazed fired object looks good but makes a "ping" sound instead of a full-bodied sound when you knock on it, then you may have a problem, and there may be a weak spot or crack in the clay glazed body. This can result in detachment, which means that you need to handle these works very carefully. The edges of the detached sections are very sharp and can easily cut you.

Glaze that is too thick or has not been left to dry before firing could cause any of the following problems: the glaze could pull away from the clay body; create gaps and cracking in the glaze coating; or create cracks in the clay – causing an unstable print, which could easily break apart or fully detach from the clay print.

The consistency of the glaze applied was too thick and did not give the clay body the space it needed to expand - This resulted in the clay cracking and breaking apart at the coil layer lines / Hendrien Horn / 2022.

CLAY CRACKS

Potters have long sought "the best" technique for fixing cracks in their works. When cracks occur, and trust me they will, you must either choose to live with them or start all over again.

Clay printed objects are most vulnerable in the leather hard and greenware stages. Special care needs to be taken when lifting and moving prints off the bat. The clay print must be dry enough not to warp to the touch, and if lifted, not to stretch between the coil layers. Cracks will not always be noticeable in the greenware stage. Once fired for the first time, a crack may appear in the weak spot, and if not, there is still the chance that it might develop during the glaze firing process.

As a clay work is fired in the different stages of the pottery process, the clay body will shrink and expand. With each firing, a crack will simply get bigger, and there is nothing you can do to stop that from happening.

In my early days as a potter, I tried various tricks to fix cracks in my clay objects with no understanding of the chemical reactions and processes that take place during the kiln firing process. One of the "brilliant solutions" I considered at one time was to apply a thick layer of glaze, thinking it would cover up the crack forever, never to be seen again.

And... as you have guessed, the high temperature of the kiln melted the glaze and that "solution" went right out the door! The crack became more visible because at higher temperatures cracks open up further, with the thick glaze separating from the clay body and making the gap look even worse!

Clay crack filler - the clay solution that is used to fill in the cracks on the surface of the clay body, (usually in the greenware or bisque stages) has varying results – in some cases, it may work beautifully. However, I have stopped using crack filler because it is time ill spent trying to fix something which has a good chance of cracking again.

The crack may be filled in completely with crack filler, but once glaze fired, it is more than likely to reveal itself again. I have also had works emerge intact from the glaze kiln, only to break a few days later at the same weak spot that I had so diligently filled up. Should I spot a crack at any stage in my pottery process, I refrain from working further on the print. It is unadvisable to sell a work to a client if you know that because of cracks in the clay body, there could potentially be a risk of it breaking in the future.

HEALTH & SAFETY

Working with clay can be a messy job! Once clay dries, it turns into dust. Inhaling this can be very harmful. You need to ensure that you take the right steps to keep a dust-free working space and to protect your lungs!

As a potter, keeping a clean workspace can be extra work that is often tedious. However, it is necessary. One of the biggest tips is to always have warm water in a bucket, with a wet cloth and a mop nearby for wiping surfaces, equipment, tools, and floors to ensure that dust does not fill the air that you breathe in. When the bucket of water becomes very murky and 'clayey', pour it out into a recycling container and replace it with clean warm water. Repeat this for the duration of your work process.

Wear an apron at all times in the studio to prevent dust from settling into your clothing. An apron also allows you to take it off and shake out the clay dust outside, thus freeing the particles into the air away from yourself!

Because the dust particles are harmful, you also need to remember to wash your hands regularly and thoroughly with warm water and a mild soap and to use a scrubbing brush to help remove the clay from under your fingernails. Never eat or drink anything with unwashed hands!

Be aware of the ingredients in the decorating materials that you are buying and using. Some of these give off toxic fumes which can be very harmful if breathed in. This makes the wearing of a mask in some cases a necessity. Before you start glazing or decorating with any material, rub a small amount of the decorative material onto your skin to see how it reacts. For sensitive skin, always use gloves.

Your clay 3D printer is a machine with many moving parts. The printer will run until you press the button for it to stop - so remember to keep all fingers and clothing away from any movable mechanical parts.

Keep your printer clean, removing any excess clay from all the machinery parts if you are done for the day. If you are using compressed air, always make sure that the air in your clay container has been decompressed. The air compressor must also be switched off before detaching any piping.

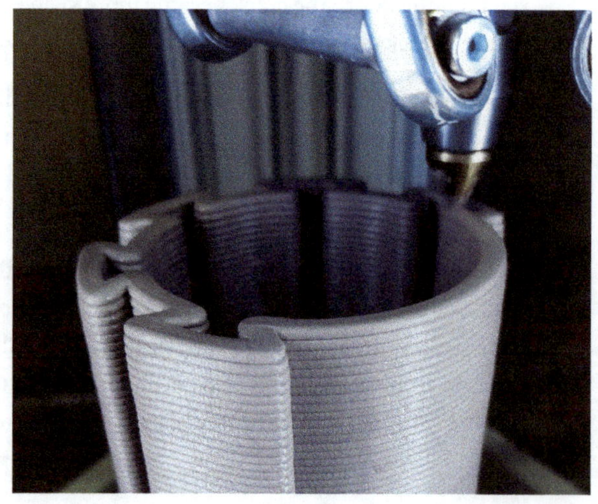

A clean nozzle means a clean 3D print!

CLAY ARTISTS FROM AROUND THE WORLD

Blending traditional pottery techniques and using the advancements of a clay 3D printer with other technologies, clay artists from around the world are exploring and pushing the boundaries of what is possible when it comes to their art.

When I think back on the beginning of my journey all those years ago, my greatest desire was to be a contemporary clay 3D printing artist, but at the time there were not many people exploring this type of art form.

Back then, I followed the work of a handful of artists. They showed me what was possible if you merely looked at clay making from a different perspective. Since then, many more artists have been added to my list. Each of them expressing their point of view, creating art that speaks to their love of using clay material to bring their designs to life in a unique way.

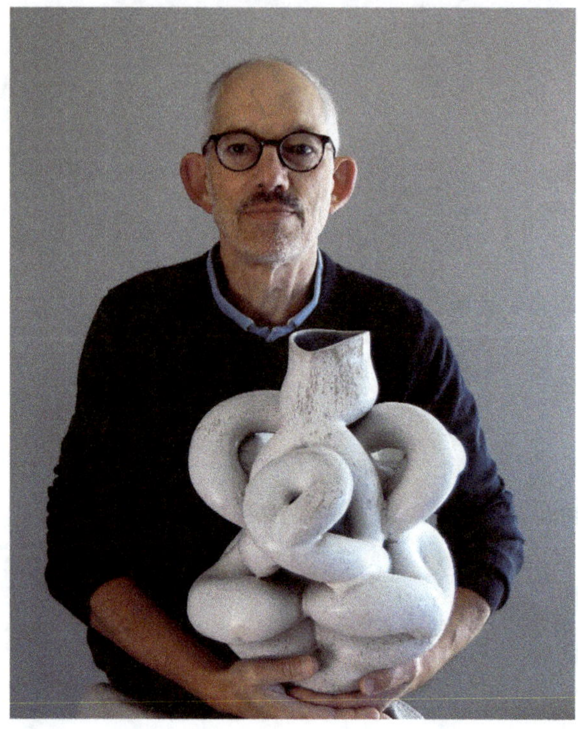

Jonathan Keep / 2022.

JONATHAN KEEP

Inspired by the "hidden numerical natural code that underpins all nature", Jonathan's clay 3D printed works interweave effortlessly between technology and art.

He strives to redefine what a 'pot' is and is excited to work with clay in new and revolutionary ways. He is of the opinion that the digital revolution has been in the pottery studio for years; that it emerged with the advent of the electric kiln, and that introducing technology into the pottery studio is unavoidable.

His focus is on the exploration of clay forms and on manipulating them by employing generative design techniques.

To him, the natural progression to computational design and 3D printing with clay are mere tools, just like the electric pottery wheel. Generative design is a design process that uses algorithms to create a large range of solutions and ideas for complex problems in a software environment. This is exemplified by changing the structure of a 3D model by the application of mathematical equations written in a computer-coded language.

In his "Curve Series", he explores the three-dimensional curve using Processing, a software used to help generate his beautiful clay forms. The series delves into planetary paths, where ratios, proportions, and relationships between structures evoke movement within the curves of the clay walls.

Curved Series / Jonathan Keep / 2017.

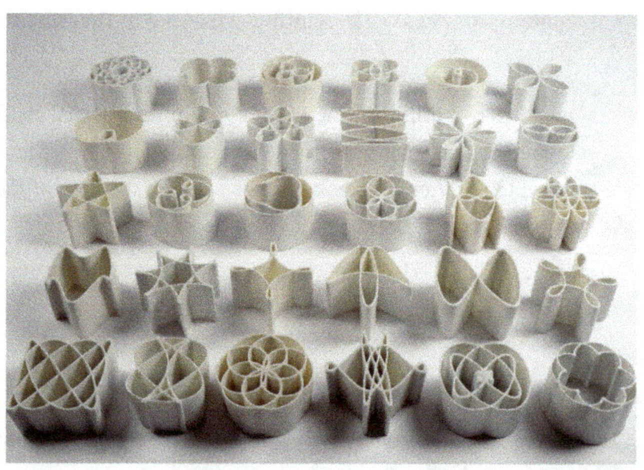

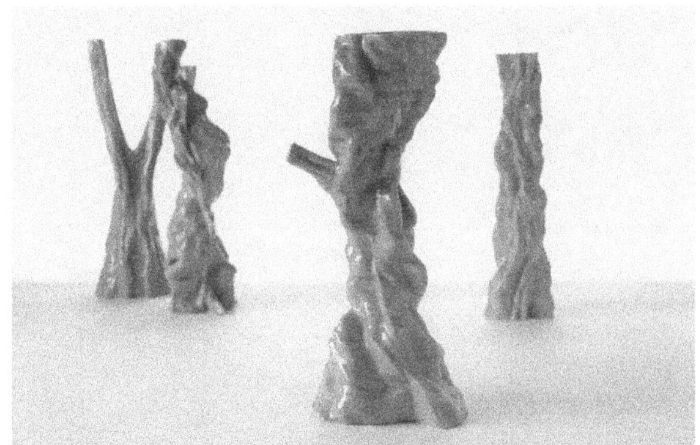

Petrified Trees Series / Jonathan Keep / 2012.

His "Petrified Trees" series on the other hand examines how humans try to obstruct or contain trees in the environment. He motivates the viewer to think about their own influence and how they are part of something much greater than themselves. The 3D printed trees appear to be other-worldly and come to life when light passes over their glazed clay bodies.

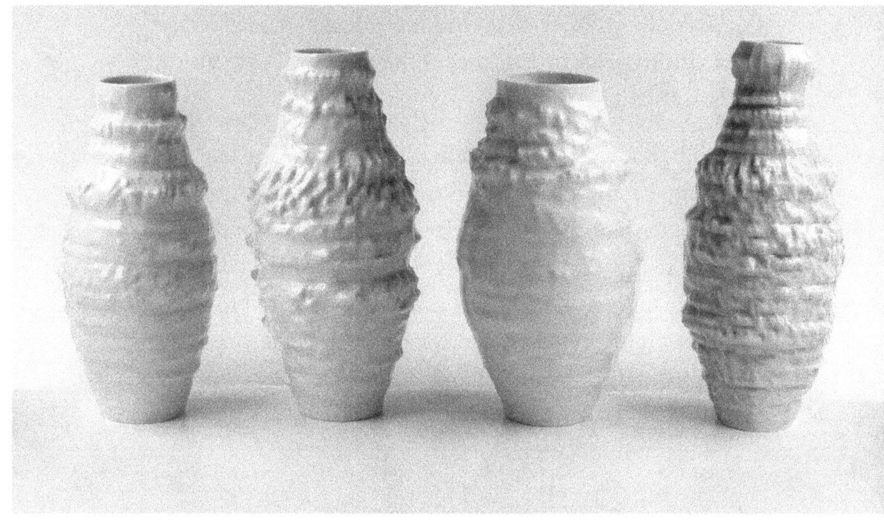

Sound Surface Series / Jonathan Keep / 2014.

"Sound Surface Series" is very interesting as the prescribed virtual shape of the vase starts out as the same vase. Each of the clay vases is then individually manipulated by code that is controlled through the sound of music. The height of the vase depends on the length of the musical interlude; and the rhythm and tone of the music are related to the surface texture of the vessels. Like a conductor would an orchestra, Jonathan creates a performance in this series of works, with each vessel becoming unique as it reaches its final state, and as the curtain falls.

Jonathan's complex 3D printed coil forms often need his skilled pottery hands to intervene for the print to hold its shape whilst drying. His designing and printing knowledge sets his artworks apart as he pushes the boundaries of what is possible with gravity-defying prints made with technical precision.

His work has been exhibited in England, many European countries, the United States of America, Australia, South Africa, Korea, Taiwan, and China. These artworks have inspired many artists to look at new ways of innovation in the design and creation process, thus pushing them to think creatively, to explore what is possible, and how technology and art can fuse together to create something beautiful.

NICOLAS TOURON

Born in France, Nicolas Touron is a New York City based artist. He was a Fullbright scholarship recipient and obtained his MFA at the School of Visual Arts in New York. He studied sculpture and ceramics at the Gerrit Rietveld Academy in Amsterdam and is currently a visiting artist in residency at the ceramics programme at Harvard University.

He is known as a storyteller with his dream-like 3D printed sculptural compositions. These sculptures are an extension of a vernacular body of work developed over many years. Examining the juxtaposition between art forms considered naive and a computerized form of creation perceived as a more concept-driven process, he captures the imagination of his audience.

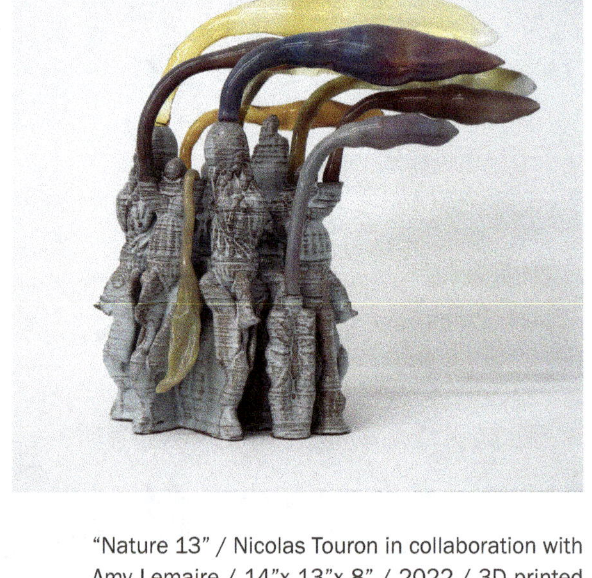

"Nature 13" / Nicolas Touron in collaboration with Amy Lemaire / 14"x 13"x 8" / 2022 / 3D printed stoneware (cone 6) and borosilicate.

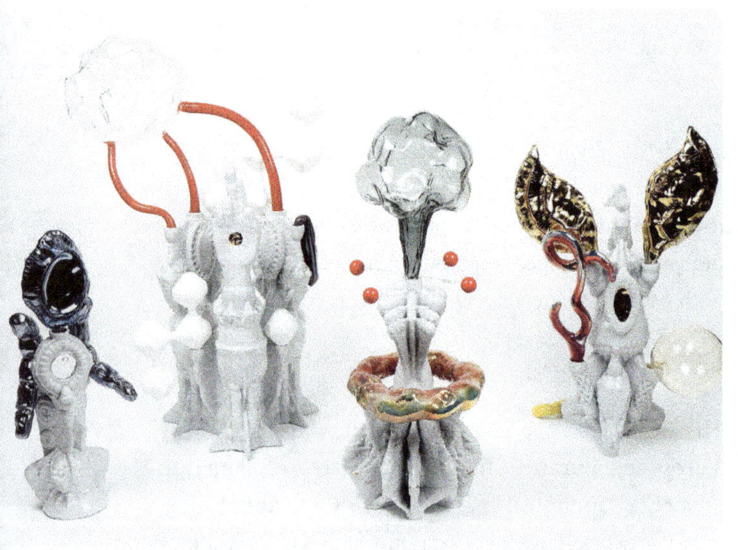

"Nature 1" ,"Nature 2", "Nature 4", "Nature 6" / Nicolas Touron in collaboration with Amy Lemaire / Various dimensions / 2022 / 3D printed porcelain (cone 10) and borosilicate.

"Second Nature" is a collaboration with Amy Lemaire, a glass artist from New York. It exhibits muted clay printed forms with the addition of bright pops of colour from sculpted glass. Looking closer you keep discovering new details that may only be visible from closeup, showcasing a beautiful complex composition, frozen in time.

Nicolas Touron's work has been featured in art galleries, museums, and public spaces around the world, with his work also found in numerous private collections. He uses 3D Potter and LUTUM® 3D clay printers to create his art works.

Working in her studio / Marlieke Wijnakker / VormVrij® / 2021.

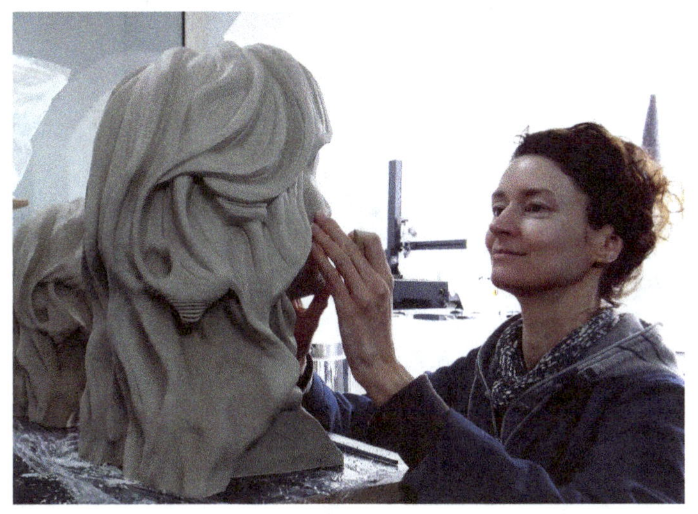

MARLIEKE WIJNAKKER

Marlieke studied at the Design Academy in The Netherlands and went on to co-found VormVrij®. She helped to develop the LUTUM® range of 3D printers, which she uses to create her sculpted portraits.

A 3D-scan is taken of a client's bust and once 3D printed in clay, her portraits initially appear to be sleeping. Because of the relatively large round nozzle that she uses, the extruded clay does not reach the deepest nor highest perimeters, which in turn softens the features of her portraits.

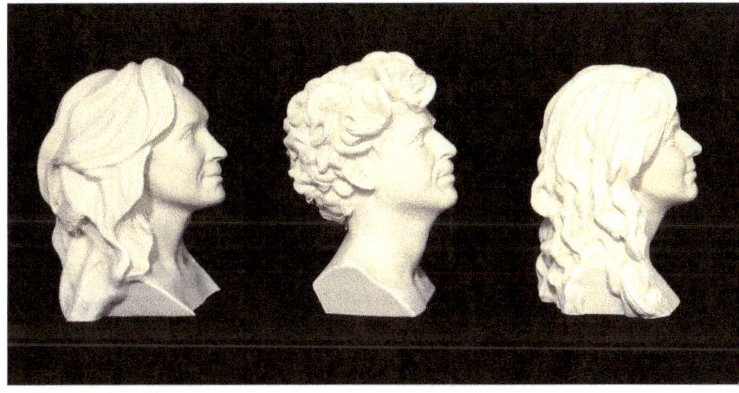

Sculpted Busts / Marlieke Wijnakker / VormVrij® / 2021.

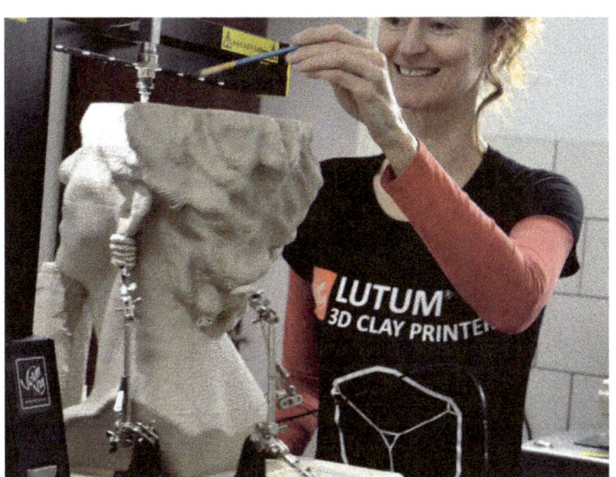

Marlieke Wijnakker / VormVrij® / 2021.

When the clay approaches the greenware stage, Marlieke sculpts the intricate details by hand. These portraits of both young and old alike capture a realistic moment in time. Her impeccable attention to detail is evident in the completed sculpted work.

Initially, her signature touch was clearly visible in her works, but currently, her pieces have on occasion taken on a more stylized surface, with a glaze or bronze patinated finish. Resembling a picture more than a painting, the final result can appear to be confronting to some.

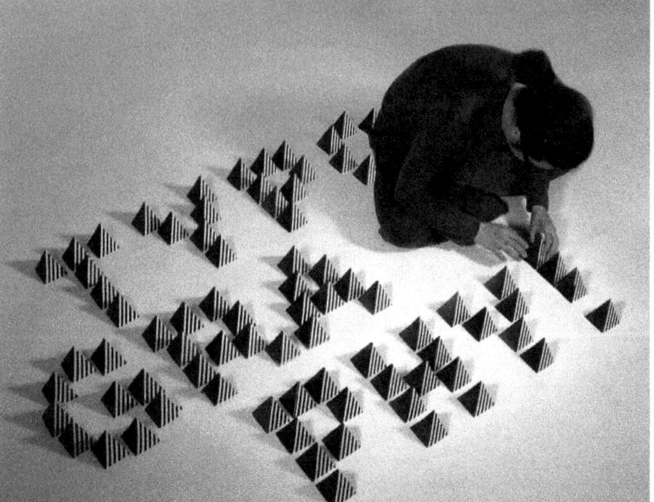

MFA Thesis Taekyeom Lee / 2015.

TAEKYEOM LEE

Born in South Korea, Taekyeom is now living in Madison, Wisconsin, and teaching Graphic Design at the University of Wisconsin–Madison. He moved to the United States of America later in life and went on to receive his MFA degree in Graphic Design from the University of Illinois at Urbana–Champaign. During his graduate studies, he had a huge health scare when diagnosed with a retinal detachment. It took months for him to recover after two eye surgeries, and this ultimately impacted his work and the way he approached graphic design.

During this time, he started taking a ceramics class, which was like therapy to him. He remarked to a friend at the time that this was "his retirement plan". The friend then turned to him and said, "Why would you want to wait, you are working with it now?". Not long after that, Taekyeom emailed his advisor and changed the topic of his thesis to use ceramics material for typography. He only discovered clay 3D printing after his graduation, when he no longer had access to a ceramics facility.

Inspired by his father, who was a vehicle mechanic, and his grandfather, who was an aeroplane mechanic in the Korean war, Taekyeom decided to build his own printer using DIY printer kits and the RepRap.

His healthy curiosity for fixing gadgets as a child came in handy as he recalled the difficult path he took by building a delta 3D printer and extruder in 2015.

Because of his love of typography, he wanted to 3D print various letterforms with clay. He soon realised that a special type of auger mechanism would be needed for his extruder. This would give him the ability to retract the clay material mid print rather than to have a continuous extrusion. He took advantage of 3D printing technologies by designing various extruder designs until he was happy with the final mechanism.

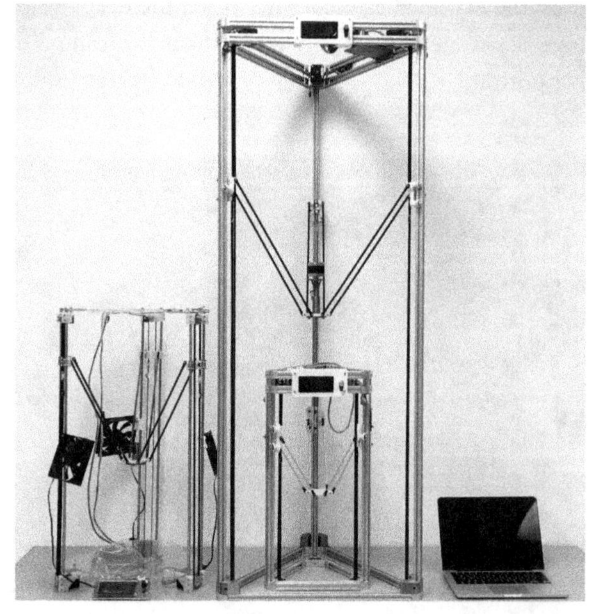

Ceramic 3D Printer by Taekyeom Lee / 2016.

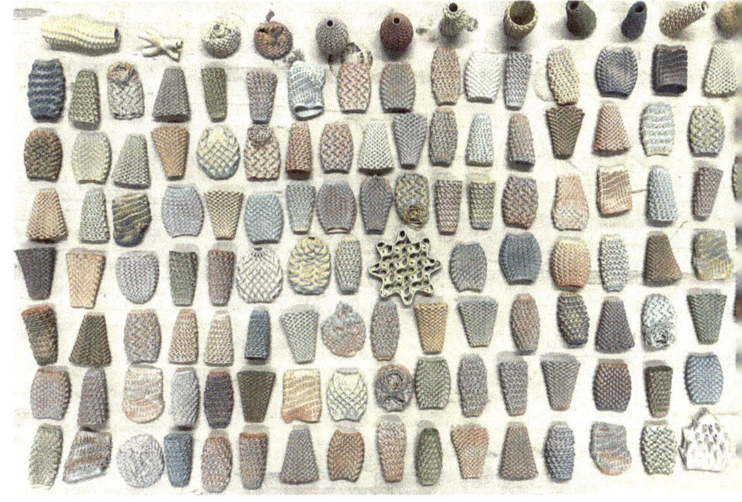

Collection with Gravity / Taekyeom Lee / 2022.

Taekyeom attended an Artist in Residence Programme at the Internet Archive, a non-profit digital library that gives free universal access to online books, movies, and music. Here, Taekyeom recorded the process of building a ceramic 3D printer based on the Kossel RepRap printer and made his build instructions public. Much to his surprise, others have started building their own 3D printers using his instructions. As an educator who loves teaching, he admires those who are willing to teach themselves.

As he started to explore 3D printing with clay, he found people were constantly asking him why he was printing typography? He explained that clay is one of the first materials to be used in history as the spoken word. As a graphic designer he sees clay as ink, and noted how we print on paper and screens. So why not turn back the cycle to the physical printing of words, a type of tangible typography?

He observes that between the clay and his hands there is a tool, a clay 3D printer, that adds another layer. The clay can at times be challenging to work with because of the care taken to ensure the right consistency for a print. An experienced potter knows when the clay is ready just by touching it. That it can be difficult to explain the exact measurements of water and clay to someone else is something that I completely agree with.

Besides typography, Taekyeom also enjoys the 3D printing of clay vessels. One collection, "Collaboration with Gravity", consists of vessels that were deliberately collapsed after they had been 3D printed. These intriguing contemporary pieces perfectly capture a specific moment in time.

Taekyeom enjoys glazing his works by airbrushing them with assorted colours. His decorating style is unique. Precision and consistency of colours each play a role, especially in his two-toned works. Depending on the viewer's perspective, these works change colour and resemble a magic trick. He also enjoys slip trailing, which is adding decorative raised surface texture to a clay body by using clay slip. This can be a slow and tedious process, but the final product is alluring.

Another project that Taekyeom embarked on includes the use of a 3D printer as an embosser. Inspired by braille, he essentially printed business cards without ink, using only his 3D printer. He also teaches a class about accessibility in graphic design as it relates to individuals who have impaired vision.

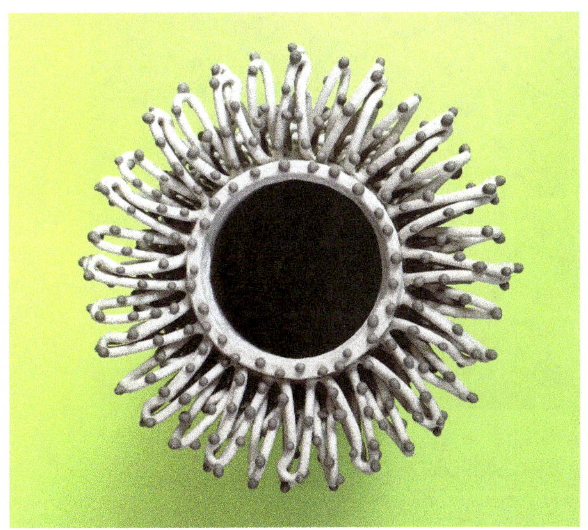

Slip trailing / Taekyeom Lee / 2019.

When I asked him for his perspective on clay 3D printing and art, he said, "A clay 3D printer is a tool, much like our hands. Our hands use a knife to cut, which means a knife is also a tool. There are still those that think art needs to be done completely by hand and this can be quite disrupting. Don't you think that if Da Vinci had access to new tools that he would not have used them?"

At the end of the day, artists are the decision makers, often building their own tools to create things. Taekyeom hopes that in the future the many creative communities, including those committed to creating ceramics, would be more inclusive and diverse, and appreciate new ideas and tools.

Lastly, we chatted about how 3D printing has also been born in the spirit of opensource information. Both of us have experienced that creators do not often give credit where it is due.

Should you 3D print a design that is not your own or that you have not paid for, tell others who you were inspired by, or acknowledge the person who designed the original 3D piece. In my opinion, such community honesty will allow for progression and growth, promoting creativity and innovation.

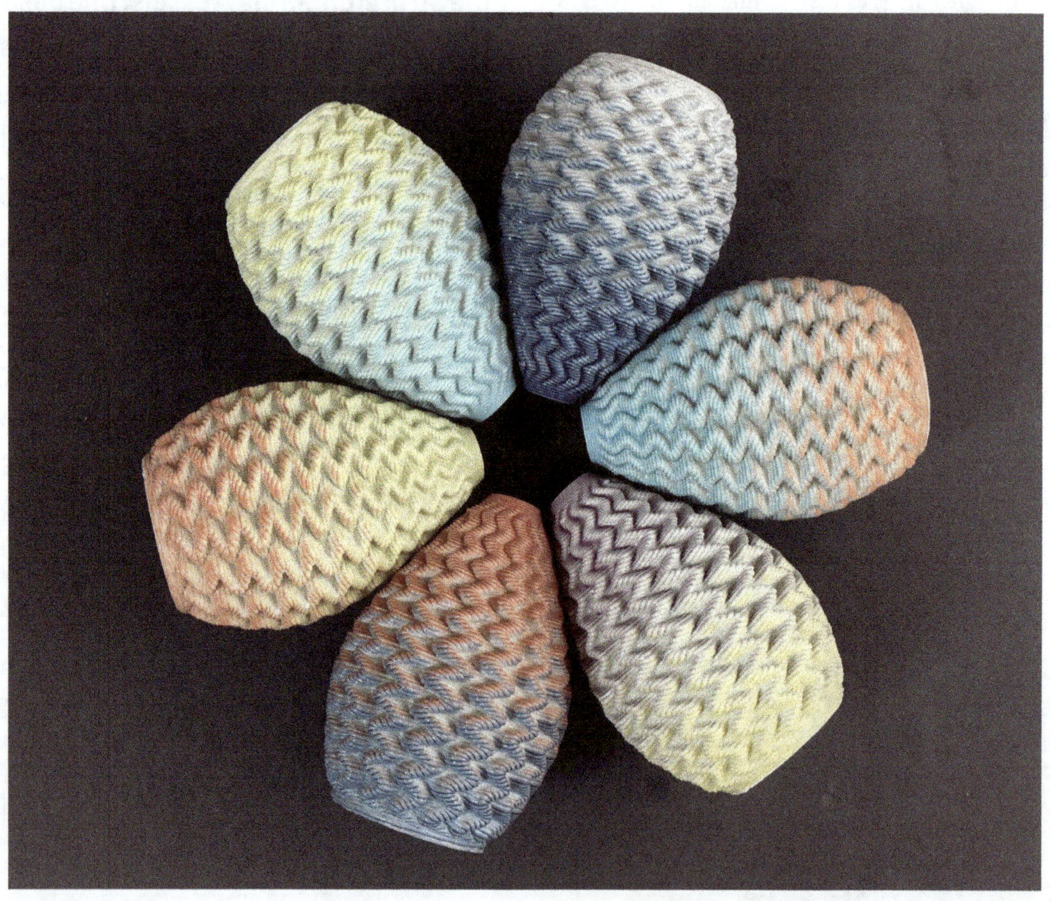

Airbrushed clay printed vases / Taekyeom Lee / 2020.

JULIANNA DOUGHERTY

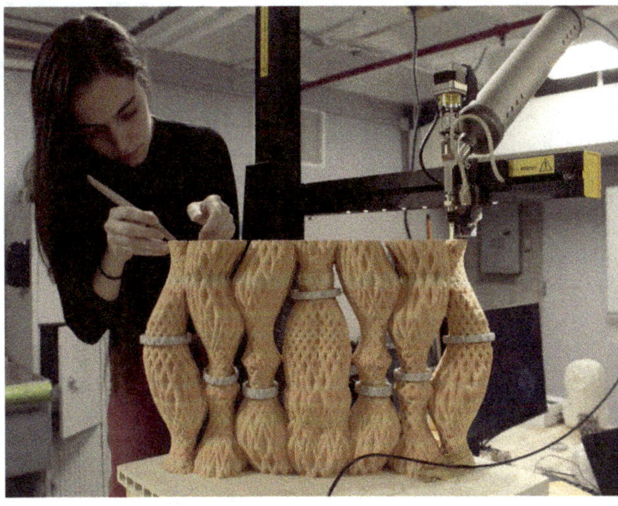

Julianna Dougherty / Photo by Julia Lauer / 2022.

Julianna Dougherty is a ceramic artist who discovered clay 3D printing during her studies at Alfred University in New York, where she earned her BFA and worked in the digital lab assisting fellow students.

Her artwork is known for its vivid colours, textures, and intricate compositions. She uses pre-printed interlocking elements such as bisque fired rings during the 3D printing process. This allows her to be more present during the printing process for further artistic intervention. Symmetry is a common element implemented in her designs to provide balance and visual appeal. The geometries of her designs often use angles that may be on the point of collapse, but rather defy gravity in an elegant and purposeful way.

Julianna uses LUTUM® clay 3D printers in her practice, leveraging their dual extrusion capabilities to craft aesthetically pleasing, multi-coloured compositions.

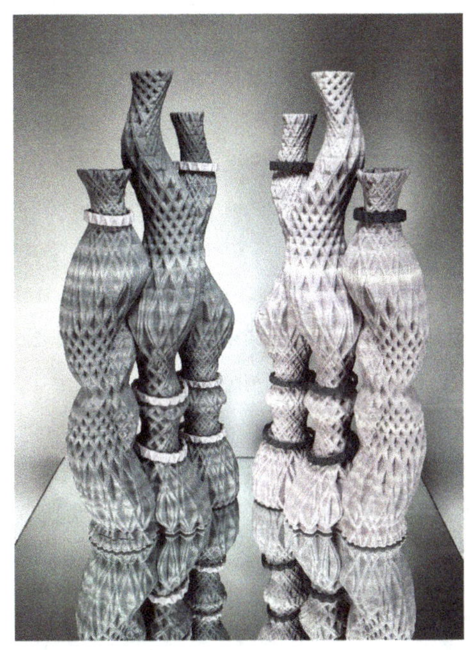

Untitled / Julianna Dougherty / 2023.

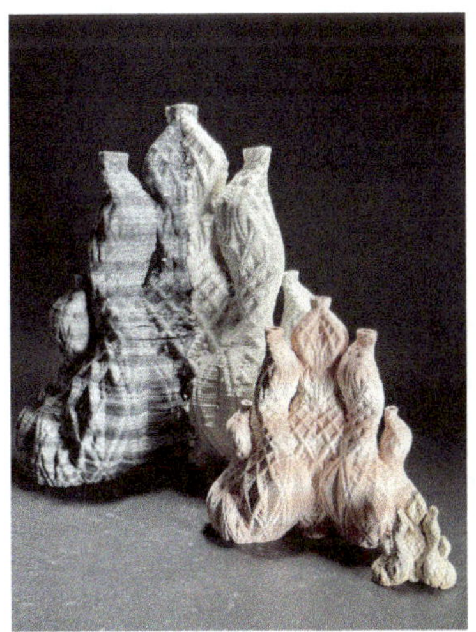

Ring Composition 2 / Julianna Dougherty / 2022.

In the future, as she works to develop her own customised clay printer, she hopes to further explore and extend her research in CAD modelling and clay 3D printing.

She challenges preconceived ideas of what the possibilities of clay 3D printing are in the contemporary art space. Julianna demonstrates how new ideas can be inspired by others but evolve into an individual and unique perspective which in turn stimulates further innovation.

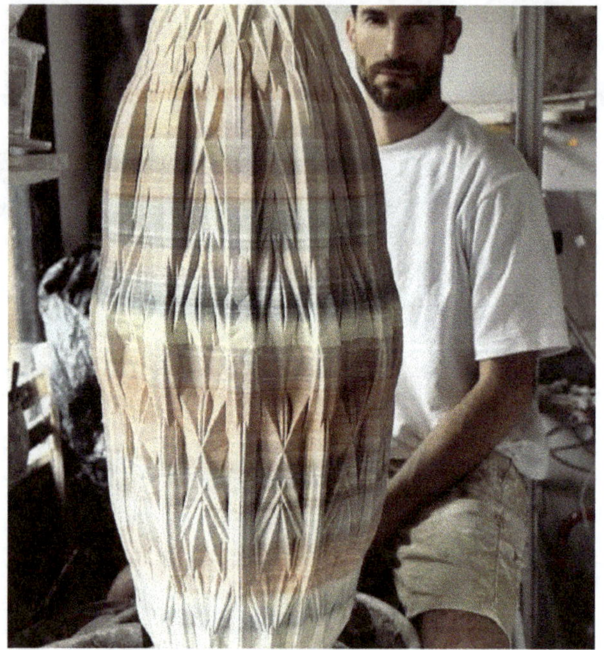

Ryan Barrett / 2023.

RYAN BARRETT

Ryan is a Goldsmiths University Fine Arts textile graduate from Ipswich, United Kingdom. He started exploring ceramics in 2013. As a self-taught potter, he won "The Great Pottery Throwdown" in 2017, a series hosted by the BBC which focuses on traditional pottery techniques. He later went on to build his own clay 3D printer, which he uses to push the boundaries of what is possible in ceramics, as he fuses the digital and physical worlds.

His porcelain pieces often range between 10 000 and 20 000 layered coils, showcasing his unique and, at times, eccentric point of view. Sublime intricate constructions, natural form and sculptural art are the foundation of Ryan's creative inspiration.

Ryan's ceramics are bold, breathtakingly beautiful, incorporating movement and flow in his digitally designed tapestries. His work combines textiles and ceramics that express brilliant textures, form, and surfaces, while maintaining a careful balance. Influenced by modern and mid-century abstract art he maintains tactility within his digital and virtual forms which is critical to Ryan's technique. He customises his practice to maintain total creative control and treats every 3D printed work as a new idea. Furthermore, he enjoys the nuance of one piece never being an exact replica of another.

With his work constantly evolving, his large-scale exquisite clay prints are jaw dropping as they display his expert use of colour, clearly evident in his clay coil layers.

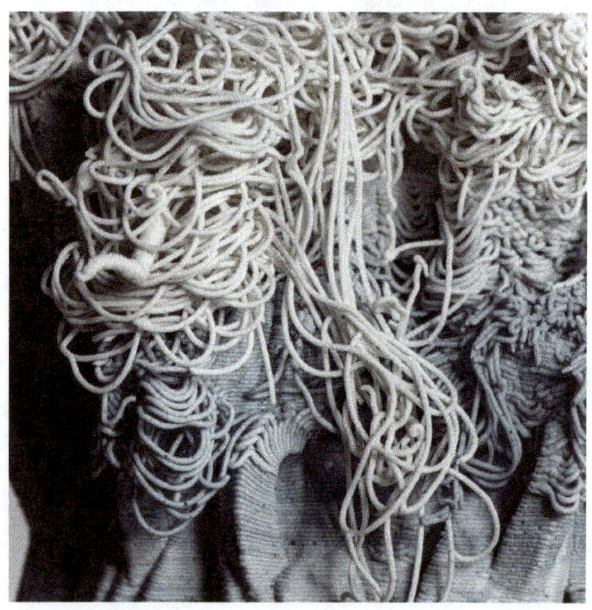

Porcelain coiled layers / Ryan Barrett.

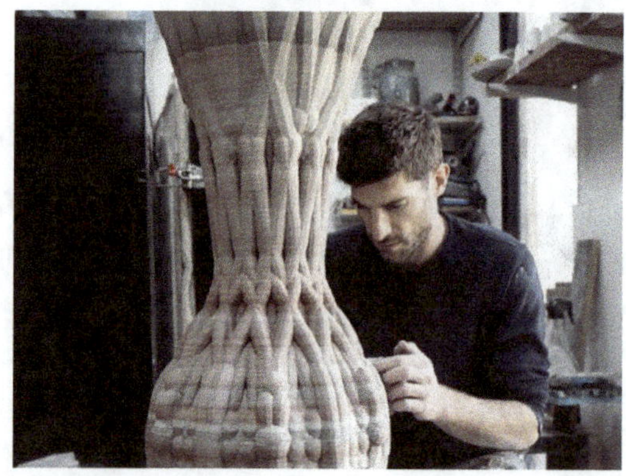

Working in his studio / Ryan Barrett / 2023.

GUY LEVAKOV

Guy is a ceramic designer who blends old-world techniques with 3D printing technology. He studied industrial design at the Holon Institute of Technology and currently lives in Jaffe. Drawn to the tactile nature of clay, he built his own ceramic 3D printer with a feature that allows him to disrupt the printing process to add colour, texture, and character to his pieces. Guy's work has been featured in numerous galleries and artbooks. He also exhibited at the prestigious Paris Design Week in 2022.

He sets himself apart with his emphasis on human intervention during the printing process, believing that the magic of art lies in its imperfections.

His pieces are a testament to his creativity and passion, exhibiting attention to detail and a commitment to unique designs. He hand-finishes each piece, blending technology with tradition to create beautiful and thought-provoking works.

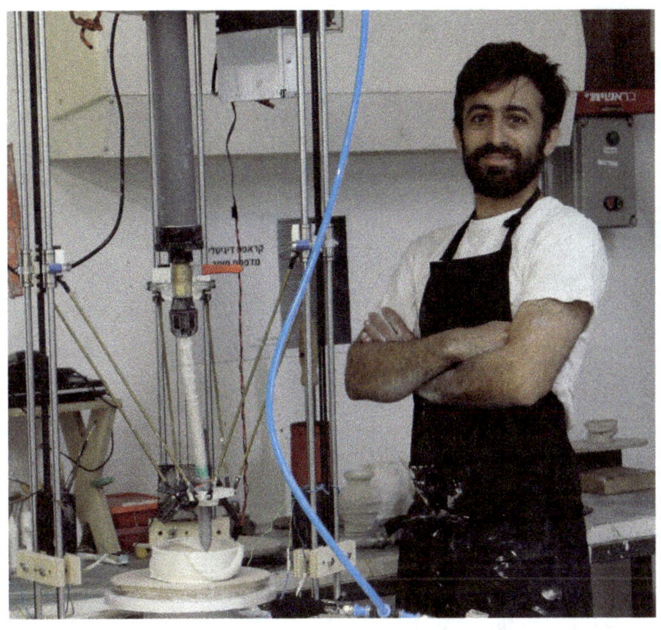

Guy Levakov with his ceramic 3D printer.

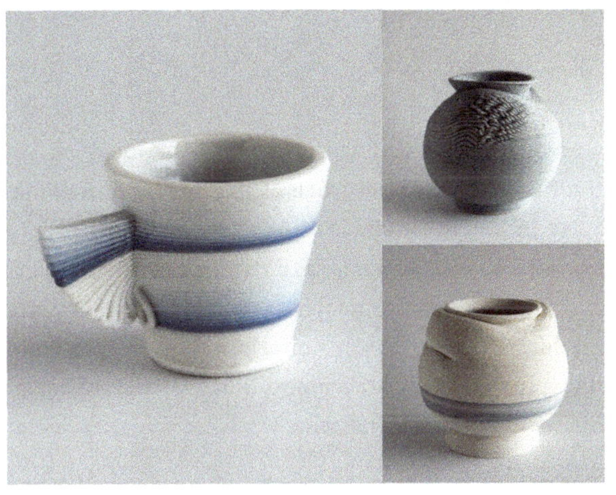

A good example of his elegant design decisions is his espresso cup (top left), which is a personal favourite of mine.

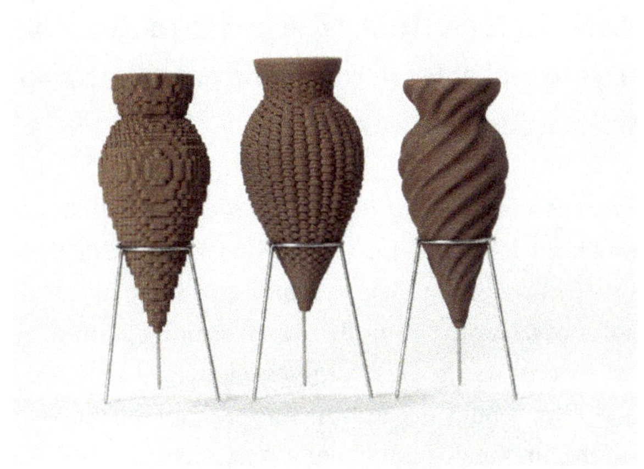

Amphoras / Guy Levakov / 2023.

"Amphora" is the name of his latest line of clay printed urns inspired by the designs of the ancient Greek and Roman amphoras. These printed pieces add classical charm to his modern designs, with the delicacy of these clay vessels evident in the coiled layers. The curves and angles that he achieves in his 3D printed clay forms, despite the notoriety of the material to collapse, are inspirational.

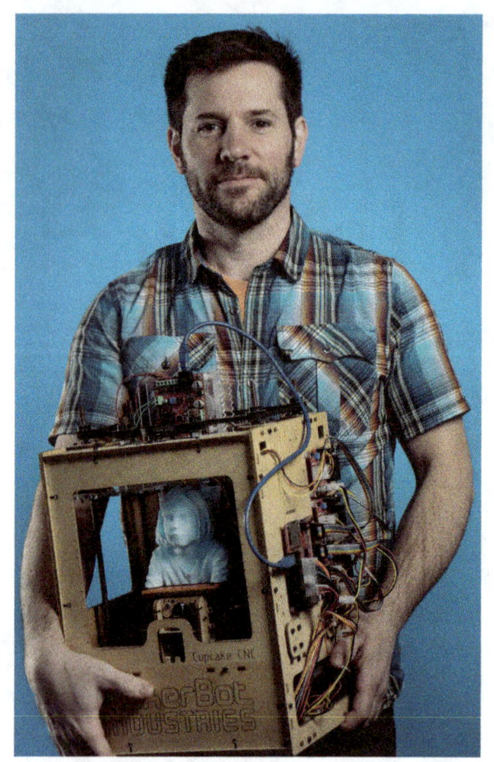

Tom Lauerman / 2022.

TOM LAUERMAN

Growing up in Chicago, Illinois, Tom focussed on traditional forms of art such as painting and drawing. Later in life, as he studied for his bachelor's degree in fine arts, he took ceramics as a required elective subject and found the class and topics very impactful. For Tom, the idea that clay as a material could be sculpted and manipulated was a welcoming thought, and so began his passion for all things clay.

He went on to study at the Cranbrook Academy of Art in Michigan where he specialised in ceramics. During this time, he met fellow artists and architects who inspired him to learn how to use 3D modelling software.

He noted at that stage that digital fabrication equipment was expensive and hard to come by. The first plastic object he ever printed was in 2008; it was a small tile that cost him around 100 dollars (USA). He saw the potential in using these printed forms for casting and went on to teach mould making, working towards precision plastic 3D prints and all the while keeping an eye on clay 3D printing as it started to develop around the world.

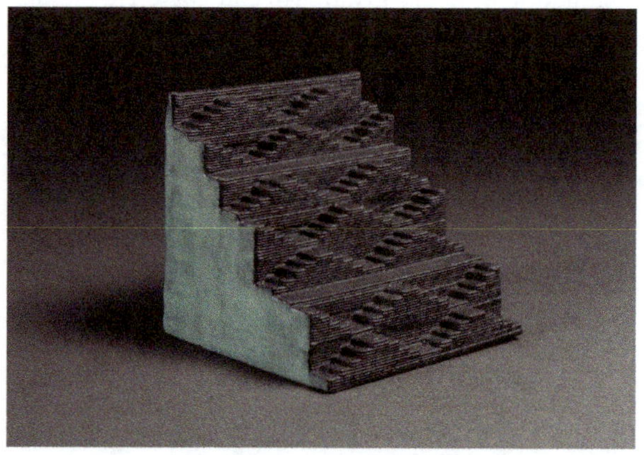

Two tone clay 3D print / Tom Lauerman / 2021.

When he started teaching at Penn State University, he lobbied for the purchase of plastic 3D printers for the design department in 2012.

With the arrival of the 3D printers, he soon accustomed himself with dismantling and modifying them. With the help of the engineering department at the university, he was able to build his own clay 3D printer.

The Learning Factory Program was a project that was established in 2014 for engineering students in their final year of study. Here, a handful of students would collaborate with Tom by experimenting with clay extrusions. As the years progressed, both the students and Tom would expand on the progress of the year before, the final result being a dual extrusion clay 3D printer that used a direct extrusion auger system.

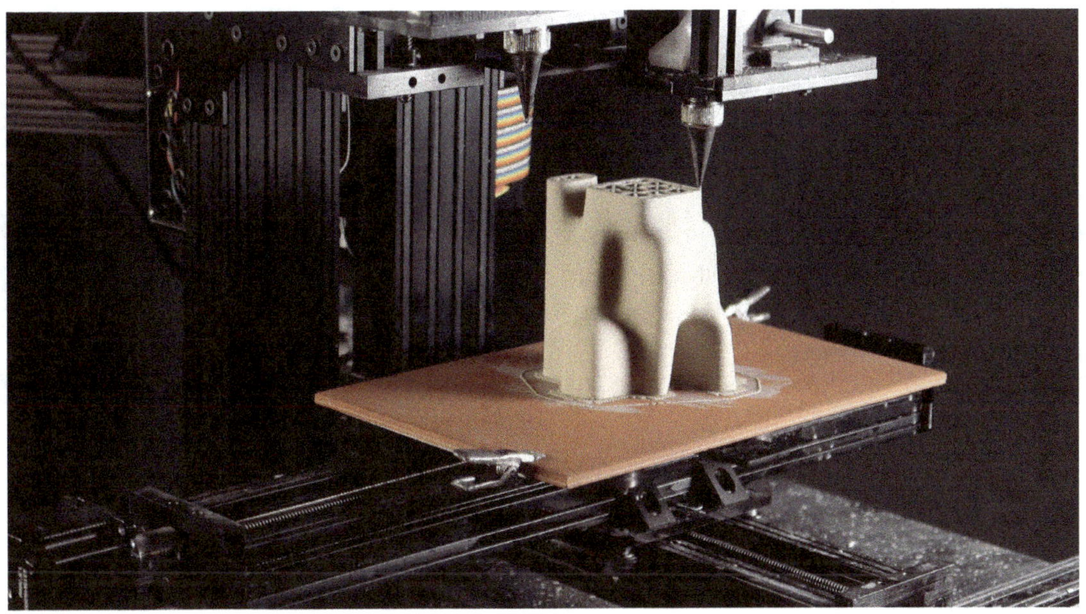

Dual extrusion clay 3D printer / Tom Lauerman.

This concretisation of their initial concept, developed through time, could be used to print with clay, together with another material that could essentially be fired away in the kiln (e.g. newspaper shavings), leaving behind an amazing structure. Tom noted that to calibrate the printer was a major challenge as endless tests had to be run before a printing procedure could even be started.

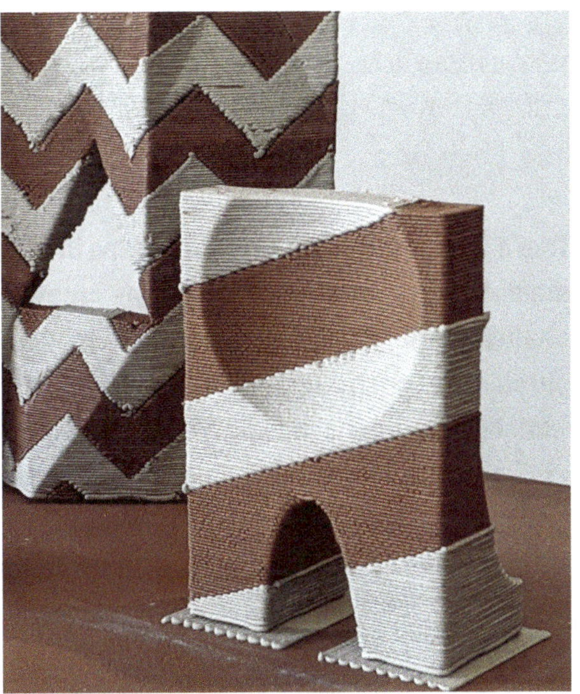

Tom worked to create clay 3D printers that could also produce high-quality clay prints to the level of a plastics filament printer – a most difficult task to achieve. It was a personal obsession of his which grew during the Covid-19 pandemic as he continually modified his clay 3D printer. His fascination with the built environment and his interest in architectural design were his main inspiration for ultimately attempting to produce clay 3D prints that replicate plastic filament printers.

The dual extrusion clay 3D printer has two nozzles that can move up and down at different computer-programmed intervals, extruding different colours and types of clay.

Marvelling at what slicing software is capable of, Tom used these to effectively design his bridging forms, which where revolutionary. This highlighted the possibilities of precision printing and how the maker could have more control over the material with which they print. Tom prefers a cartesian printer setup and has no interest in printing clay vessels.

An example of a bridged form with a two tone colour / Tom Lauerman / 2021.

His background in sculpture has inspired his distinctive cubist style, that is reflected in his small-scale prints, with many of his clay printed works deliberately incorporating infills and supports.

One of his projects, which I find most impressive, is his stop motion animations, which involve an adapted pen plotter. A pen plotter is a computer programmed robot, that can draw any graphic on a piece of paper, with one or multiple pens, pencils, or markers. Tom's idea was originally inspired by one of his students, Audrey Ann, who, using a pen plotter that had a pottery needle tool, instead of a marker, attached to it, experimented with writing on a clay tile.

Tom's love for animation further motivated him to use Blender® as a generative design tool when creating his animations. Once completed, the animation is exported in frames (single photos of each step in the animation). These files are then sent to the adapted pen plotter that uses a needle tool. Instead of paper, a slab of clay is used. The plotter then draws out the captured frame into the clay, whereupon a high-resolution photo is taken. The clay slab is then smoothed, ready for the next frame to be drawn on it. It can be a messy process. However, the result of many painstaking hours of capturing and processing images materialises into a few seconds of the most fascinating stop motion animation possible!

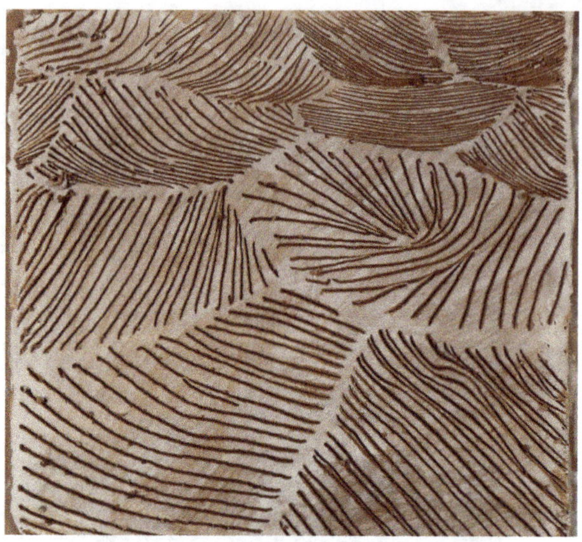

Stop motion animation / Tom Lauerman / 2023.

I find this innovative mindset very inspiring. Using all the tools in your arsenal and acquiring a new perspective on clay and what you can make with it is so exciting! The evolving knowledge of clay artists as they venture into exploring new technologies and material techniques is exactly how clay 3D printing started.

Given the many manufactured clay printers currently on the market, Tom advises that if you can afford to buy one, do so. For those with smaller budgets, Jonathan Keep's original design for a low-cost printer is a good stepping-stone for any interested in building their own.

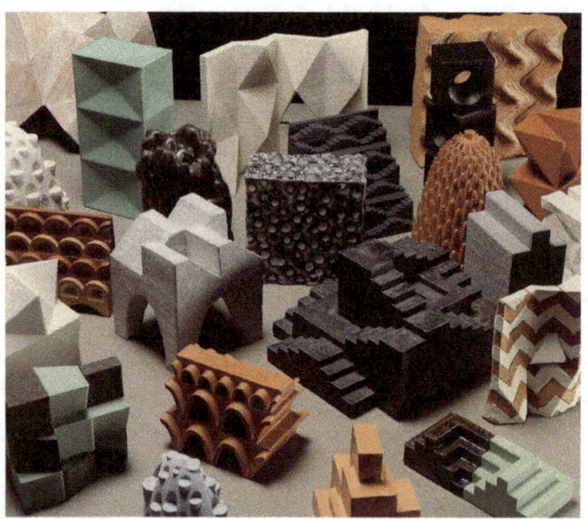

Tom's love of "tripping over territories in new media" is an ever dynamic changing creative challenge. His vision for the future is to keep pursuing his crisp and detailed small designs, whilst exploring the modularity and assembly of clay printed forms, as summed up by him, "in essence, coming full circle, back to where I started as a sculptor."

- Tom Lauerman / 2023.

3D prints / Tom Lauerman.

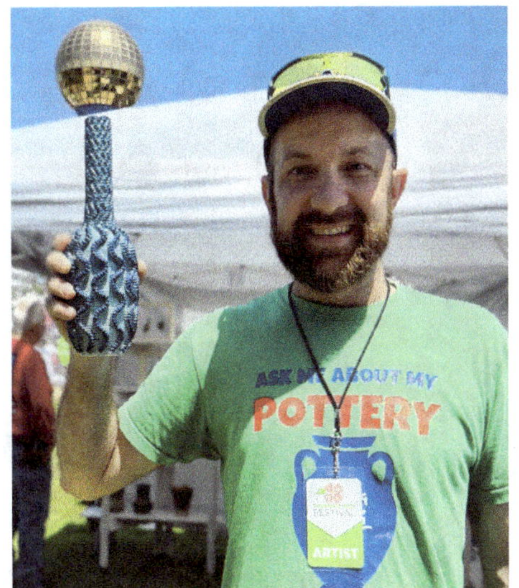

Garrett Durland / 2023.

GARRETT DURLAND

Currently residing in Tennessee, USA, Garrett went from working as an engineer at Oak Ridge National Lab in 2018 to running a well-established 3D printing business. Considering materials other than plastic, he modified and converted a plastic printer into a clay 3D printer. He was awarded the "Emerging Artist of the Year" award at the American Handcrafted Show in 2023, where both modern and traditional crafted works are celebrated.

Garrett also fabricates 3D printed vases that are converted to moulds and then used in casting intricate concrete planters. With his experience in using a variety of materials, he explores how 3D printing can be used across multiple industries, not just pottery art. Another great example is his inclusive 3D printed bathroom signs, of which to date he has sold well over 5 000 prints.

Garrett enjoys experimenting with different glaze compositions when decorating his expressive vessels. Bright colours and intricate details are evident on his forms. He also creates porcelain light fixtures that use parametric techniques to precisely position clay coils and loops, imitating the fractal beauty built into natural and fantastical objects.

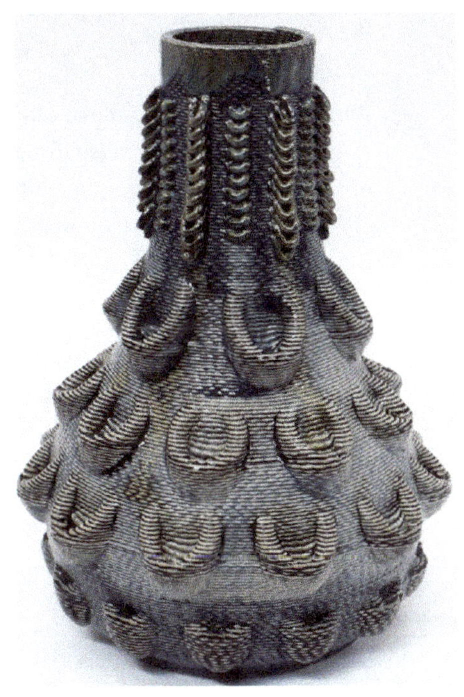

Vase / Photo by Maker exchange / 2022.

Adding unique features to his vessels, he transforms a familiar shape into pottery that is exciting and inventive – truly, a reimagination of what a pot is.

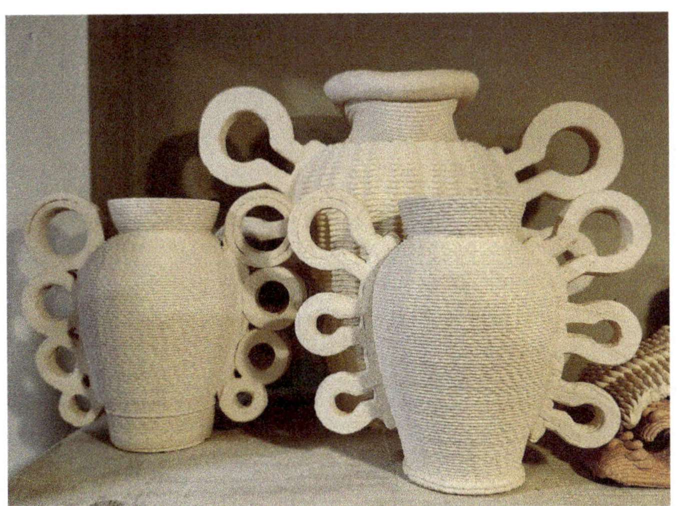

Large vessels / Garrett Durland.

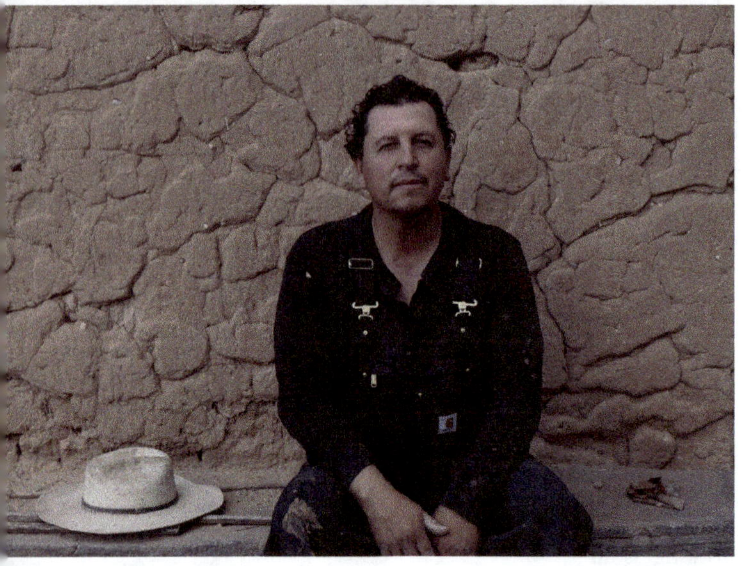

RONALD RAEL

Ronald Rael / 2023.

Ronald is currently a professor in Architecture as well as the Head of the Art Department at the University of California, Berkley. As the co-founder of Emerging Objects, a company that specialises in providing innovative solutions from various industries by using 3D printing technologies, his academic and work life are often interwoven.

His passion lies in 3D printing with adobe materials such as soil, mud, and clay to create low impact structures and concepts for the 21st century. His background as a traditional adobe builder and architect is projected in his book, "Earth Architecture", published in 2008.

He had already speculated in 2007 that 3D printing with earth may be a way forward in the field of architecture. Trying to think of ways to further this idea, he asked Mark Ganter, a professor from the University of Washington, and the first person to 3D print an object with ceramic powder, to teach him the basics of ceramics and 3D printing on a small scale.

Ronald had no intention of becoming a ceramic artist but found that his background allowed a natural progression into that artform. At the time he was exploring the possibilities of plasticity and gravity related to new patterns and textures formed in the clay during the 3D printing process.

He noticed how this was emulated by others and ultimately decided that rather than keep the technology to himself, he would make it available to all. Initially, he asked 25 ceramic artists to participate in a workshop to test a software programme, which led to the 3D printing of over 200 vessels. And so, Potterware, was born. The software has to date been used widely all around the world as a tool to educate and help build the toolkit of everyday clay makers.

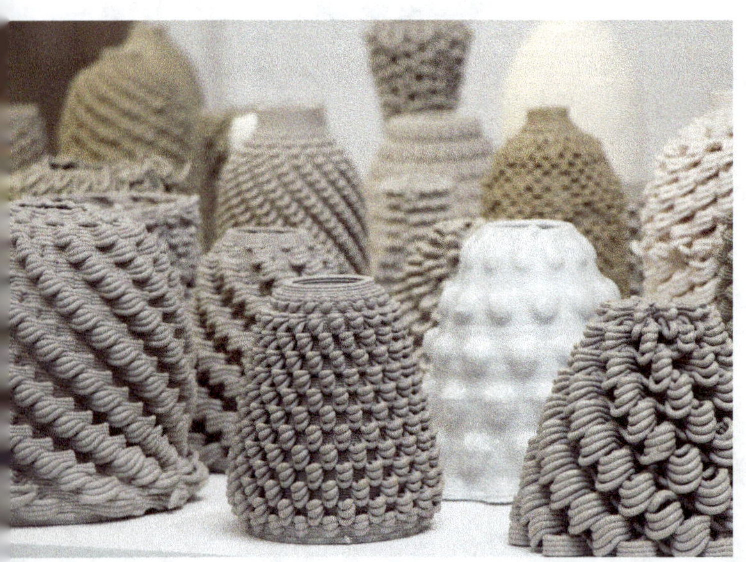

"g.code clay" / Various clay vessels created with Potterware / Emerging Objects..

Ronald further experimented with other materials, such as wood, cement, rubber and car tyres, but the desire to 3D print large scale structures using earth was never far from his mind. He finally divulged his dream to Danny Defelici from 3D Potter, and the idea of a large-scale 3D printer came to fruition. Ronald had previously built his own extrusion printer but admitted that by no means did he have the skills to build a large-scale robot.

To date, Ronald still uses the first version of the Scara 3D Printer from 3D Potter, along with other 3D printers, to print his large-scale mud houses, a dream come true.

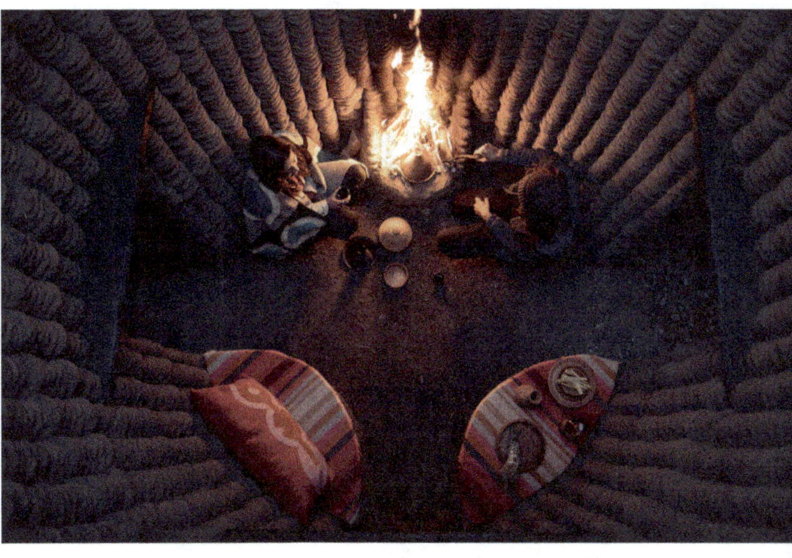

Casa Covida (above and below) / PROJECT TEAM: Emerging Objects: Ronald Rael, Virginia San Fratello, Mattias Rael, Sandy Curth, Logman Arja / 3D Potter: Danny Defelici / Textiles by Joshua Tafoya. Special thanks to Christine Rael, Johnny Ortiz (Shed Project) and Maida Branch (Maida Goods) / Photography by Elliot Ross and Emerging Objects.

"Casa Covida" is a cohabitation house that is the first large-scale 3D printed adobe building of its kind created with sand, silt, clay, water, and straw. With the advent of the Covid-19 pandemic, Ronald had time to rethink the scale and design of the project, which was eventually completed in 2020. Situated in the San Luis valley of the Colorado desert, special attention was given to the space provided for the cooking, sleeping, and sitting areas. So prestigious was the "Casa Covida" creation that it received the - 2023 Jeff Harnar Social Justice and Environmental Award.

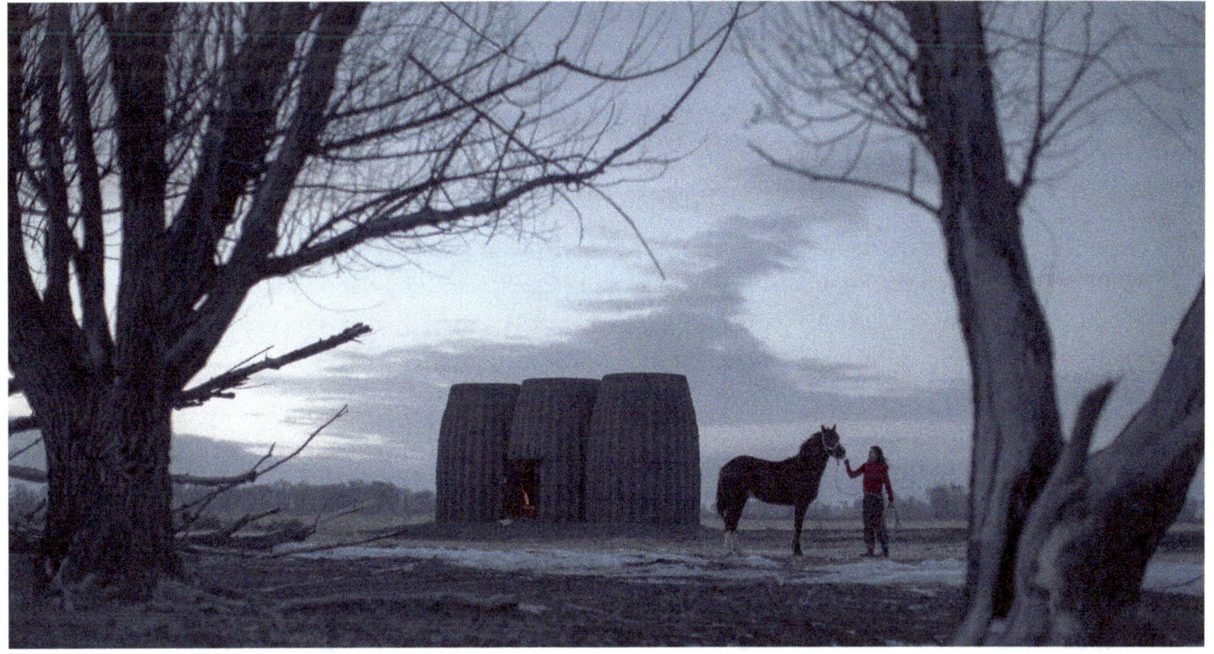

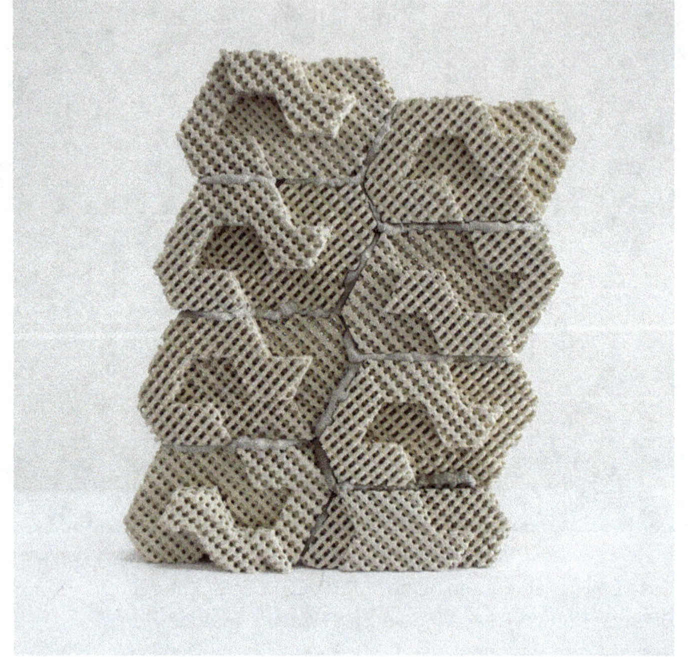

The clay 3D print, "Cool Bricks", consists of individually 3D printed clay bricks that are designed with an inner matrix. The design allows for air to flow through the bricks, which are sprayed with water, thus cooling the interior of the structure. The idea was inspired by a trip Ronald took to sub-Saharan Africa. He witnessed how the mud huts of the locals were kept cool through large ceramic vessels filled with water and placed in each hut. These vessels were cool to the touch, with the porous clay creating a cooling effect within the space.

Cool Bricks / Emerging objects.

"Bad Ombres" is a series of clay vessels that are made from a variety of clays that when 3D printed in one extrusion, create a colour gradient across the vessel. Expertly designed, the flowing clay coils create a unique texture to these already beautiful vessels. "Bad Ombres V2" is displayed in the permanent collection of the Smithsonian American Art Museum in Washington D.C.

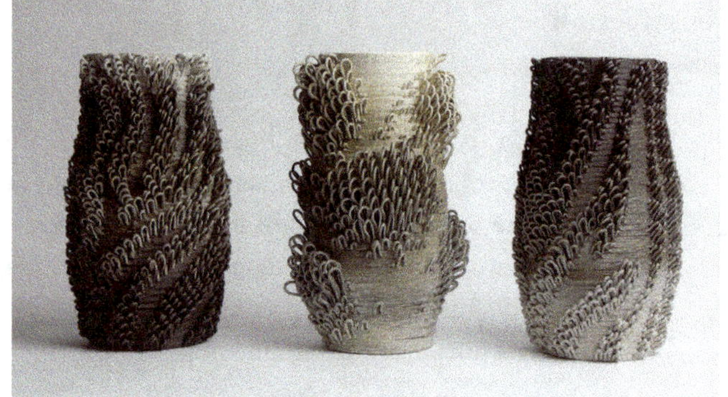

Bad Ombres / Emerging objects.

Ronald's book "Printing Architecture; Innovative recipes for 3D printing" was published in 2018. It largely motivated me to move into clay 3D printing. I can personally recommend it to anyone who is interested in learning more about innovative design concepts in the field of 3D printing.

Ronald hopes that for the future, architectural design will look at incorporating other parts of a building in the additive manufacturing process in an elegant and efficient way. He specifically mentions plumbing, electricity, and heating. Currently, he is teaching a course at UC Berkley that is focused on these areas and how, as different cultures start to embrace new forms of construction, they can be guided and be responsive to using technology.

He cannot get his head around the fact that concrete, plastics and resins are possibly representative of the future of architecture, in that they are presently detrimental to our health and the environment.

"We need to build in smart ways", he says. "Architecture must be clean and beautiful but also respond to a modern lifestyle." He is very curious to see how people in his home country (USA), choose to embrace concrete 3D printing, as most structures there are built using wood.

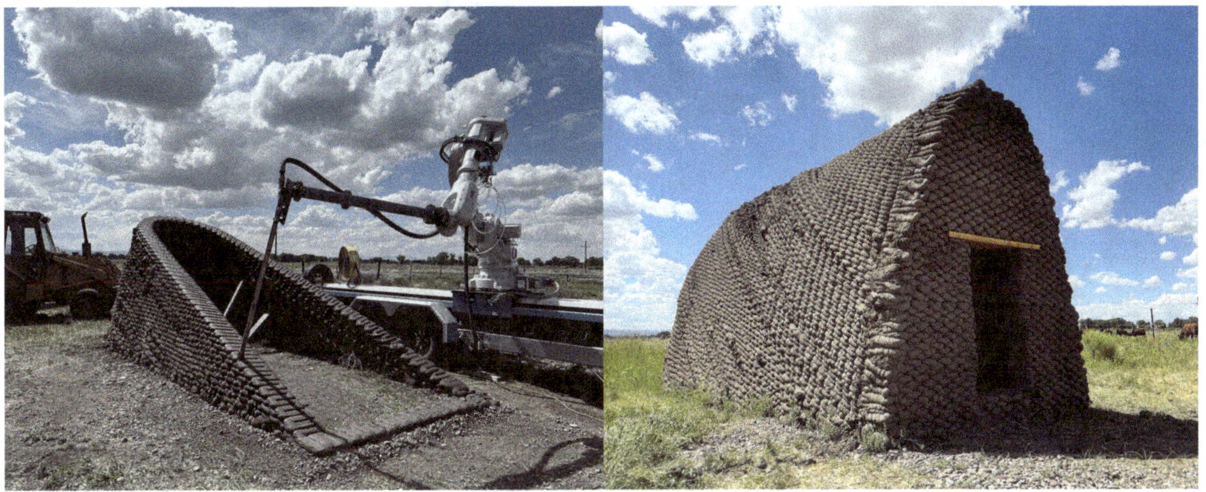

From Walls To Roofs: In-progress 3D printed Nubian Vault during construction.

From Walls To Roofs: Front view of the completed formwork-free, 3D printed adobe Nubian Vault.

In architecture a Nubian Vault is a type of curved surface, forming a vaulted structure. The above construction is called "Terrano" and was 3D printed in 2023. It is the first structure in the world to have a roof 3D printed on site using adobe materials. With the use of a robotic arm that has been mounted on the back of a trailer, the 3D printer can be moved anywhere. The robotic arm is also able to move back and forth on a rail on the trailer, allowing for a greater build area and volume.

Adobe materials have widely been used by different cultures throughout history. Ronald explains how new tools have almost forced these cultures to move into the modern way of building in that they have to use materials such as concrete, instead of retaining traditional heritage techniques and building customs using earth materials.

In the same breath, he admits that additive manufacturing can also be disruptive to cultures that take great pride in their traditions, beliefs, and symbols, and we need to be careful not to force technology onto those who do not yet accept it.

"Much like the pottery wheel was used to help speed up production of clay vessels, why not look at how 10 000 years of tradition using earth to build houses can't be reintroduced in a 21st century capitalist society?"

- Ronald Rael / 2023.

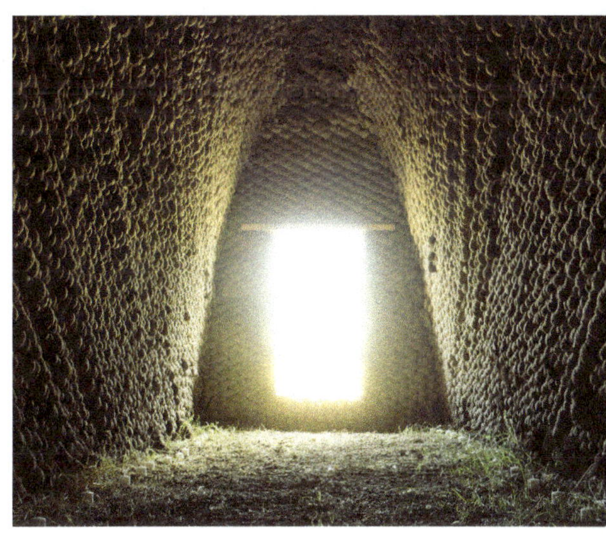

Terrano on the inside / Emerging Objects.

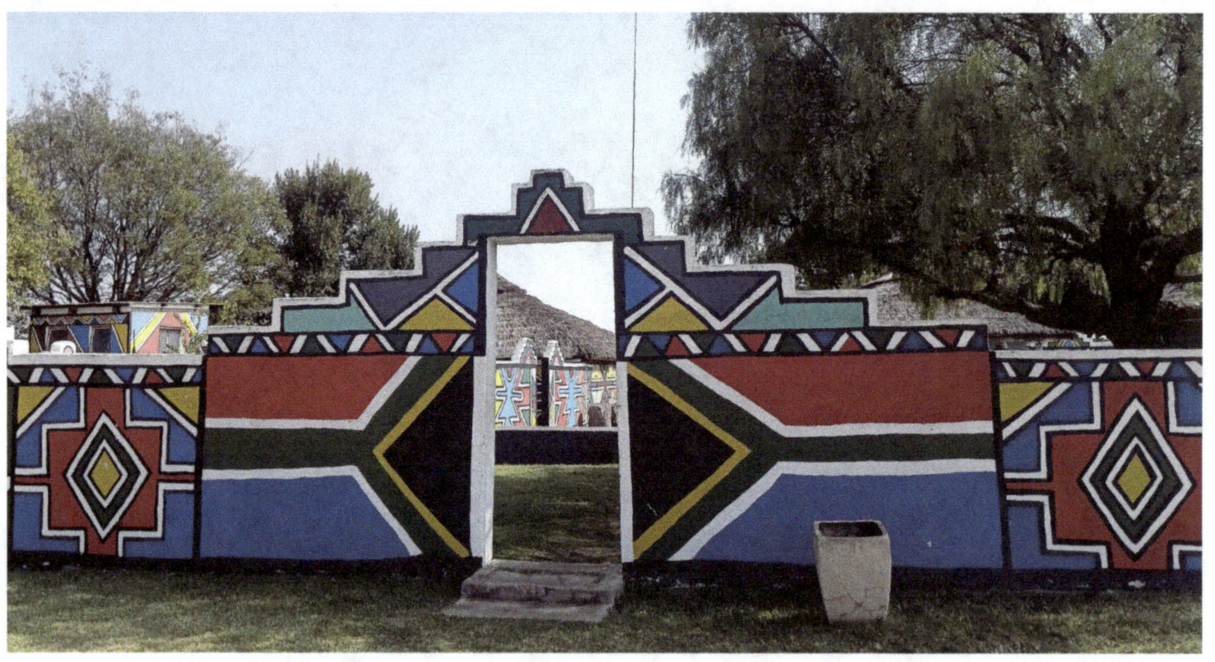

Ndebele Cultural Village walls depicting the South African national flag in, Mpumalanga / South Africa / Photo by Hendrien Horn / 2024.

Ronald predicts that new forms and shapes will emerge in cultures as architecture continually advances and changes, not just in the 3D printing industry. An appropriate example he gives is of the Ndebele people of South Africa who are widely known for their beautiful geometrically painted designs on the walls of their houses. These patterns are essentially illustrating a story. Embedded with meaning, the houses have evolved over time, with modern influences, such as logos, nowadays popping up on Ndebele house walls.

He envisions how people can take command of the design of their own houses, creating an identity and looking at "producing difference and not sameness" – an idea that I can identify with!

As our interview ended, the sun was rising in my world and was setting in his. I was touched by his humility, considering the impact his work has had, not only on me, but also on many in the 3D printing industry around the world.

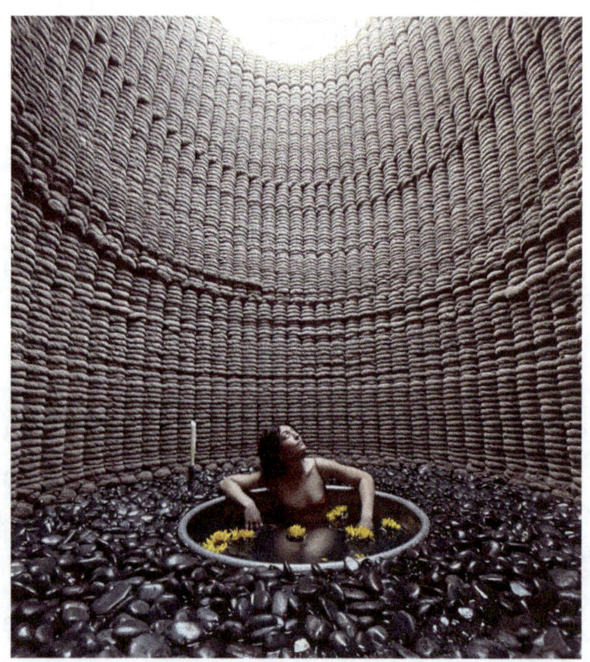

Casa Covida / Emerging objects.

A SOUTH AFRICAN PERSPECTIVE

HANS FOUCHÉ

A few years ago, when I started exploring clay 3D printing, I could find only one person in my country who had any knowledge on the subject, and thank goodness, he was only a 45-minute drive away from me.

He is a man of few words, but the projects he has worked on speak for themselves. After completing his Honours degree in Mechanical Engineering, he worked as an Aerospace engineer and at the age of thirty, moved to England to work as Chief Aerodynamicist for the Lola and Brabham Formula One racing teams. There, he built 3D printers that were used to print race car concept designs for aerodynamic testing in wind tunnels.

Hans eventually moved back to South Africa where he started Fouché Chocolates, a company that operated for over thirty years. He started by building 3D printers that used ABS plastic granules and named his machine model the "Cheetah". Gradually, he modified these machines, experimenting and printing, using a large variety of food stuffs such as caramel, custard, jam, icing sugar, ice-cream and potatoes, to name but a few.

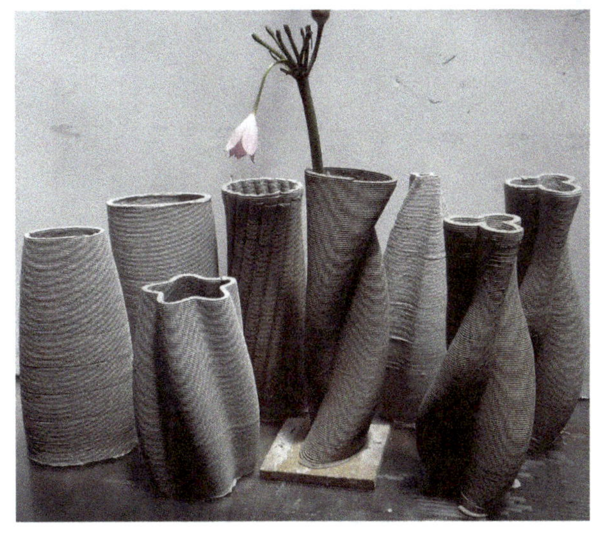

Clay prints / Hans Fouché.

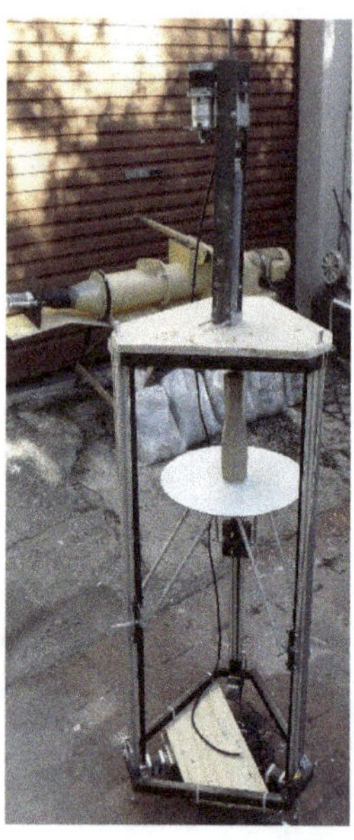

The "Warthog" prototype.

Along with his colleague, Wally Langsford, the two began to experiment with clay as an extrusion material. He confessed that it was a rather messy start, with air pressure being used to push the clay from a bucket to the printer, and resulting in many burst pipes.

All his experiments ultimately led him to design a plunger system. This was adapted multiple times in tandem with his experiments as to how the weight of the clay could influence the machine, ultimately resulting in his final delta design. This enabled the large extruder to be stationary, with only the bed plate of the printer moving. He explained that he started using a pugmill to help prep the clay for printing which made the process easier.

Hans called the clay printer the "Warthog". It could be adapted to 3D print using various amounts of clay. He admits that its appearance resembled a prototype and as an engineer he is not very good at adding all the "bells and whistles" to his printers.

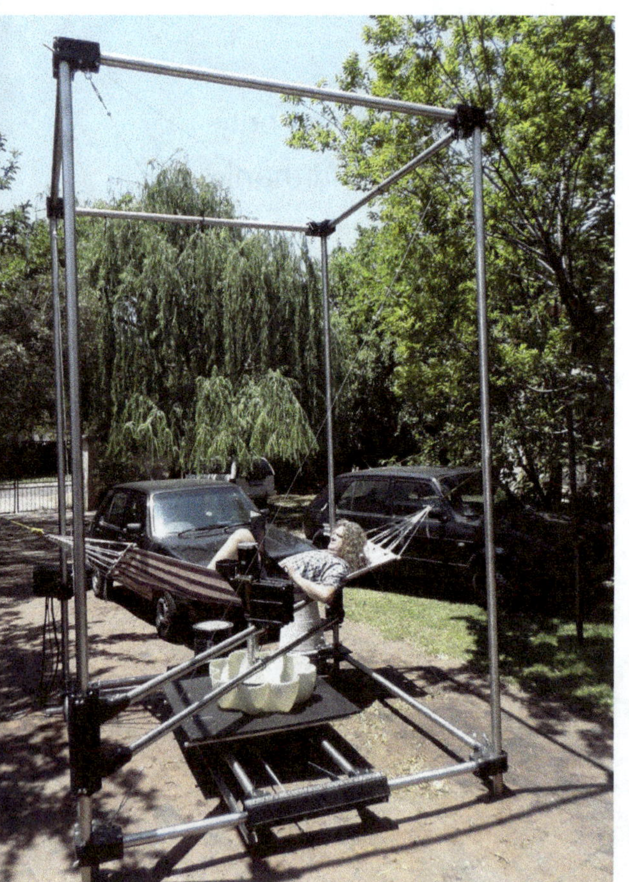

Hans soaking up the South African sunshine as he 3D prints with his "Cheetah" printer.

When I asked which people had influenced his clay 3D printer build and clay prints, he remarked, with a wide smile on his face, "The same people that influenced you!".

His advice for new makers, is to think practically. If you want to sell something, how can you make it so appealing that someone would want to buy it? With such an attitude, one can in fact successfully build a small business. An example he used was of the lawnmower that he 3D printed, which was not heavy, it was easy to manoeuvre, and did not take up a lot of storage space.

Hans is working on a concept that involves 3D printing low-cost houses, emphasising that they differ vastly from what is currently available on the market. As intrigued as I was, I did not ask any more questions, acknowledging that he will reveal his invention once he is ready to.

Hans's achievements are inspirational, and I am thankful that he was willing to share some of the details of his earliest work in clay 3D printing with me. The first clay 3D print I ever made was with the aid of Warthog. As a potter, I remember looking at the print and thinking, "Wow, anything is possible now!".

DRIP ADDITIVE MANUFACTURING

If you want to learn more about what it takes to build your own clay 3D printer, here is a company doing exactly that!

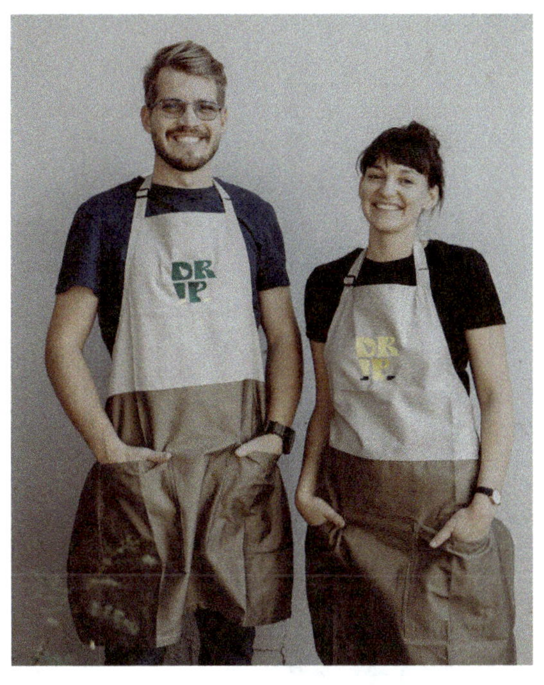

Jason Kearney & Marié Snyman / DRIP AM© / 2023.

DRIP is a new start-up established by Marié Snyman and Jason Kearney. These two friends decided to combine their skills to explore and experiment with both the mechanical and practical aspects of 3D printing with different extrusion pastes.

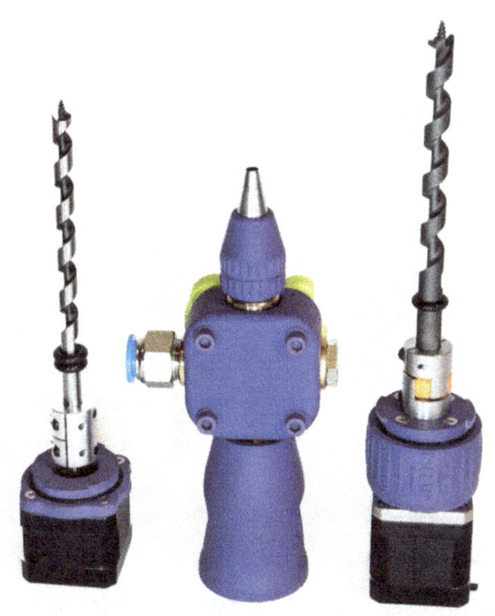

Extruder and auger screws / DRIP AM© / 2024.

Marié, who has a Master's degree in Architecture from the University of Cape Town, indicated that 3D printing found her when she was researching topics to write about in her thesis. She wanted to explore the opportunities that 3D printing could have on construction in South Africa. With that in mind, she decided to import a small clay 3D printer, which she used to test print structural design concepts for architecture on a small scale.

Jason, a civil engineer from the University of Pretoria, completed his Honours degree, focussing on fused deposition modelling and how it could be used to create concrete moulds. He started by buying up all the filaments that he could when he visited the United States of America and bringing them home. Thereupon, he bought a plastic filament 3D printer that he then modified to print and test different types of materials.

When it came to the design of their first clay extruder, the team admitted that it was able to do the job, but that there was much room for improvement. Some of their first extruders were built from 3D printed fittings made from PLA filaments. However, unable to handle the force of the air pressure, but at the same time not allowing for a proper airtight seal with the bolts, the PLA caused some problems – it would burst and break.

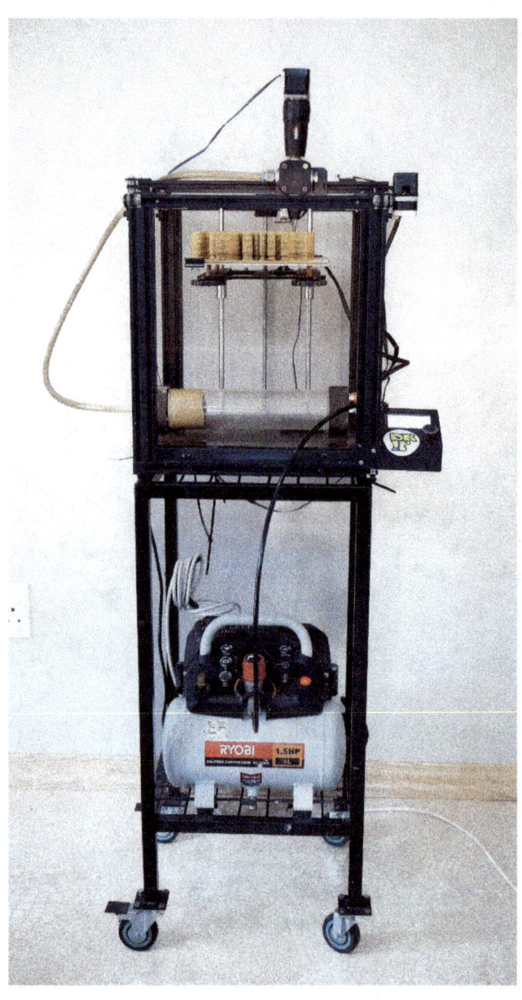

Their modified clay 3D printer with a portable trolley housing the air compressor / DRIP AM© / 2024.

Their first manufactured aluminium extruder could be dismantled and cleaned with ease. The team decided to do a soft launch, by showcasing their converted plastics printer at the Rondebosch Potters Market in Cape Town. They were worried about the perceptions of their machine by the traditional potters, but the overall response was positive.

The feedback they received motivated them to experiment with the continuous feeding of clay to the printer. Currently, this is not possible with the DRIP system. It does, however, allow the maker to pause the print, swap the empty clay cylinder with a new full one, enabling the print to continue. This adaptation allows for the printing of larger objects.

The team is currently conducting experiments towards the creation of a modular extruder. This will allow the maker to 3D print with dual extrusion pastes at the same time. In doing so, materials are blended within the extruder before being deposited. The objective here is to experiment with the material and even to invent, thus giving the maker the opportunity to explore the different methods for making clay 3D prints.

Their Tips for Building a Clay 3D Printer

A relatively cheap plastic printer can be converted to print with different pastes. Consider how you are going to feed this material to the printer. Start with the basics, use a syringe, mount it, and push it manually. The biggest challenge is whether to use a mechanical system or an air compressor when moving the material from point A to point B. Ultimately, the team found that airflow worked well for what they wanted to achieve and proceeded to develop their extruder.

Locating the correct parts for their tubes and cylinders occasionally poses problems. Thus, background knowledge and industrial skillsets can be used to good advantage. Tinker and experiment with different ideas. Just because everyone else is doing things one way, does not mean that you can't find a better way.

Consider the weight of the extruder and the material, ensuring that the bracket you are mounting it on is stable. If the printer is top heavy, it may lean to one side and could possibly fall over, or, if the bracket moves during the printing process, it may result in uneven printing.

Lastly, do the things that you have a passion for and that you consider to be important; don't just print a random design. Design it so that it has meaning for you, even if you think it is elementary and irrelevant... "That is where the magic happens."

– Marié Snyman /2023.

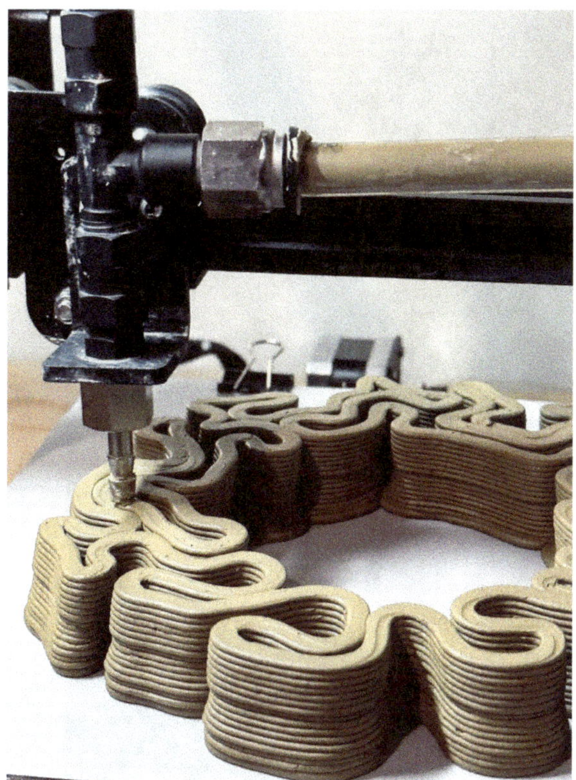

Photo by DRIP AM© / 2023.

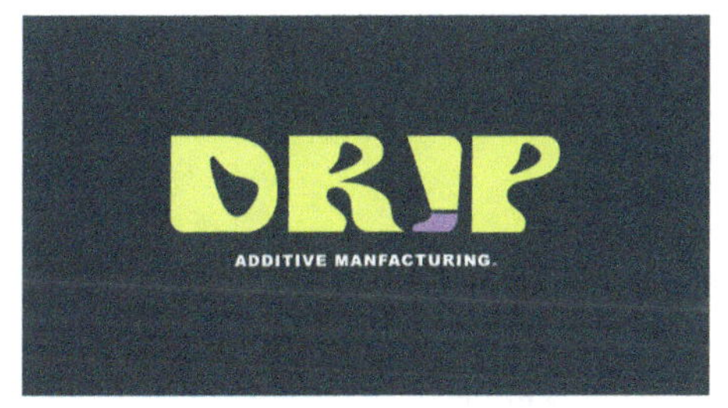

The DRIP team is currently working on building bigger printers as they explore concepts of how, with the aid of large-scale 3D printers, to improve the infrastructure and housing in South Africa. Printers that work autonomously should not be included in the plan; rather use the printer for what it is good for, namely, for building complex parts at a faster rate. In this way, the large labour force that we have in our country can be trained to build infrastructure and houses by assembling 3D printed building components.

Apart from clay and other viscous materials, the DRIP team is exploring ideas of printing furniture parts, along with looking at the advantages and disadvantages of printing on a larger scale. Placing a strong emphasis on innovation, supported by the motto, "Bet we can print that!", the focus is not solely on the material, but also on the technology it requires to print something well.

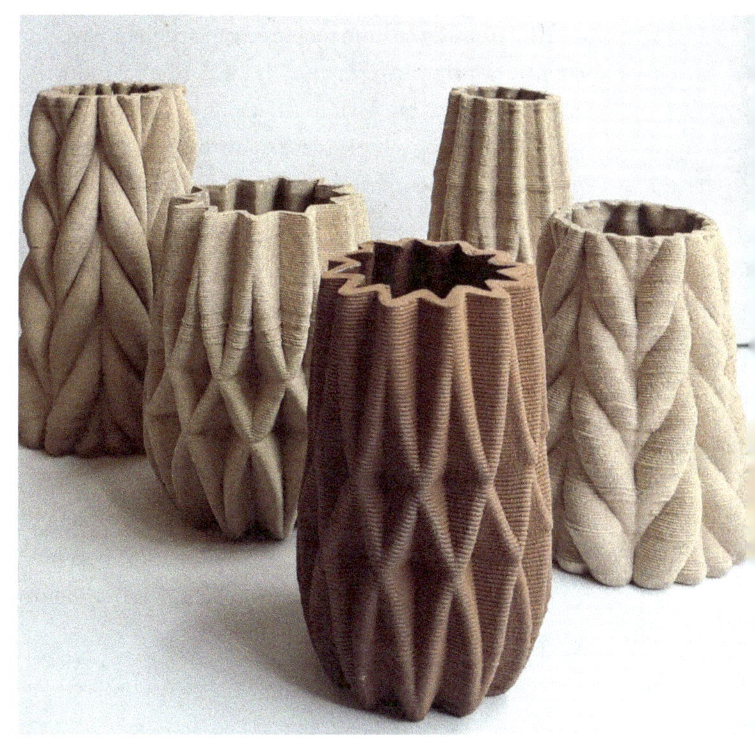

Clay Vessels by DRIP AM© / 2024.

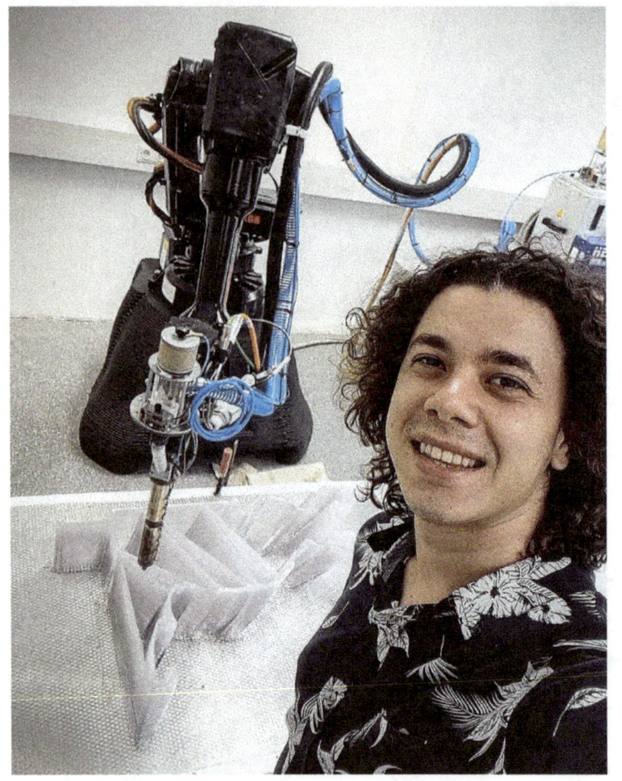

Dino Kartoudes / 2023.

Sometimes you find yourself in the right place and at the right time. A chance meeting at my friend's pottery studio led me to learn more about the interesting work performed by this inspiring architect.

DINO KARTOUDES

Over the past several years, Dino worked for multiple companies whilst completing his studies. Some of his projects and collaborations include rapid prototyping and 3D printing custom tools and replacement parts for engineers, printing resin moulds for the dental industry, and using an x-ray scan to 3D print a highly accurate model of a dog's broken leg – to help veterinarians prepare for a complex procedure before attempting to operate.

Having purchased and used one of DRIP's small-scale clay 3D printers, Dino explored hyper efficient 3D printing of façade systems for his Master's thesis, entitled, "Modular, scalable and programmable façade systems: a sustainable and scalable framework to create unique, lightweight and adaptable panel array systems optimised for clay-based 3D printing".

The façade systems are computationally designed (CAD) in Grasshopper®, from which Dino used to programme and build his own toolset.

The software considers the set parameters of a particular building and then creates algorithms that produce custom G-code for each façade system. This G-code is then used to programme and run a clay 3D printer to fabricate the design in parts. Once dry, these prints are sent off to be fired in a kiln.

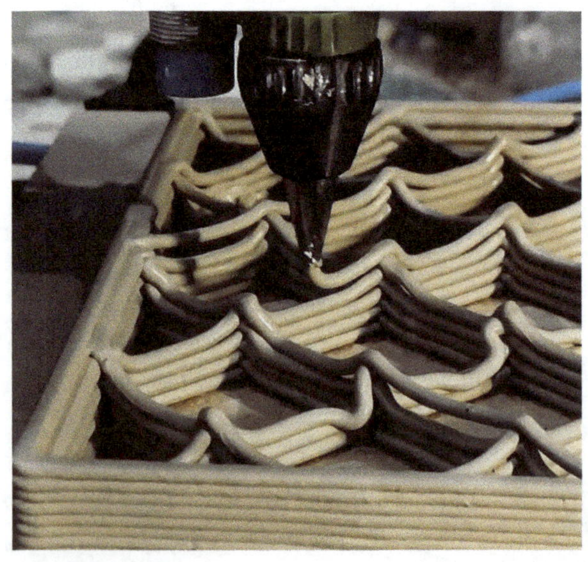

Clay fabrication / Dino Kartoudes / 2023.

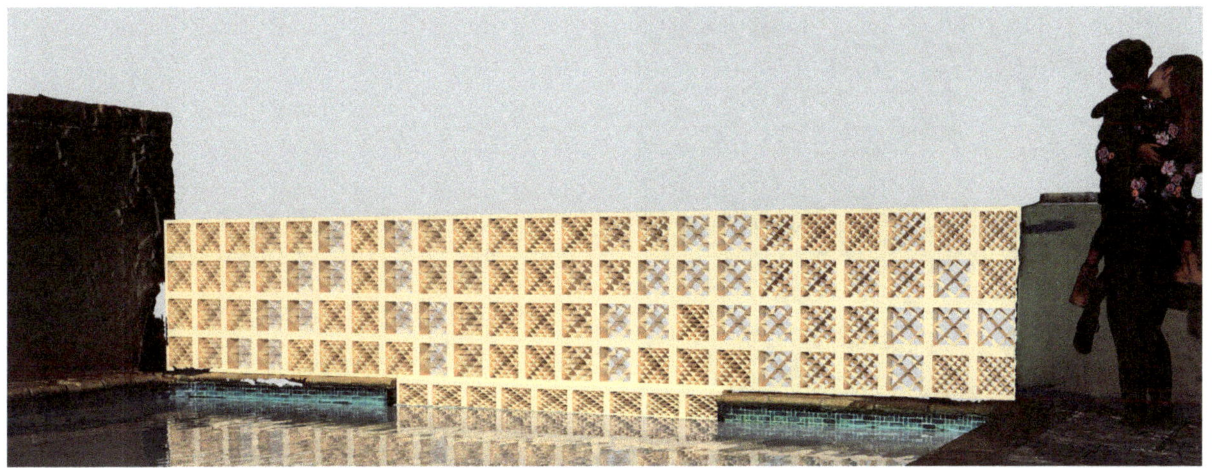

Panel Array Visualization / Rhino3D® 8 Digital Render / Dino Kartoudes / 2023.

Considering the local climate conditions and how the façade can be designed to accommodate these, the basic framework parameters may be easily adapted in the software. For example, in warmer climates, the natural ventilation of a building is important. Openings are designed to incorporate the circulation of fresh air; but in cooler climates, insulation is the main consideration.

The overall look and feel of the final design as opposed to the design of the façade system should also be considered and should match the features of the building. This also allows for mass customisation, ensuring an optimal solution that is unique in both appearance and performance.

To optimise the modular façade systems by using this computational tool and introducing clay for such designs necessitates an exploration into lightweight and efficient materials. Steel and glass are often the most popular materials. They are, however, more expensive to design and build with whilst not being a sustainable option over the long term in a world with diminishing resources.

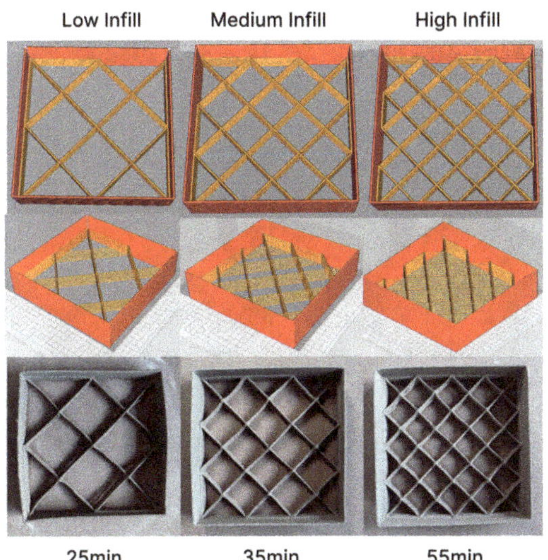

By focusing on the workflow, as well as the product, Dino hopes to introduce an "all in one" solution that can solve multiple problems, whilst overcoming multiple complex design challenges.

A growing overlap in design within the different industries is very exciting as makers try to find solutions within their own field of expertise whilst using the different 3D printing technologies. Designing façades more efficiently is not necessarily a new concept in the architectural landscape, but Dino demonstrates how an individual maker can take the same idea, build, and modify it, ultimately developing a new perspective in an ever-developing architectural space.

Infill pattern analysis / Ultimaker Cura® 3D model with photographs / Dino Kartoudes / 2023.

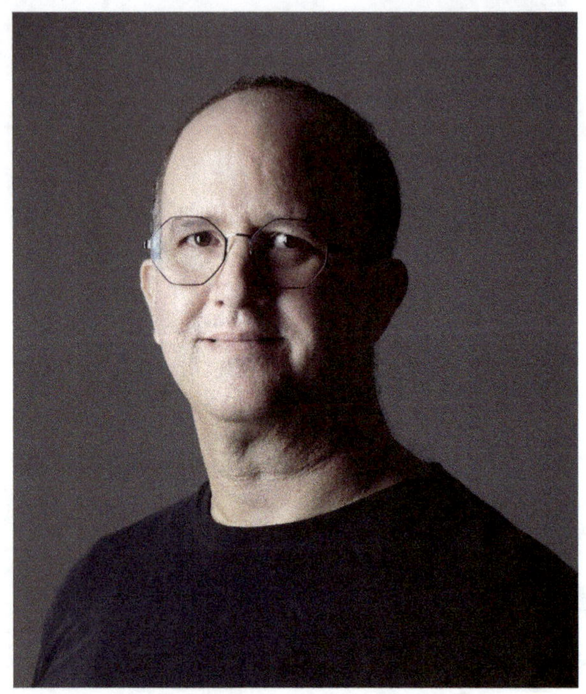

Daniel Brand / 2023.

With the resurgence of pottery globally over the past few years, I wanted to hear how pottery in South Africa is adapting to new types of technologies, techniques, and trends... and possibly get some tips too!

DANIEL BRAND

Daniel Brand is the chairperson of the Gauteng committee of Ceramics Southern Africa and is a well-renowned pottery artist. I was happily surprised to learn that he had a background in coding that was cultivated from a young age.

As a child, he often played in his mother's pottery studio and was also encouraged to explore computer technology. Daniel recalls how he was given programming exercises with his first Apple IIE Computer, aimed at introducing children to coding technology. Once an exercise had been completed, the programme would respond (e.g. a small, animated man would jump up and down) "which at the time was very impressive" – Daniel Brand.

As the years passed, he found himself drawn back to a material that once allowed him to explore physical creative forms. In 2012, he started to further extend his hand-made pottery skills by exploring different techniques and developing his own unique and recognisable style.

"The ceramic industry has always embraced forms of tech; look at the pottery wheel, kiln, pugmill, and even a jigger machine that is used to make plates. These are all expensive types of equipment, with the next step being the 3D printer." – Daniel Brand / 2023.

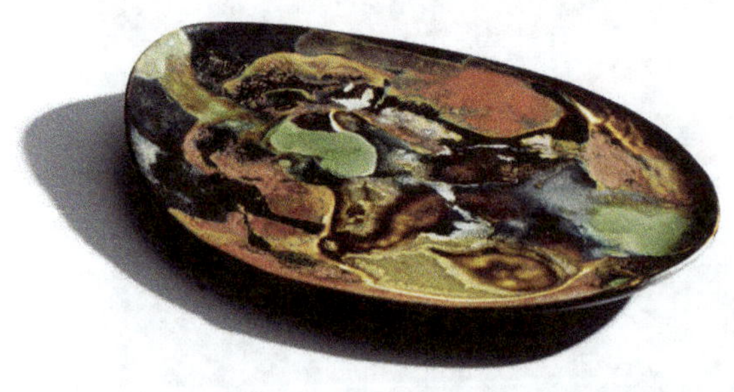

Untitled / Daniel Brand / 2023.

Daniel quoted another great example of technology related to ceramics – when transfers were introduced. It was a breakthrough for potters in terms of how they could decorate a clay object. Transfers created an entire new pottery technique that has become a feasible alternative to hand painting and glazing.

Daniel is excited at all the prospects that clay 3D printing can bring into the ceramics industry. He adds that currently there is a slow progressive movement in that direction. With the influx of the new generation of ceramic artists, it won't be long before it becomes the norm. He told me of a ceramics workshop that he attended with a woman who loved working with clay but hated the feeling of this medium between her fingers; so, she would always wear gloves. He believes that introducing someone like her to clay 3D printing would be "a match made in heaven" and I couldn't agree more!

Daniel's "Sculptural Murals" are thin flattened porcelain clay disks that are manipulated, with sections of the clay purposefully elevated, creating organic forms and curves.

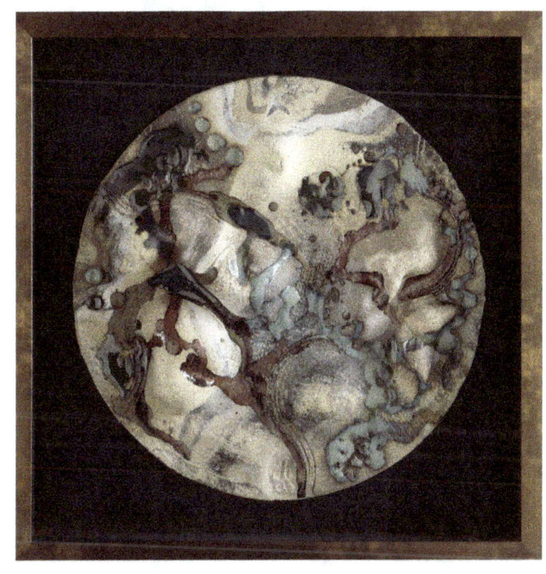

Sculptural Mural / Daniel Brand / 2023.

Glazing tips from Daniel

Daniel uses AMACO glazes which are available worldwide. His favourites are the "Potters Choice" range of glazes, which he sometimes alters by adding other raw materials, which would then change the overall effect of the glaze. He advises that potters should not be afraid of exploring and experimenting with their glazes.

"Disregard what it is going to look like in the end and just see what it will do! Sometimes it will reward you and sometimes your pottery will become a filler for your backyard!"– Daniel Brand.

Don't be afraid to be wild with your glaze brush strokes! Daniel often uses brush-on glazes as he feels he has more control over their application. However, if you want one tone colours, buy pouring or dipping glazes as they are faster to apply and more cost effective.

For smaller vessels that need to be glazed, place a balloon inside and blow it up inside the vessel. The inflated balloon will be 'stuck' inside, and you can easily hold it by the knot, and then dip it in the glaze. As you pull it out you will have an even layer of glaze on the outside of your vase, clear of any finger marks. Once the glaze is dry, you simply 'pop' the balloon, and then add a colour on the inside, or leave it as is.

As discussed, clay 3D prints often have glaze body fit problems. To overcome this, Daniel suggests that you glaze only one part of the clay object, either on the inside or on the outside. This will then ensure that the clay object can easily expand and contract during the kiln firing.

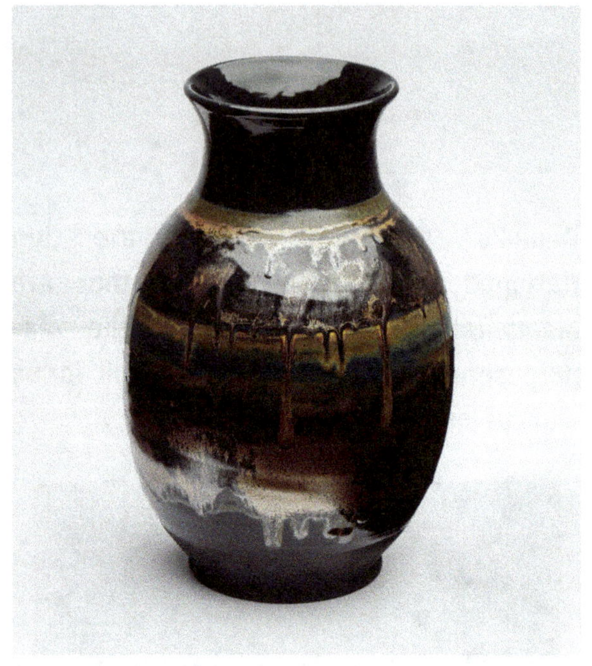

Glaze reactions in the kiln can cause the glaze to run / Vase by Daniel Brand / 2023.

Looking at the big revival of pottery around the world, Daniel is of the opinion that it is a reaction from people who feel disillusioned with technology. They want to work with a material that is slow and unpredictable. The ability to 3D print with clay invites those who may previously not have considered the artform as a creative outlet, to explore clay making in a new and exciting way.

Masking tape is a popular choice when you want to achieve a clear glaze line. To ensure that the line is at the desired angle, Daniel will always first draw it out in pencil before sticking the masking tape on the clay object.

Running and dripping glazes during kiln firing have been a problem that he has often encountered as he layers the glaze. To overcome this, he paints AMACO Velvet Underglaze on the bottom portion of his vessels, ensuring that the area is clear of applied glazes. During the kiln firing, the glazes will run until they are partially halted because of the groggy consistency of the underglaze.

Looking at current trends within the ceramic industry in South Africa, Daniel explains how alternative firing processes have become increasingly popular. With South Africa's current economic climate, and the advent of virtually daily power cuts, potters have had to explore new decorative techniques such as Raku and traditional pit firing.

These are quite invasive as potters must deal with scorching temperatures as they manage the heat flow and decorating additives during the firing process. In a sense, these techniques celebrate spontaneity within the pottery process as there are many unpredictable circumstances that contribute to the overall outcome.

Nerikomi is a technique that Daniel often uses. It is a Japanese technique which involves taking different colours of clay and layering them in a pre-determined pattern. He observed that many potters only decide how they want to decorate their clay forms after a kiln firing. Nerikomi forces the potter to decide what the finished work must look like in advance, before starting the clay making process. This is much like the clay 3D printing design process.

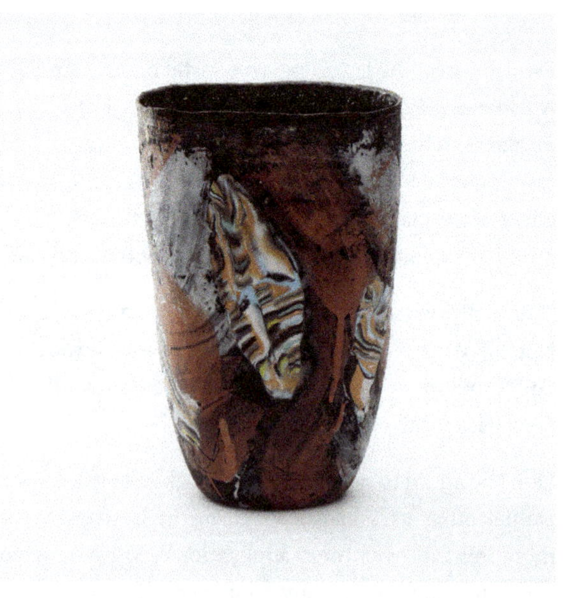

Nerikomi vase / Daniel Brand / 2021.

FINAL THOUGHTS

LEARNING CURVE

I have never come across a clay 3D maker who said that it was easy to master the clay 3D printing process the first time. It can be quite intensive because of the many unfamiliar factors that need to be considered. That is why having a game plan from the start is key to accomplishing your goals.

From the beginning, although I understood the pottery process, it was the 3D design element that I knew I would have to focus my energies on. Ultimately, it came down to repetition. The more I repeated the steps that I had jotted down in my 3D design booklet, the sooner I became comfortable with designing my own works.

Remember this word... "REPETITION!".

My traditional pottery experience gave me a pretty good understanding of clay. What I didn't account for, was the continuous testing for the consistency of the clay. Initially, I planned to do two months of testing, but it eventually took me four months.

As an artist, there were different ideas that I wanted to explore and cultivating these took much longer than anticipated. Your timeline may be completely different from mine and will depend on the direction and industry you have chosen to move into. Set goals, and if you find the timeline you have set for yourself is not reasonable, be flexible in your approach as you reach your projected outcomes.

Set aside a good amount of time to explore and learn. Any learning curve is like a mountain that needs to be climbed, and it is important to be patient with yourself and the process. Learn at your own pace and never compare your progress with that of others.

EXPERIMENTATION

Experimentation and testing are integral to the creative process and, as I mentioned before, they will require patience.

Do not allow the testing to stop you from experimenting. I purposely have a three-print rule - If it collapses three times in a row, I either adapt and change the 3D design or I move on to something different.

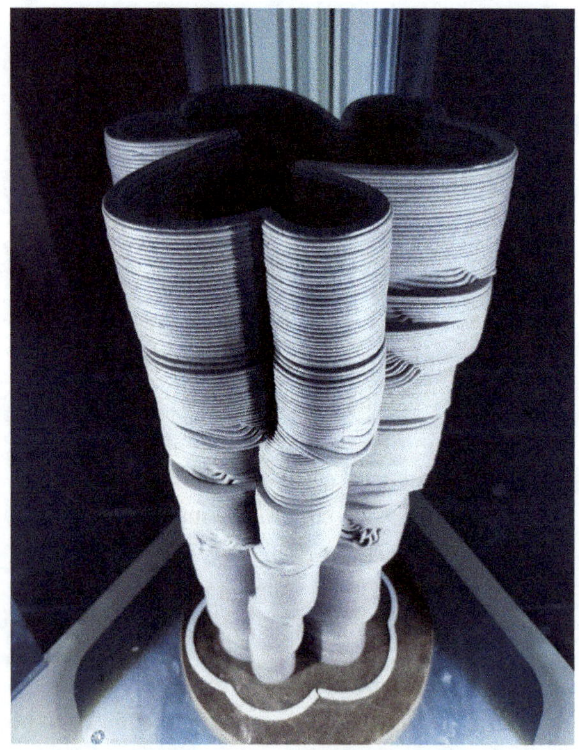

An experimental clay design that is on permanent exhibition at the Pretoria Art Museum / Hendrien Horn / 2022.

You will find your work evolving over time as you learn and develop your skills. New methods of creating will start to replace old ones and your confidence will grow as time moves on and you start producing items that are the product of your own visualisations.

I have also found that a "happy mistake" (as I like to call it) can sometimes occur during a print. I recall an instance when the combination of an angle and the clay extrusion parameters influenced my envisioned design for the better. It always happens when least expected and can often direct you down a different path from that leading to your initial designs.

Remember, a specific clay form may collapse from using a particular sized nozzle over another. Your instincts for the structural capabilities of your clay design will develop over time as you explore how to manipulate your clay forms.

Don't hesitate to investigate fresh ideas (e.g. testing how the clay reacts when different materials are added, introducing colour during the 3D printing process, and how to achieve sharp angles that do not warp). A strong belief in your own capabilities will keep you going when things get tough. Understanding that failure will form part of the testing process is important and should be viewed as a challenge that must be worked through!

GOOD LUCK!

With room for growth, clay 3D printing has the potential to contribute new innovative ideas in many industries.

The advantages that this type of technology can afford a small-time maker are endless. Figure out your "WHY?" as you start developing your ideas.

Clay is notoriously known as a tricky material, that at times, has a mind of its own. Taking a step-by-step approach may be a more efficient way of teaching yourself the 3D design and pottery processes. Throwing yourself in the deep end as you try to learn everything all at once, may in this case, not be the best strategy.

During these developmental stages of your journey direct your energy where your passion lies. If you are unable to 3D design using a CAD software, use the various applications currently available as you learn about digital design and the implementation thereof. Explore clay as material, learning how it must be prepared, handled and kiln fired to produce the results that you require.

Pottery can be an expensive hobby. Taking the time to determine how much you are willing to spend will directly influence the material, software, equipment and machinery that you will ultimately buy. Do not buy expensive equipment (e.g. a kiln) if you do not need too. Cutting down expenditures where you can and making use of a well-established pottery studio as you build up your skillsets will be advantageous.

Seek advice from those who have experience. A simple solution may be all that it would take to solve the problem at hand. Always take a step back if needed and remember your big picture!

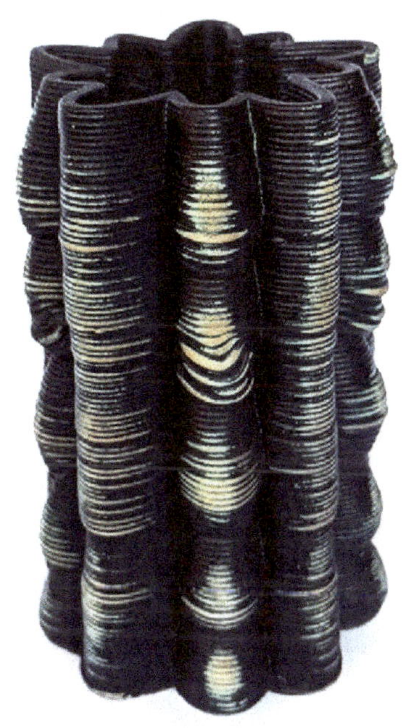

Fossil 4 / Hendrien Horn / 2023.

Good luck and welcome to a whole new world of exciting possibilities in the clay 3D making space!

ADDITIONAL RESEARCH

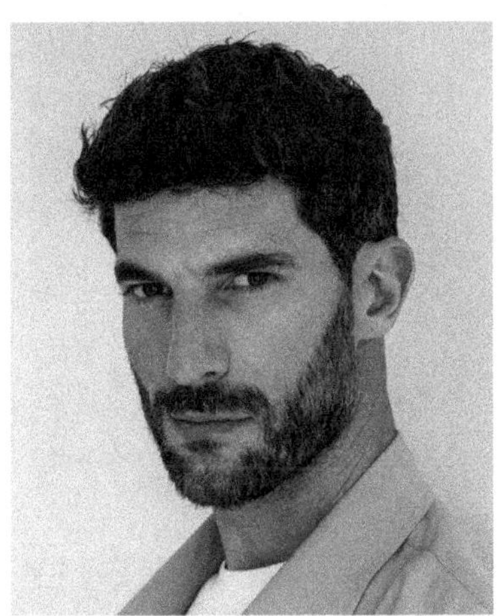

RYAN BARRETT

@ryanbarrettceramics

www.ryanbarrettceramics.com

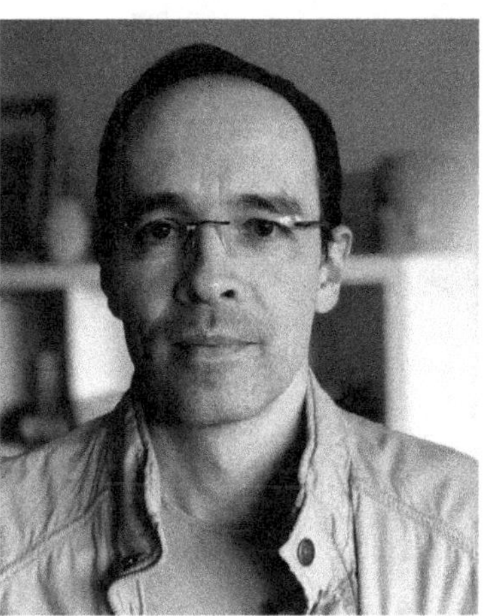

ANATOLY BEREZKIN STONE FLOWER

@stoneflower3d

www,stoneflower3d.com

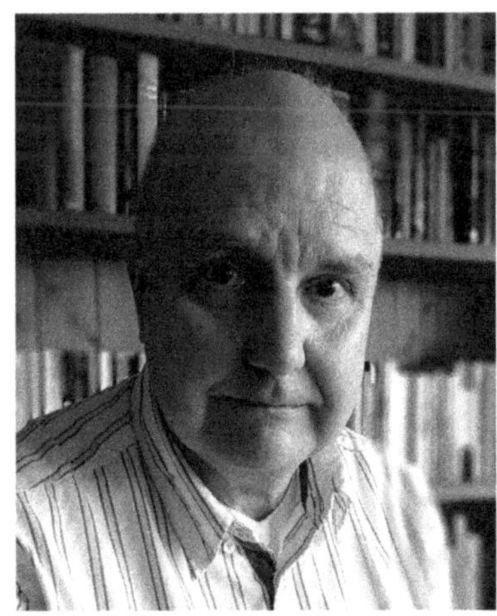

DR ADRIAN BOWYER REPRAP

www.reprap.org

https://adrianbowyer.com/wp/publications/

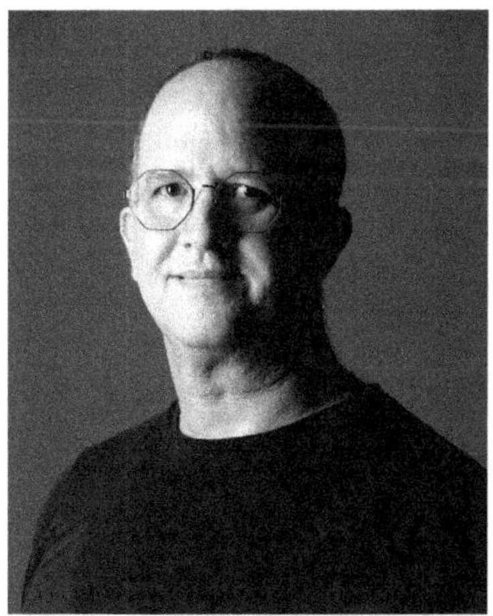

DANIEL BRAND

@danielbrandceramics

www.dbceramics.co.za

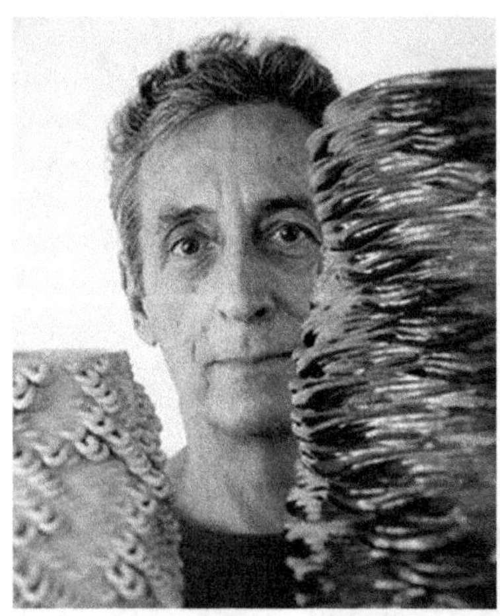

DANNY DEFELICI
3D POTTER

@3dpotter

www.3dpotter.com

Facebook: https://www.facebook.com/3dpotter/

YouTube: https://www.youtube.com/@3DPOTTER

Tech Support: https://www.youtubecom/@3DPotterTech

Probuild3D: https://www.probuild3d.com/

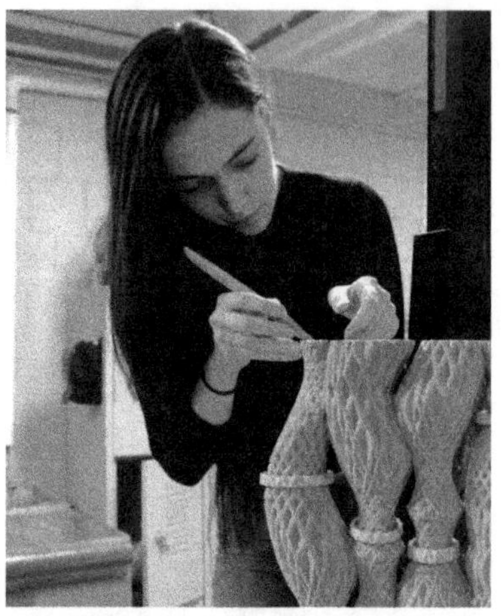

JULIANNA DOUGHERTY

@juliannadoughertyart

www.juliannadougherty.com

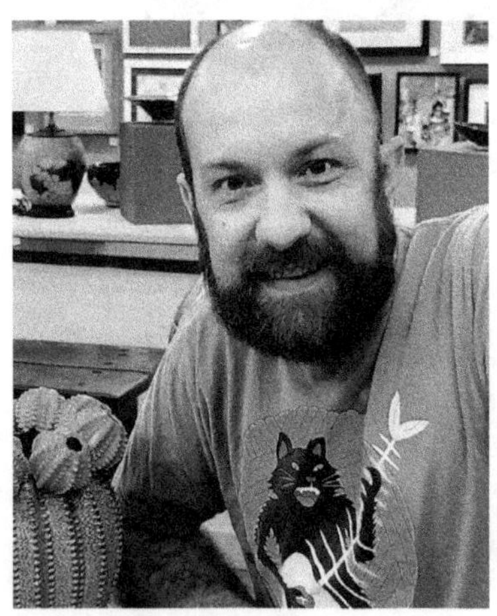

GARRETT DURLAND

@tinkerandprint

www.layerupceramics.com

sassycentaur.com

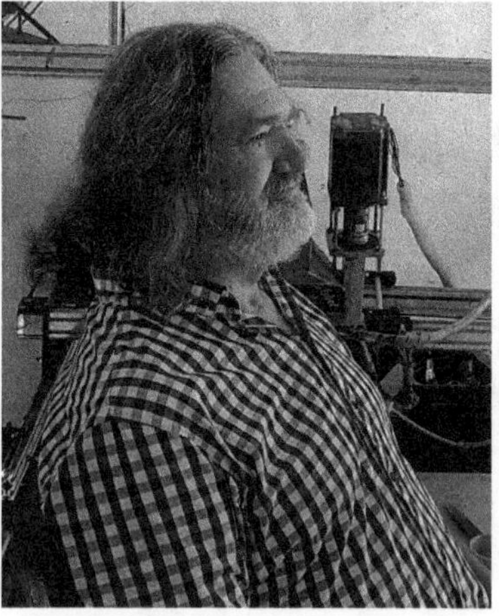

HANS FOUCHÉ

Linkedin: https://www.linkedin.com/in/hans-fouche-23489638/

3DPRINT.COM: https://3dprint.com/146202/hans-fouche-i-makers-lab/

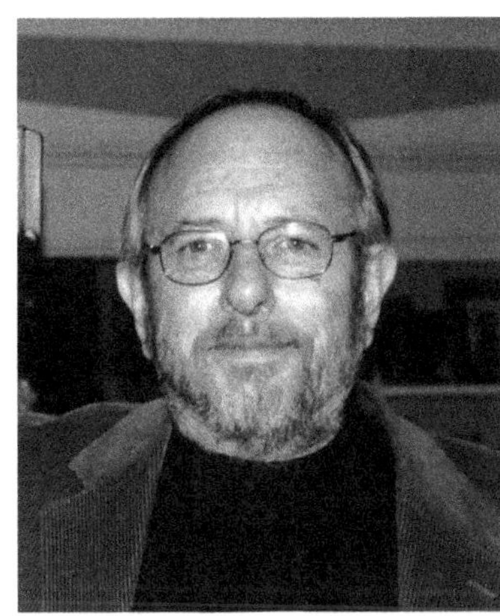

DAVID HERROLD

Catalogue: David Herrold - A retrospective Exhibition:

https://www.depauw.edu/files/resources/david-herrold.pdf

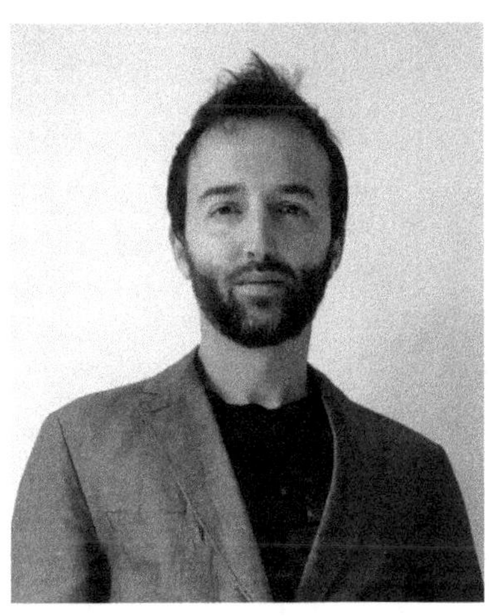

DIEGO GARCIA CUEVAS CONTROLMAD®

@professorcuevas

www.controlmad.com

Linkedin: https://www.linkedin.com/in/dgcuevas/

Book: Advanced 3D Printing with Grasshopper® Clay and FDM; Authors: Diego Garcia Cuevas and Gianluca Pugliese

YouTube: https://www.youtube.com/channel/UCkOdJ1VpvDGJvnRcIg_RBBA

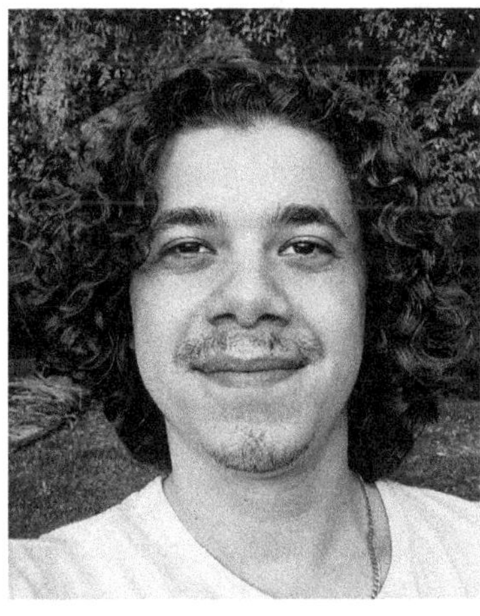

DINO KARTOUDES

@deazyne

MetaHedra: https://2023wip.cyens.org.cy/exhibition/control-vs-material/metahedra/

MetaHedra Workshop https://bit.ly/MetaHedra2023

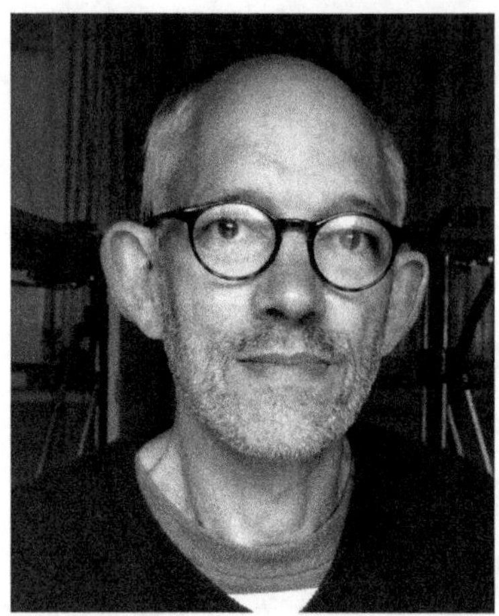

JONATHAN KEEP

@jkeep_artpottery

www.keep-art.co.uk

A Guide to Clay 3D Printing: http://www.keep-art.co.uk/Journal/JKeep-Guide%20to%20Clay%203D%20Printing%20-%202020.pdf

Formulating and testing a Clay Body for Extrusion Clay 3D Printing

Testing of Six Clays for Extrusion 3D Printing

Testing the relationship between Nozzle Size, Layer Height, Print Speed and Material Consistency for Clay Extrusion 3D Printing

http://www.keep-art.co.uk/journal_1.html

Traditionalist and Innovator: https://www.youtube.comwatch?v=N2AaZR13Kj g&t=1s&abchannel=JonathanKeep

10 years of extrusion Printing (Part 1): https://www.youtube.com/watch?v=x7al7b2u XMM&ab_channel=JonathanKeep

10 years of extrusion Printing (Part 2): https://www.youtube.com/watch?v=MS8IEn dyHcQ&ab_channel=JonathanKeep

Ceramic 3D Printing Teaching – Playlist: https://youtube.com/playlist?list=PLD_uR9vw07u_TAFIN7m5TPE7olhRs BfdR& feature=sharedw

Ceramic Review Issue 240 Nov/Dec 2014; The Fourth Way: http://www.keep-art.co.uk/Journal/JK_CR204_The_Fourth_Way.pdf

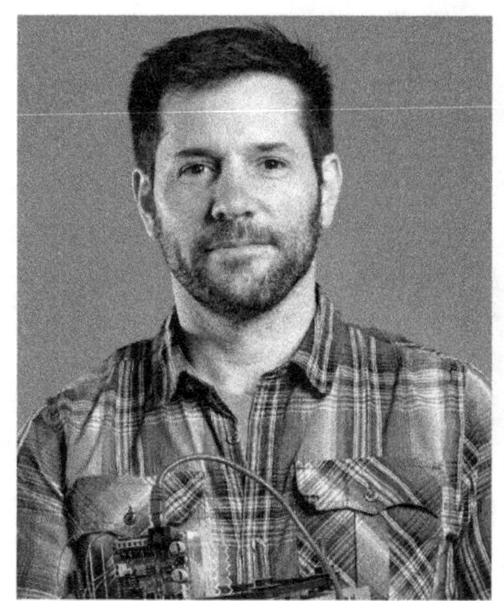

TOM LAUERMAN

@tom_lauerman

www.tomlauerman.com

YouTube: https://www.youtube.com/@TomLauerman

YouTube: https://youtu.be/ksyDqFblJGE?si=Bm-SbaU8x99uC44h

Book feature: Tracing the Line. The Art of Drawing Machines and Pen Plotters. Vetro Editions and Generative Hut: https://vetroeditions.com/products/tracing-the-line

Book contributor: The 3D Additivist Cookbook devised and edited by Morehshin Allahyari and Daniel Rourke: https://additivism.org/cookbook

Maake Magazine: https://www.maakemagazine.com/tom-lauerman

Studio Potter: https://studiopotter.org/what-do-you-want-be-clay

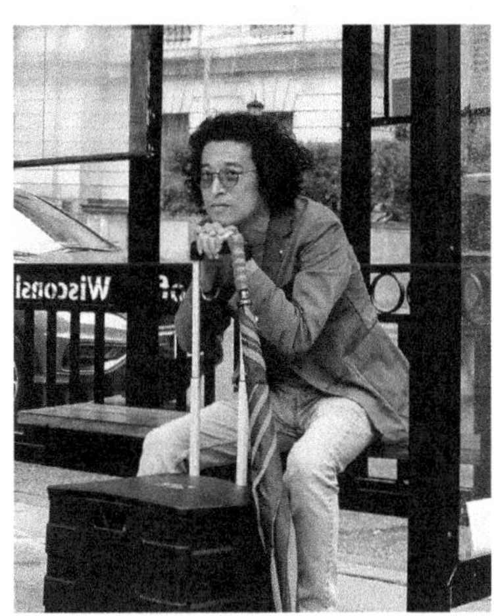

TAEKYEOM LEE

@taekyeom

http://portfolio.taekyeom.com

DIY ceramic 3D printer instructions:

https://docs.google.com/document/d/1cxzm2Zv575Ldp3vXclYurYDGf_Gu2Q7 tX 4ixDO5vAL4/edit?usp=sharingg

YouTube: Building a DIY ceramic 3D printer: : https://www.youtube.com/playlist?list =PLcYkbdrqZJf_u4xgj_zYr6wPriauxqYYK

The Great Discontent: Interview: https://thegreatdiscontent.com/interview/taekyeom-lee/

Make: https://makezine.com/article/digital-fabrication/3d-printing-workshop/3d-printing-ceramics-self-built-3d-printer/

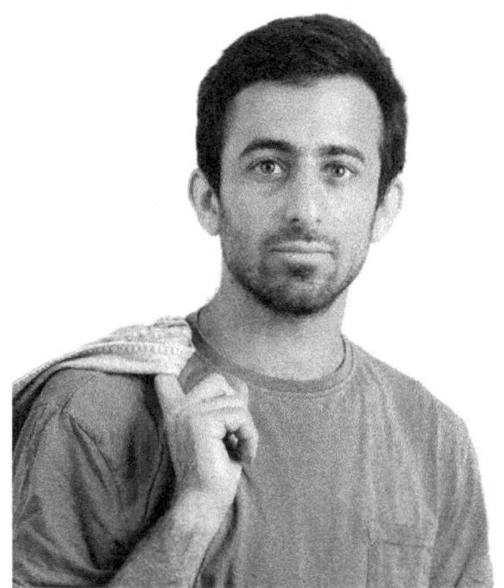

GUY LEVAKOV

@levakov.ceramics

https://levakov-ceramics.com

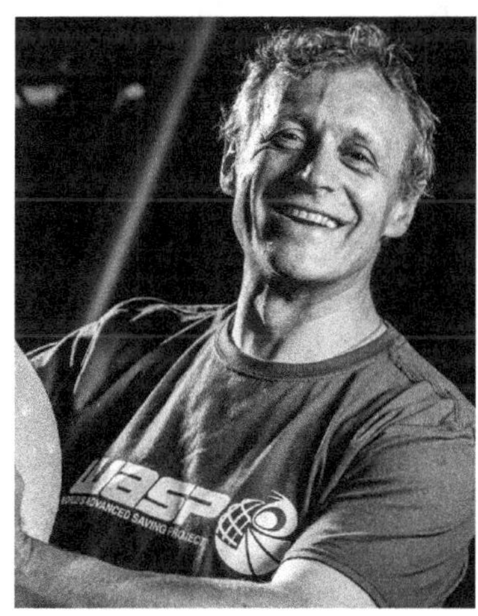

MASSIMO MORETTI WASP®

@3dwasp

www.3dwasp.com

YouTube: https://www.youtube.com/@waspprojecteam

Blog: https://www.3dwasp.com/en/blog/

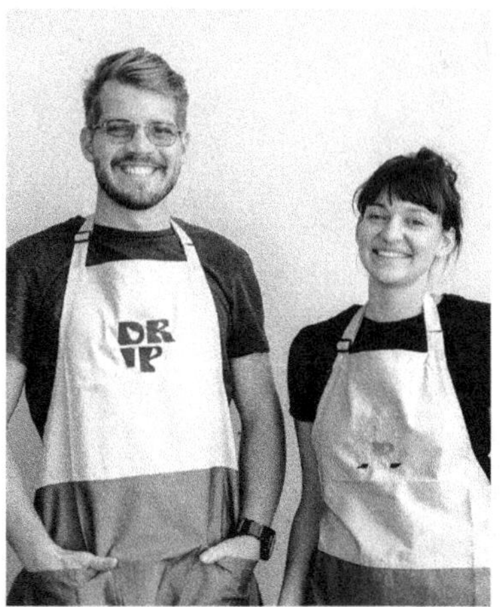

MARIÉ SNYMAN & JASON KEARNEY
DRIP ADDITIVE MANUFACTURING

@drip.am

www.dripam.com

Designing Ways; Issue 271: https://designingways.com/Digi/2023/271/index.html

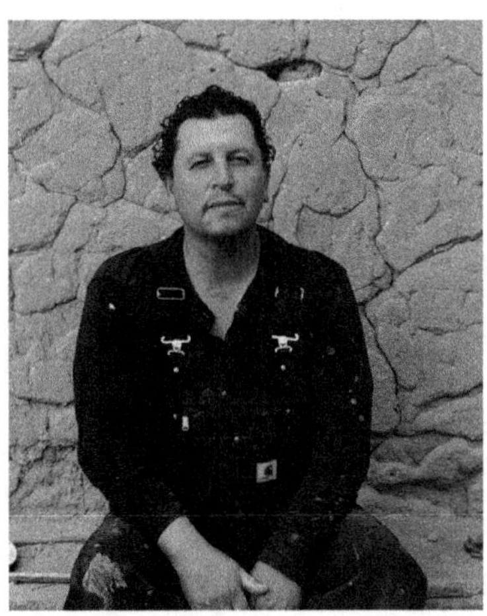

RONALD RAEL
EMERGING OBJECTS & POTTERWARE

@rrael

https://www.rael-sanfratello.com/

Books:

Earthen Architecture

Printing Architecture: Innovative Recipes for 3D Printing

Borderwall as Architecture: A Manifesto for the U.S. - Mexico Boundary

Emerging Objects: https://emergingobjects.com/

TED Talk: https://www.ted.com/speakers/ronald_rael

YouTube: 3D Printed Earth Architecture: Ronald Rael: https://www.youtube.com/watch?v=Py0aE_t4cbU&ab_channel=DigitalFUTURESworld

Potterware: https://www.potterware.com/

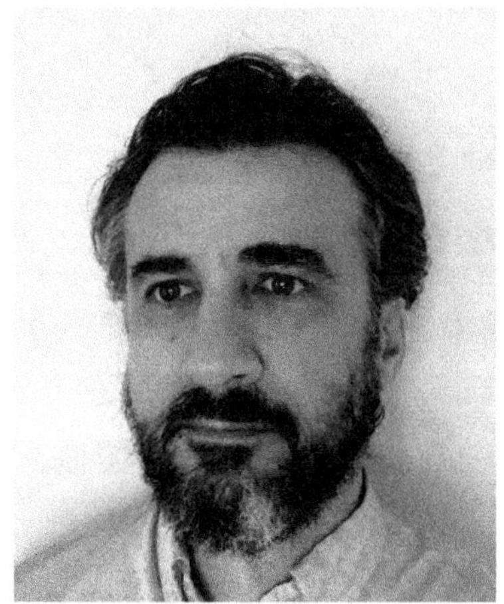

NICOLAS TOURON

@nicolas_touron

https://nicolastouron.com

School of Visual Arts, New York: http://www.sva.edu/faculty/nicolas-touron

Pratt Courses: https://www.pratt.edu/courses/digital-ceramics/

Harvard University: https://ofa.fas.harvard.edu/people/nicolas-touron

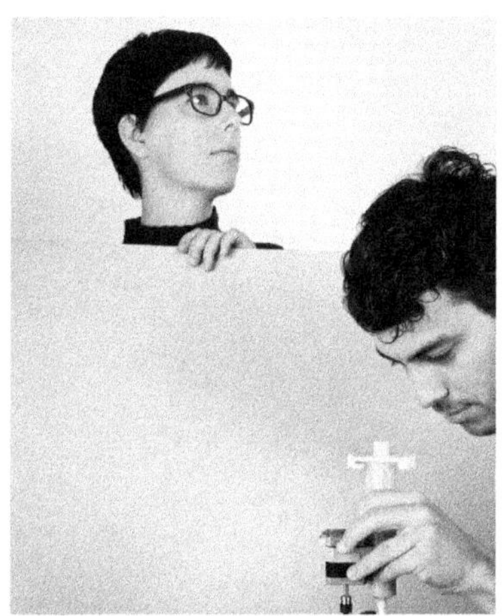

CLAIRE WARNIER & DRIES VERBRUGGEN UNFOLD

@unfoldantwerp

www.unfold.be

Book: Printing Things - Visions and essentials for 3D Printing, Authors; Claire Warnier, Dries Verbruggen, Robert Klanten, Sven Ehmann

Domestika course: https://www.domestika.org/en/courses/3459-introduction-to-ceramic-3d-printing/unfold

The Digital Craftsman and their Tools: http://unfold.be/pages/the-digital-craftsman-and-his-tools-essay.html

"X>CTRL+P An interview with Unfold by Bryan Czibesz Studio Potter 47": https://www.dropbox.com/s/0pcu6fswqau2i34/Studio%20Potter%2047-1_x-ctrlp-interview-unfold.pdf?dl=0

RepRap Magazine: Paste extrusion: https://issuu.com/garyhodgson/docs/reprap magazine_issue_3?mode=window

Instagram page about ceramic 3d printing: https://www.instagram.com/ceramic 3dprinting/

Blog:

https://unfoldfab.blogspot.com/2010/01/hello-slurry-world.html

https://unfoldfab.blogspot.com/2010/02/futures-here-baby-first-successfully.html

https://unfoldfab.blogspot.com/2010/02/hello-blogosphere.

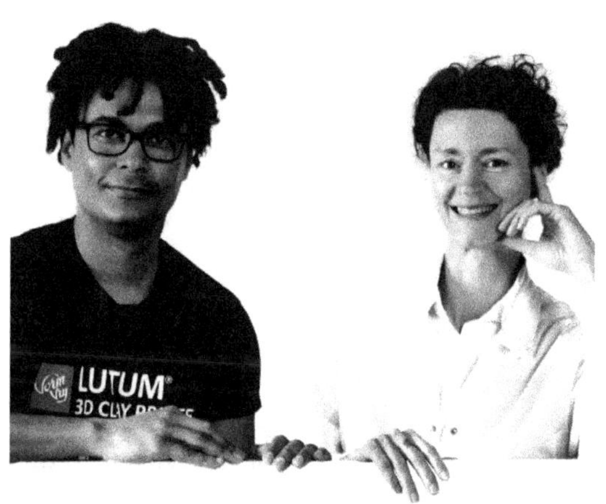

MARLIEKE WIJNAKKER & YAO VAN DEN HEERIK VORMVRIJ® & LUTHIFORM®

@vormvrij3d

www.vormvrij.nl

Full length feature: New Digital Craft; A new 21st Century Craft: https://vormvrij.nl/3dclayprinting/?p=1007

KEY TERMINOLOGY

ABS (Acrylonitrile Butadiene Styrene) - Type of filament used in 3D printing.

Accelerants - Substances added to alter material. In this case some may serve to strengthen the clay body or help the clay dry faster.

Additive Manufacturing - Technique used to create objects by adding material layer by layer. This is in contrast with traditional subtractive manufacturing methods, where material is removed to create a shape.

Adobe - Building material made from earth and organic materials.

Canister/Container - Container that stores clay and requires either air pressure or a mechanical force to push the clay from the container and through the extruder mechanism.

Analogue - Term often used to describe non-digital technologies or processes.

Auger - Clay 3D printers that use auger systems typically work by feeding clay through a rotating auger (in the extruder mechanism), which pushes the material through a nozzle to create the desired shape. It allows for precise control over the flow of clay.

Bat - Thin slab of wood or plaster tile used to hold a clay form whilst building and/or sculpting it.

Bisque Firing - The first kiln firing of pottery that is dried.

Bridging Forms - Creating structures that span between two points without support.

Build Volume - Maximum size an object can be 3D printed; it is dependent on the size specifications of the 3D printer.

Cartesian - Coordinate system that uniquely specifies each point in a plane by a set of numerical coordinates.

CAD (Computer Aided Design) - Use of computer systems to aid in the creation, modification, analysis, or optimization of a design.

Clay Consistency Testing - Mixing different consistencies of clay and water into a paste that is suitable for 3D printing.

Clay Slab - Flat piece of clay used for building or decorating pottery.

CNC (Computer Numerical Control) - A process used in manufacturing that involves the use of computers to control machine tools.

Computational Design - Using computer algorithms to generate and optimize designs.

Continuous Material Flow Systems - Systems that enable a continuous flow of material in a manufacturing process.

Delta - 3D printer design where the print head moves on three arms.

Digital Fabrication - Creating physical objects directly from digital models.

Dual Extrusion - The use of two extruders to print with two different materials or colours.

Embosser - Tool used to create raised designs on a surface.

Extruder - Device used to push material, often used in 3D printing, also known as a print head.

FDM (Fused Deposition Modelling) - 3D printing technology that uses a thermoplastic filament.

Filament - Material used in FDM 3D printers to create objects.

Flow - Movement of material, such as clay or glaze, in a controlled manner.

FFF (Fused Filament Fabrication) - Another term for FDM, describing the process of building objects by extruding filaments of material.

Generative Design - Using algorithms to generate design options based on specified parameters.

Glaze Firing - Second firing of pottery after applying a glaze/surface coating.

Glaze Runs - When glaze melts and runs down the sides of a pottery piece during a kiln firing.

G-Code - Computer programming language used to control the set parameters of a 3D print during the 3D printing process.

Grog - Refractory clay that has been fired and ground to various particle sizes.

Hotend - Part of an FDM printer that heats and melts the filament for extrusion.

Kiln - Furnace or oven used for firing pottery.

Layer Height -Thickness of each layer of material laid down in 3D printing.

Maker - Person who creates or produces things, often used in the context of maker culture.

Mechanical Ram Extruder - Used to push material through the extruder with mechanical force.

Mobile Manipulator - Robotic arm mounted on a mobile platform.

Nozzle - Part of an extruder that deposits material onto the print bed.

Parametric Design - Design that is driven by parameters or variables that can be adjusted to generate different outcomes.

Paste Materials - Materials used in 3D printing that are in a paste-like consistency.

Pen Plotter - Device that uses a pen and computational code to draw images on a surface.

PLA (Polylactic Acid) - Type of filament used in 3D printing.

Porous - Having small holes that allow liquid or air to pass through.

Print Bed - Surface on which objects are printed by a 3D printer.

Print Builds - Objects or structures created through 3D printing.

Print Fail - When a 3D print is not completed successfully.

Print Head - Device used to push material, often used in 3D printing, also known as an extruder.

Print Run - Process of printing a batch of objects.

Raku - Type of pottery firing process that involves removing pieces from the kiln while they are still hot and placing them into a material (e.g. sawdust) which creates varying decorative results.

Rapid Prototyping - Process of fabricating physical prototypes from digital designs.

Safety Valve - Valve that opens to release air pressure in a system to prevent damage or failure.

Sieve - Utensil consisting of a wire or plastic mesh held in a frame, used to separate materials based on particle size.

Slicing Software - Software used to convert 3D models into instructions for a 3D printer.

Slip Casting - Ceramic production technique where liquid clay is poured into a mould.

Slip Trailing - Decorating technique done by adding lines of liquid clay (slip) to a clay object, usually done in the leather hard stage of the pottery process.

Slurry - Thick, creamy mixture of material and water.

Speed - Rate at which the 3D printer runs whilst printing.

Stepper Motor - Type of motor used in 3D printers to control the movement of components.

STL File - Computer file format used for 3D models in 3D printing.

Stopper - Plug used to close an opening tightly.

Thermal Expansion - Tendency of material to change its shape, area, and volume in response to a change in temperature.

Tester Tiles - Small ceramic tiles used to test pottery glazes.

Tool Paths - Paths followed by the 3D printer in relation to the parameters set by the G-code.

Wedging - Kneading clay to remove air bubbles.

BIBLIOGRAPHY

3D POTTER., [no date]. Printers [online]. Available from: https://3dpotter.com/printers [Accessed 30 June 2022].

AUTODESK®., [no date]. Autodesk [online]. Available from: https://www.autodesk.com/products/fusion-360/overview?term=1-YEAR&tab=subscription&plc=F360 [Accessed 15 September 2021].

BOWYER, A., [no date]. Adrian Bowyer [online]. Available from: http://www.adrianbowyer.com/wp/ [Accessed 21 July 2021].

CARLOTA, V., 2019. 3D Potter's Technology Facilitates Clay 3D Printing [online]. 3D Natives, 3D Software. Available from: https://www.3dnatives.com/en/3dpotter-interview-281120195/#! [Accessed 11 July 2023].

CARLOTA, V., 2019. The top CAD software for all levels [online]. 3D Natives, 3D Software. Available from: http://www.3dnatives/com/en/top10-cad-software-180320194/ [Accessed 5 September 2022].

CAROLO, L., 2022. What is a 3D slicer – simply explained [online]. All3DP. Available from: http://www. all3dp.com/2/what-is-a-3d-slicer-simply-explained/ [Accessed 8 September 2022].

CAROLO, L., 2022. What is FDM Printing? -Simply explained [online]. All3DP. Available from: http://www.all3dp.com/2/fused-deposition-modeling-fdm-3d-printing-simply-explained/ [Accessed 8 September 2022].

CERAMICS NOW., [no date]. Jonathan Keep [online]. Available from: https://www.ceramicsnow.org/jonathankeep/#:~:text=Jonathan%20Keep%20is%20an%20artist,College%20of%20Art%20in%202002 [Accessed 25 July 2023]

CLAY BOTTRESS., [2020]. Image Maps in Potterware® 4.0 [online]. Clay Bottress. Available from: https://claybottress.com/image-maps-in-potterware-4-0/ [Accessed 17 September 2023].

CZIBESZ, B., 2019. An interview with Unfold. Studio Potter, 7 August 2022, pg. 43-50.

DEJAN., [no date]. G-code explained [online]. How to Mechatronics. Available from: http://www.howtomechatronics.com/tutorials/g-code-explained-list-of-most-important-g-code-commands/ [Accessed 9 September 2022].

EMERGING OBJECTS., [no date]. Available from: https://emergingobjects.com/ [Accessed 10 December 2023].

FORMLABS., [no date]. Digital Fabrication 101 [online]. Available from: http://www. formlabs.com/blog/digital-fabrication-101/ [Accessed 10 August 2022].

FORTNUM, K., 2019. Where does clay come from? [online]. Available from: http://www.katherinefortnumceramics.com/post/wher-does-clay-come-from [Accessed 6 September 2022].

GARCIA CUEVAS, D., 2020. Diego Garcia Cuevas – Winning the lottery with Grasshopper® [online]. https://www.youtube.com/watch?v=_2BEqwh6hno&ab_channel=diegogarciacuevas [Accessed 15 September 2023].

HANSEN, T., [no date]. Drying Shrinkage [online]. Monthly Tech- Tip – Reference Library. Available from: http://www.digitalfire.com/glossary/drying+shrinkage / [Accessed 25 July 2022].

HANSEN, T., [no date]. Grog [online]. Monthly Tech- Tip – Reference Library. Available from: https://digitalfire.com/material/grog#:~:text=Grogs%20are%20added%20to%20bodies,%2C%20impart%20visual%20character%2C%20etc [Accessed 11 June 2023].

HERROLD, D., 2008. A retrospective exhibition. DePauw University.

KEEP, J., [no date]. Resume [online]. Available from: http://www.keep-art.co.uk/resume_intro.htm [Accessed 24 May 2021].

KEEP, J., [no date]. Potting in a digital age [online]. Studio Potter. Available from: http://www.studiopotter.org/potting-digital-age [Accessed 15 July 2022].

KEEP, J., 2016. Jonathan Keep- Studio Potter[online]. Available from: https://studiopotter.org/digital-issue/1075 [Accessed 28 February 2023].

KEEP, J., 2016. Jonathan Keep- Traditionalist and innovator [online]. Available from: https://www.youtube.com/watch?v=N2AaZR13Kjg&ab_channel=JonathanKeep [Accessed 16 November 2019].

LEE, T., [no date]. Taeykeom Lee [online]. Available from: https://portfolio.taekyeom.com/about.html [Accessed 15 September 2023].

LESLEY., [no date]. Decorating pottery - 21 Great ways to decorate clay [online]. The Pottery Wheel. Available from: https://thepotterywheel.com/decorating-pottery/ [Accessed 21 January 2023].

LESLEY., [no date]. Types of clay for pottery – The 5 main types of clay [online]. The Pottery Wheel. Available from: http://www.thepotterywheel.com/types-of-clay-for-pottery/ [Accessed 6 September 2022].

LESLEY., [no date]. What is pottery glaze made of? Understanding pottery glaze [online]. The Pottery Wheel. Available from: https://thepotterywheel.com/what-is-pottery-glaze-made-of/ [Accessed 14 September 2023].

LESSER, C., 2018. Why ceramic artists are so good at dealing with failure [online]. Artsy. Available from: http://www.artsy.net/article/artsy-editorial-ceramic-artists-good-dealing-failure [Accessed on 25 February 2021].

LOCKER, A., 2022. Top 20: Best 3D printer slicer software (most are free) [online]. All3DP. Available from: http://www.all3dp.com/1/best-3d-slicer-software=3d-printer/ [Accessed 8 September 2022].

MASHAMBANHAKA, F., 2019. 3D Print.com [online]. Interview with Hans Fouche on his African large scale pellet 3D printer the Cheetah. Available from: https://3dprint.com/258249/interview-with-hans-fouche-on-his-african-large-scale-pellet-3d-printer-the-cheetah/ [Accessed 3 July 2022].

MORETTI, F., 2021. Wasp 3D prints a unique concept store in collaboration with Dior. Available from: https://howfashionworks dotcom.wordpress.com/2012/06/12/design-school-the-origin-of-diors-cannage-design/ [Accessed 12 April 2022].

MUNN, J., 2023. Slip Trailing for Beginners. A Primer on a Great Ceramics Decorating Technique [online]. Ceramics Arts Network [online]. Available from: https://ceramicartsnetwork.org/daily/article/Slip-Trailing-for-Beginners-A-Primer-on-a-Great-Ceramics-Decorating-Technique/ [Accessed 17 September 2023].

OBJEKT., [no date]. Tom Lauerman [online]. Available from: https://objkt.com/profile/tomlauerman/created/ [Accessed 15 July 2023].

POTTERWARE., [no date]. Available from: https://www.potterware.com/about/ [Accessed 15 September 2023].

REPRAP., [no date]. Welcome to RepRap [online]. Available from: http://reprap.org/wiki/RepRap [Accessed 22 July 2021]

SHER, D., 2015. Hans Fouche: 3D Printed vacuum cleaner is the tip of the iceberg [online]. 3D Printing Industry. Available from: https://3dprintingindustry.com/news/3d-printed-lawnmower-just-tip-hans-fouches-iceberg-39905/ [Accessed 3 July 2022].

SIMPLIFY3D®., [no date]. Available from: https://www.simplify3d.com/ [Accessed 23 October 2021].

STONE FLOWER., [no date]. Available from: http://www.stoneflower3d.com [Accessed 18 January 2023].

TRACTUS 3D., [no date]. Advantages of 3D printing [online]. Available from: http://www.tractus3d.com/lnowledge/learn=3d=printing/advantages-of-3d-printing [Accessed 5 September 2022].

TRACTUS 3D., [no date]. 3D printing technology – Delta versus Cartesian [online]. Available from: http://www.tractus3d.com/lnowledge/learn=3d=printing/advantages-of-3d-printing [Accessed 3 September 2022].

VERBRUGGEN, D., 2010. An Englishman in Antwerp [online]. Unfold©- Labs. Available from: http://unfoldfab.blogspot.com/2010/11/englishman-in-antwerp.html [Accessed 10 August 2022].

VERBRUGGEN, D., 2012. Print, print, print… [online]. Unfold©- Labs. Available from: http:// http://unfoldfab.blogspot.com /2012/ 06/print-print-print.htmlhtml [Accessed 24 February 2023].

VORMVRIJ®., [no date]. LUTUM® [online]. Available from: http://www.vormvrij.nl/lutum/ [Accessed 21 January 2023].

VORMVRIJ®., [no date]. Portret [online]. Available from: http://www.vormvrij.nl/portret/ [Accessed 21 January 2023].

WALKER CERAMICS., [no date] Glossary of ceramic terms [online]. Available from: http://www.walkerceramics.com.au/resources/glossary-of-ceramic-terms/ [Accessed 15 August 2022].

WASP®., [no date]. Delta Wasp 2040 Clay [online]. Available from: https://www.3dwasp.com/en/clay-3d-printer-delta-wasp-2040-clay/ [Accessed 11 April 2023].

WASP®., [no date]. Continuous feeding system [online]. Available from: https://www.3dwasp.com/en/wasp-continuous-feeding-system/ [Accessed 11 April 2023].

WASP®., [no date]. Crane Wasp [online]. Available from: https://www.3dwasp.com/en/3d-printer-house-crane-wasp/ [Accessed 11 April 2023].

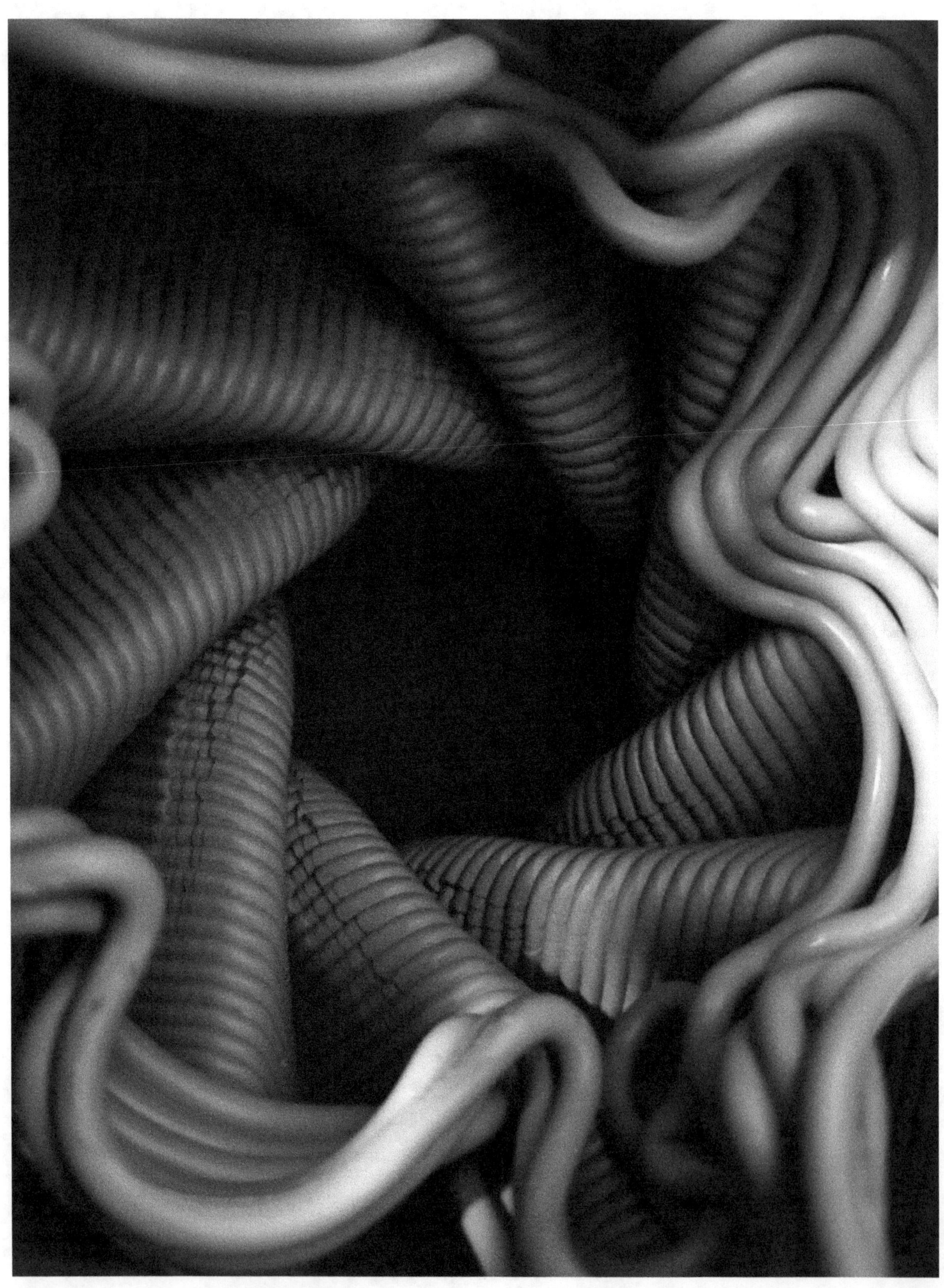

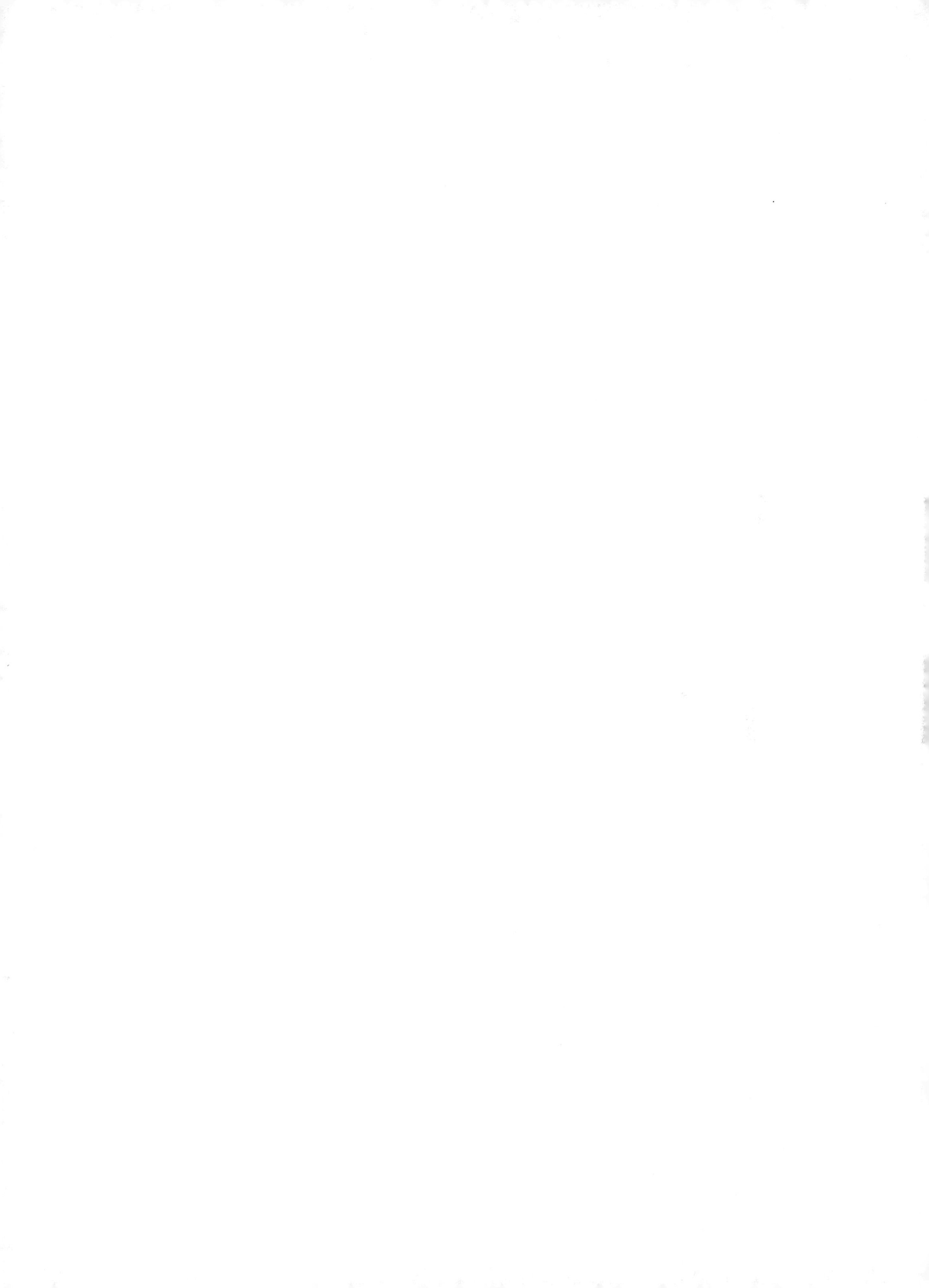

www.ingramcontent.com/pod-product-compliance
Lightning Source LLC
LaVergne TN
LVHW081251100826
845148LV00009B/1196
9780796195104